T0041994

From the first poignant vignette through many [...]
its inspiringly compassionate conclusion, Dr. [...]
a gripping medical chronicle infused with wisdom, science, and deep
humanity.

> GABOR MATÉ, MD, author, *In the Realm of Hungry Ghosts: Close Encounters with Addiction*

You couldn't find more authoritative tour guides of rural America
than Dr. Cooke and Laura Ungar, who have lived and worked among
its people—their people—for decades. The pair's medical savvy
and crackling prose can compete with the best out there. . . . This
gripping, heartbreaking, and ultimately hopeful book is about far
more than a tiny town and its hardscrabble people, many of whom
were affected by one of the biggest HIV outbreaks in US history. It's
a look at where so much of America has been heading when so many
others weren't watching.

> JAYNE O'DONNELL, health policy reporter, *USA Today*;
> cofounder, Urban Health Media Project

A very powerful and immensely moving must-read for anyone
working to end the syndemics of opioid use disorder, poverty, and the
HIV/hepatitis C epidemics among people who inject drugs in rural
America. . . . This book is a major contribution that challenges us to
see the humanness in everyone and inspires us to care and work to end
the suffering caused by the opioid crisis!

> CARRIE FOOTE, sociology professor, Indiana University–Purdue University
> Indianapolis; chair of the HIV Modernization Movement–Indiana

What a fantastic, inspiring, and informative book on how one person
made the difference in leading a rural community from a devastating
HIV outbreak and opioid addiction problem to a community of
hope and healing. Dr. Will Cooke superbly tells the story of how
he, the only physician in the community, guided a small rural town
in southern Indiana to recovery by focusing on compassionate,

person-centered care. This book is a must-read for all medical students and other health-care professionals. Once you start reading it, you won't be able to stop.

DR. WILLIAM L. YARBER, senior director, Rural Center for AIDS/STD Prevention; Provost Professor, Indiana University School of Public Health

I found this book to be an inspiring autobiography of how one committed physician truly made a difference in addressing an urgent public health problem through partnerships, persistence, and compassion.

JIM CURRAN, dean, Rollins School of Public Health, Emory University; former head of the Division of HIV/AIDS Prevention at the Centers for Disease Control and Prevention

People who use drugs haven't changed. What has changed is the way physicians and society have become more willing and able to see the humanity of people instead of only their disease and substance use. In his book *Canary in the Coal Mine*, Will Cooke reaches inward and articulates the steps of his change in a personal treatise of a family physician working to care for an onslaught of opioid injection–related HIV and hepatitis C infection in a small rural town. A black doctor in Chicago reminds Dr. Cooke that blacks have been in the midst of a heroin and HIV epidemic for years. Society was too ready to see this as a problem of "other" and embark on a drug war instead of a treatment war. Dr. Cooke's care transforms to embrace the tenets of treatment and harm reduction that characterize the care of most diseases, and he articulates their application to mental health and addiction. Primary care serves as the de facto mental health and addiction treatment system in the US. *Canary in the Coal Mine* reminds us how woefully unprepared and under-resourced these front-line clinicians are. His book provides a wake-up call to the structural violence suffered by too many and should serve as a humanitarian roadmap to address these challenges.

DAVID A. FIELLIN, MD, professor of medicine and director of program in addiction medicine, Yale School of Medicine

WILLIAM COOKE, MD
WITH LAURA UNGAR

CANARY
IN THE
COAL MINE

A FORGOTTEN RURAL COMMUNITY,

A HIDDEN EPIDEMIC, AND A LONE DOCTOR

BATTLING FOR THE LIFE, HEALTH,

AND SOUL OF THE PEOPLE

TYNDALE
REFRESH™

Think Well. Live Well. Be Well.

Visit Tyndale online at tyndale.com.

Tyndale and Tyndale's quill logo are registered trademarks of Tyndale House Ministries. *Tyndale Refresh* and the Tyndale Refresh logo are trademarks of Tyndale House Ministries. Tyndale Refresh is a nonfiction imprint of Tyndale House Publishers, Carol Stream, Illinois.

Canary in the Coal Mine: A Forgotten Rural Community, a Hidden Epidemic, and a Lone Doctor Battling for the Life, Health, and Soul of the People

Designed by Dean H. Renninger

Published in association with the literary agency of Steve Ross Agency, LLC, 70 Hillcrest Avenue, Park Hill, NY 10705.

For information about special discounts for bulk purchases, please contact Tyndale House Publishers at csresponse@tyndale.com, or call 1-855-277-9400.

ISBN 978-1-4964-4648-0 (hc)
ISBN 978-1-4964-4649-7 (sc)

Printed in the United States of America

29 28 27 26 25 24 23
7   6   5   4   3   2   1

To my parents for sharing your love,

my wife for sharing your life,

my brother for sharing your laughter,

my kids for sharing your wonder,

my mentors for sharing your wisdom,

my patients for sharing your stories,

my staff for sharing your dedication,

my God for sharing Your sacrifice,

and to my friends . . .

in recovery for sharing your courage,

in ministry for sharing your faith,

in service for sharing your passion,

and last, to those who've experienced isolation, disease, and death

because of a social status you did not choose.

Your suffering has been shared by too many.

Contents

Author's Note

I WROTE THIS BOOK as a tribute to Austin, Indiana, and to the people who've inspired me by their spirit, heart, and resilience. All of the events in this book really happened. As I wrote, I relied not only on my memory but on my personal correspondence, media reports, and notes. To protect the privacy and identity of my patients, I have not only changed names and identifying details but created composite characters. The stories are taken from interactions and interviews with actual patients, and their dialogue is almost exclusively quoted in their own words.

FORGED BY FIRE

THE COVID-19 OUTBREAK that gained momentum throughout the United States in 2020 highlights how socioeconomic and racial disparities impact the health of people. This fact goes beyond genetics or limited access to medical care. The roots of disease can consistently be traced along a tragic history of toxic stress experienced—often generationally—by marginalized and impoverished people. Socioeconomic stress has been well established as a contributing factor in the development of chronic diseases like diabetes, heart disease, and asthma.[1] According to an article in the medical journal *Lancet*, "The negative consequences of health disparities . . . in the US were already a problem before the pandemic." The article goes on to explain that the sickness and death resulting from COVID-19 disproportionately affects "already vulnerable US populations. . . . The deeply rooted social, racial, and economic health disparities in the country have been laid bare."[2] In other words, COVID-19 simply put the already existing problem in sharp relief.

My patients taught me just how devastating the health impact of socioeconomic hardships can be. In March 2015, I was the only doctor in Austin, Indiana—a city of 4,300 people in Scott County, just off I-65 between Louisville, Kentucky, and Indianapolis, Indiana—when it became ground zero for two unprecedented health-care disasters with roots in the 1980s. One was the national opioid epidemic. The other was the worst-recorded HIV outbreak among people who use drugs in the nation's history. These two deadly epidemics that had been brewing alongside one another for decades boiled over in Austin.

Whole families were injecting prescription painkillers together, and since state laws made sterile syringes so hard to obtain, desperate people locked in a deadly dance with addiction resorted to sharing syringes, and with them, diseases.

Within a few months, our HIV incidence climbed to one of the highest globally. Experts, researchers, and journalists flocked to Austin from around the world. But since no one had ever seen anything like what was happening in my small town, no one knew what to do.

I told reporters that this wasn't a freak occurrence. The conditions that made Austin ripe for this crisis existed in towns all across America. We had to act immediately and decisively to prevent other communities from being harmed. I told Dean Reynolds of *CBS Evening News* as we walked through the hardest hit area of Austin, "I've described this community as a canary in the coal mine. This could happen anywhere. We are all Austin, Indiana."[3]

Dr. Anthony Fauci, director of the National Institute of Allergy and Infectious Diseases, agreed. "I expect we will likely see similar outbreaks of injection drug-related HIV. There's nothing particularly different about the Indiana community than other communities throughout the country."[4]

In 2016, after studying what had happened in Austin, the CDC issued its own dire warning, identifying 220 counties across 26 states that were primed for outbreaks of HIV.[5] Unfortunately, in May 2019, four full years after the crisis hit our town, the *New England Journal of Medicine* reported, "The outbreak in Scott County may have been a warning sign, but the message hasn't been heeded in many parts of the country." Despite the importance of harm reduction in curbing the epidemic in Austin, the article concluded that the US government didn't appear poised to "do what is necessary to address the spread of HIV and HCV [hepatitis C virus] in rural America."[6] Echoing the growing concern of public health experts nationwide, Alaska's director of the Division of Public Health, Jay Butler, said, "The nightmare that wakes me up at 3 a.m. is a Scott County–level HIV outbreak happening here."[7]

Unfortunately, Austin's warning to America has not been heeded, and the ramifications have been tragic. New transmission clusters of HIV among people who inject drugs have emerged in Florida, Kentucky, Massachusetts, Minnesota, North Carolina, Ohio, Oregon, Pennsylvania, Tennessee, Washington State, Alaska, and West Virginia.[8]

Some people have asked me why they should care about HIV transmission among people who inject drugs. I believe our common humanity demands that we defend every human life, especially those we view as different. Additionally, HIV is transmitted in ways other than injection drug use. If we don't take measures to stop its transmission, it will eventually find its way to someone we know or even love.

The opioid epidemic continues to rage out of control. Overdose now claims more lives than motor vehicle accidents, breast cancer, kidney disease, or colon cancer.[9] In fact, the death toll has become so great that life expectancy in the United States decreased for three straight years—from 2014 through 2017. This was the first time life expectancy in the US decreased so drastically in a hundred years, dating back to the years when the country was embroiled in a world war and the Spanish flu pandemic from 1915 to 1918.[10]

"A whole constellation of conditions" affects life expectancy, according to Dr. Howard Koh, a Harvard professor of public health leadership. "It is not just medical conditions, but also the social drivers that appear to be at play, like income inequality and mental distress."[11]

I have witnessed, up close, the breakdown of a community and the toll it takes on every resident, as generations remain trapped in cycles of poverty, abuse, and addiction. For decades leading up to the health-care disaster in 2015, flames of disease, despair, and death had torn through Austin, consuming whole families. I sometimes felt like a helpless spectator to the horror. If I'd known how much pain and darkness awaited me along the way, I doubt I would have dared begin this journey. It would have been impossible to comprehend the immeasurable suffering I'd witness or the depth of loss I'd endure.

The good news is that we have all the tools we need to end both epidemics. These tools can bring healing to any community, just as they did in Austin, while preventing outbreaks of death and disease. But they're not what most people expect.

I discovered them as, in time, a fellowship rose from the ashes, forged by fire to find new ways to offer healing and hope. I am honored to stand with my community on the other side of this valley of death's shadow. Our journey left us irrevocably changed. It's hard to say if the scars we carry on our hearts will ever fully heal. But the resulting change in Austin has undeniably been healing.

The world took notice in 2015 when the national opioid, hepatitis C, and HIV epidemics all converged in Austin, Indiana. Yet the story of Austin predates this convergence of interdependent epidemics. To understand what happened here and how these lessons apply to other communities, it's essential to get to know the town and the story of her people. And because my family was rooted in a place very much like Austin, I tell part of my own story so you can see how my upbringing prepared me to love and fight for this community.

My hope is that by sharing the story of Austin and our efforts to address the HIV/opioid crisis in 2015, I'll convince your mind, capture your heart, and compel your hands to join in the struggle against substance use disorder and the factors that fuel it and other devastating epidemics taking root in communities across America. Who knows? You may be the one to bring life and hope back to your own community.

William Cooke, MD,
FAAFP, FASAM, AAHIVS

CHAPTER 1

WELCOME TO LITTLE HAZARD

. . . .

Whose work is it but your own to open your eyes?

GEORGE MACDONALD

HEALTH-CARE DISASTERS DON'T JUST HAPPEN; they develop right before our eyes, unseen or ignored until it's too late. That's what happened in Austin, Indiana, and what is currently happening in communities across America.

In my case, idealism blinded me to the crises already taking root in Austin when I opened my practice there in 2004, fresh out of medical training. A small town nestled among rolling hills and fertile farmland about thirty-six miles north of Louisville and eighty miles south of Indianapolis, Austin had been without a practicing physician since the mid-1970s. I believed I could make a difference by improving the health and well-being of this community that, other than lacking adequate medical care, seemed to epitomize the quiet tranquility of rural America.

Standing under the pure blue sky, which spreads out wide and open over Austin, I felt the longings for freedom and the pursuit of infinite possibilities. Then, as I explored country roads wandering

7

through miles of farmland, dotted with old farmhouses and modest homes, I felt the spark of nostalgia mixed with a timeless image of the American dream. After all, this *is* where John Mellencamp's Little Pink House still stands.[1]

Ironically, a dark and deadly secret lurked just behind Austin's outward beauty. Once I began to get to know some of the struggling people I hadn't noticed at first, my initial impressions of this iconic all-American town were shattered. One morning I stopped at the gas station next to the liquor store and the town's only traffic light. While I was filling up my car, a young woman jumped into my passenger seat, announcing she needed a ride. I told her I was only going about a mile to my office.

"That's fine," she said. "I'm going that way."

I paid for the gas and awkwardly got back into my car. Not knowing what to do or say, I began to drive nervously with both hands on the steering wheel.

After a minute of silence that felt like an hour, she said, "I'm looking for work. Is there anything I can do for you?"

"No," I responded politely. "I only have a couple of people working for me and we aren't looking right now."

"Are you *sure* there isn't something I could do for you . . . *personally?*" she pressed.

"What kind of work are you looking for?" I asked, hoping I could at least connect her to the right people.

"Anything. I'm willing to do *anything*," she said.

I mentioned a place or two I thought might be hiring. She seemed confused.

"No, that's not the sort of thing I'm looking for," she replied. "But . . ." she said, moving a little closer to me, "I could do something for *you*."

I told her again I wasn't hiring and suggested a temporary work agency, at which point she rolled her eyes and sighed. There was a moment or two of tension before she shifted in her seat to face me more directly.

"Look, I'd be willing to do something for you. Anything. Just tell me, and I'll do it."

I tried to think of anything she might be able to help out with around the office, but nothing came to mind. "I'm sorry," I said apologetically. "I really don't need any help."

She sat back with another sigh and crossed her arms. After a few more blocks of awkward silence, we passed the half-century-old walk-up Dairy Queen, and I knew we were getting close to my office. So I thought I'd try one more option.

"You know, the LifeLong Learning Center in Scottsburg has programs to help you learn new skills. They can even help you find people who may want to hire you."

She just stared at me.

Oh well . . . I tried.

When we finally got to my office, she silently shook her head, hopped out of the car, and walked off without saying a word.

I found the only two staff I had at the time waiting as I entered.

"Who was that?" asked Elizabeth, my receptionist.

I told them what happened. Then they both looked at each other and started laughing.

"What?" I asked.

"Come on, Dr. Cooke," Amy, my nurse, chuckled. "I'll do *anything* . . . whatever you *want* . . ."

That's when it dawned on me. I felt so stupid. I blushed and laughed at my own naiveté.

I wasn't just embarrassed, though, I was ashamed.

How could I have missed that? What level of hopelessness and despair had led this young woman to try to sell her body? How many other people in Austin were so desperate that they were resorting to unimaginable means to get by for another day?

It took this encounter with a total stranger to open my eyes and see people right in front of me that I hadn't even noticed before.

I had worked hard to become a doctor, and I had learned a lot. But it was becoming clear I didn't know enough about Austin or the people. The story of Austin was more complicated than I could have imagined. Early on I felt like Samwise Gamgee from *The Lord of the Rings* when he told Frodo, "I wonder what sort of a tale we've fallen into."[2] I didn't see it then, but my early encounters with people like this young woman were harbingers of a tsunami of suffering no one saw coming until the drug-fueled HIV catastrophe struck Austin in 2015, sending shock waves throughout our nation.

· · · · · · · · · ·

From the beginning, practicing medicine in Austin challenged my way of seeing the world and people. Some experiences were eye opening, while others were jaw dropping. Many of my first patients turned out to be as unforgettable as the woman who jumped into my car.

Mr. Johnson was a sixtysomething man who checked in at the receptionist's window with his wife. My nurse took them to an exam room and came to get me.

"I put Mr. Johnson in room one," she said with a playful glint in her eye. "I think you should get in there and check him out. Apparently, his wife shot him in the neck."

I all but fell out of my chair. "Seriously?"

"Welcome to Little Hazard," she chuckled.

I grinned nervously. I knew enough of the local history to recognize our town's nickname, which originated from the many residents who hail from the Appalachian hub of Hazard, Kentucky. There's even a local saying: "A single tank of gas can get you from Hazard to a job at the Austin canning factory."

I rushed into the room, dragging my nurse along with me. Not knowing what to expect, I wanted backup. Waiting for me was a middle-aged couple, dressed in worn clothing. Both looked as though they'd been working outside most of the day.

Mr. Johnson sat on the exam table holding a bloody towel

against his neck and wearing a guilty look on his face. His wife sat in the chair across from him with her arms folded, shaking her head at him.

I grabbed some gloves. "What happened?"

"I shot his a—!" she smirked.

Stunned, I looked over at my nurse. She just smiled at me.

I began to examine Mr. Johnson, frightened by what I'd find hidden under the towel.

"Why did you do that?" I asked his wife.

"He wouldn't come in to wash when I called 'im," she said, as if it was obvious.

I located a small entrance wound on the right side of his neck, but I couldn't find an exit wound.

"What did you shoot him with?"

"She shot me with a BB gun," Mr. Johnson chimed in. Oddly, he didn't seem angry, just annoyed and almost—*amused.*

I felt around until I found the BB under his skin on the left side of his neck. Somehow the BB had traveled all the way across his neck without hitting anything important. I asked him if he wanted *me* to take it out or if he wanted to go to the emergency room.

"Heck," he said, laughing, "I woulda cut it out myself, but I figgered you were probably bored over here and maybe wanted something t'do."

"You were right." I laughed too. As I got to work taking the BB out of his neck, they told me what had happened.

Mr. Johnson was out back chopping wood when Mrs. Johnson opened the door and called him in for dinner. He told her he'd be there when he was done. So she got the BB gun, came back outside, and hollered, "Mister, you better come inside right now, or I'll shoot you."

"I told her not to aim that thing at me," he said. "And 'fore I could even finish the sentence, she went and pulled the trigger. That didn't bother me much cause she couldn't normally hit the side of a barn. Course, I ain't no barn, neither."

A few seconds later, I popped the BB out and dropped it into a small specimen jar. Then I gave it to them to keep on their mantel for a conversation piece. Little Hazard . . . er . . . Austin, I was discovering, was quite a colorful place to practice medicine.

· · · · · · · · · ·

Having grown up in southern Indiana, I knew this region felt more like Kentucky than the rest of the state. But nowhere is that more evident than in Austin. In fact, the first white child born in Louisville, William Harrod,[3] became one of the original settlers of Austin during the early 1800s. He was born during the Revolutionary War when Louisville was considered the western front as the first and only settlement on the Ohio River. The end of the war secured new lands and opportunities north and west of Kentucky for American settlers to establish homesteads.

Many of the families who later joined William Harrod's family in Austin started life hundreds of miles away in the mountains of Appalachia. During the early twentieth century, they came to work for Morgan Packing Company (now Morgan Foods), one of the world's largest food processing plants.

The town takes up just two and a half square miles in the northernmost portion of Scott County, Indiana, just off Interstate 65. Surrounded by hundreds of acres of farmland and quiet neighborhoods, Austin's single-street downtown takes you past a few churches, the fire station, and city hall, then over one of the oldest train tracks in the country to the town's only stoplight. The world's first train robbers, the Reno Brothers, perpetrated one of their heists here in 1868, inspiring generations of outlaws like Jessie James, the Dalton Gang, and Butch Cassidy. This was the original Wild West.

Just north of Main Street is a half square mile of town representing one of the most forsaken places in the country. Family homes with well-kept yards sit in neighborhoods shared with dilapidated houses and ramshackle shacks with boarded-up windows, collapsed roofs, overgrown yards, and abandoned junk.

Just across Highway 31 on the north side of town, Morgan Foods looms large over Austin's land, culture, and history. It was founded in 1899 as the Austin Canning Company by a group of local businesspeople. Not long after starting operations, some of the original investors became discouraged, and J. S. Morgan, who had to work off his $500 investment debt by serving as the factory's first president, began buying up shares. His son I. C. Morgan took over to help when J. S. came down with typhoid in 1906. Once he recovered, they proved to be a potent father-son team, eventually buying the company's remaining shares and renaming it Morgan Packing Company.

I. C. Morgan married William Harrod's great-granddaughter, Fern, uniting these two influential families. They had three children, including Ivan Harrod (Jack) Morgan, and by the beginning of World War II, Jack joined what became three generations of Morgan men working at the company.

During the two world wars, the Morgans contracted with the military to provide food to the troops. Operations expanded so quickly that it was hard to find enough laborers. However, when the Great Depression hit in the 1930s, millions of people began to flee from Appalachia in search of jobs and greater opportunities, a migration known as the Hillbilly Highway. Morgan Packing was one of the stops along the way.

Even more jobs became available during peak seasons. People flocked to Austin from across the region, arriving on foot, by bicycle, by bus, and even as stowaways in boxcars. By the mid-1930s, Morgan Packing employed about two thousand people and even convinced American Can Company to open a plant next to its own building.

During this prosperous time, I. C. Morgan built a dance hall and invested heavily in the town's development. He became known for his generosity and compassion for others. He also built a baseball stadium for the semipro team he sponsored, the Austin Packers, which was a main attraction for years. Austin's downtown came alive, and its restaurants and businesses flourished.

When laborers became hard to find again during World War II, Morgan Packing was able to rely on the foreign soldiers held in a prisoner of war camp that had been set up adjacent to Morgan Packing.[4] Following the war, Morgan Packing continued to do well, becoming one of the nation's largest condensed soup manufacturers, ranking among the top three with Campbell's.[5]

Then in the late seventies and early eighties, Austin began to suffer economic blows familiar to manufacturing-based cities and towns across middle America. Businesses began downsizing and closing. The American Can plant beside Morgan Foods shut its doors in 1986 after fifty years in business.

As I came to learn, industry wasn't the only thing to abandon the people of Austin. For the first 125 years of Austin's history, a local physician had always been available. That changed when Dr. Carl Bogardus retired in 1977, resulting in a lapse in medical care that lasted an entire generation. This ill-fated convergence of lost access to both health care and job opportunities bled into the 1980s and 1990s, when the people of Austin endured the worst economy in the state. Some people fled the town in search of better opportunities, while unemployment soared for those who remained. Deteriorating houses began to dot the streets as families couldn't afford to maintain their homes.

By the time I arrived in 2004, Austin had become a town of two faces. The majority of the population was still comprised of working middle-class families living in well-kept residential neighborhoods nestled between Main Street and the surrounding corn and soybean fields. But a significant minority, including much of the north side, was marked by extreme poverty.

While some people had the means to seek medical attention and economic opportunities in neighboring towns like the county seat of Scottsburg, many felt trapped—some families having gone generations without reliable employment or health care.

From that standpoint, Austin may not have been the best place to establish a new medical practice, but my idealistic optimism convinced me it was the perfect place to answer a calling I had first felt at fifteen and subsequently spent nearly two decades fighting for an opportunity to fulfill. Early on, the reality of Austin forced me to recognize people my limited worldview had hidden from me. But it would take years of heartache before I learned the difference between fighting for and surrendering to a calling that was bigger than myself.

CHAPTER 2
BLOOD AND TEARS

• • • • • • • • •

We are linked by blood, and blood is memory without language.

JOYCE CAROL OATES

INDIANA IS FAMOUS FOR BASKETBALL, the Indy 500, cornfields, and oddly, HIV. Growing up in Indiana during the 1980s, I felt a kinship to one of the most famous Hoosiers in history. Ryan White and I were born within a day of each other in December 1971, and although our experiences were wildly different, our stories are linked by blood.

Ryan White became a household name in the eighties when he fought hard for acceptance and the right to attend school after contracting HIV through blood transfusions intended to treat his hemophilia. Several years earlier, the Centers for Disease Control had reported the first few cases of acquired immunodeficiency syndrome (AIDS) among gay men.[1] The next year, they reported the same immunodeficiency syndrome among Haitian refugees and people who injected drugs.[2] Since modern safeguards weren't in place to protect the national blood supply, this beautiful expression of collective care became the source of heartache. Before anyone knew what was happening, 63 percent of people living with hemophilia, including Ryan White, had contracted HIV.[3]

Mass panic erupted over the rapidly spreading, fatal disease, which had no effective treatment. Frightened people focused their fears on those who had contracted HIV—predominantly gay men—blaming and even harassing them in the process. Ryan White wasn't spared such mistreatment. Sometimes it was direct, as when customers on Ryan's newspaper route dropped their subscriptions, or restaurants threw away the dishes his family had eaten from. Someone even shot a bullet through a window of their home. At other times, it was indirect, as when the reporter and publisher of a paper that supported Ryan's right to attend school were harassed.[4]

Like most Americans, I followed Ryan White's ordeal as it played out on TV. My fellow Hoosiers' lack of compassion appalled me, but I was in awe of the grace with which Ryan managed the chaos. His insistence on being treated like a person instead of a disease forced people to confront their preconceived ideas about people living with HIV. It was clear he had done nothing wrong and yet had contracted a fatal disease some had claimed was "God's punishment."[5] I recognized that his innocence and contagious smile had cracked a hole in the wall that the public had erected to isolate people living with HIV. Through this opening, a scared and confused nation began to see them as sick people in need of care instead of bad people deserving judgment.

By the fall of 1987, when Ryan and I were both fifteen, he'd finally found a school to accept him in Cicero, Indiana. Meanwhile, I sat in church about two hours away in New Albany, Indiana, listening to a guest speaker. I couldn't focus though. Something was bothering me—both in my body and in my spirit.

The ankle I had recently sprained playing basketball throbbed. For some reason it was getting worse instead of better. But there was something else tugging at my attention. My heart began to ache with a longing for something I couldn't name. I was already pretty devout for my age, having grown up in a family that attended church every time the doors were open, but it felt as though God was calling to me across time and space in a way I had never experienced before. I didn't understand what He wanted me to do, but I knew I couldn't just sit there.

I made my way on crutches to the front of the church where I prayed with my pastor and dedicated my life to this vague calling I couldn't name. I felt a sense of peace and confidence unlike anything I had experienced in my shy, awkward adolescent life.

As we rode home, the pain and swelling in my ankle continued to worsen, and I noticed red dots on my arms and legs. Around my ankle, the dots merged, forming a large bruise. Later, while I was brushing my teeth, my gums began to bleed. A little freaked out, I showed all of this to my mom.

My parents took me to an urgent care where my blood was drawn. A little later, the doctor stepped into the room looking concerned. Her voice quivered as she explained I was bleeding because my platelets were too low to measure. Like Ryan White, I was in danger of bleeding to death and was rushed to the children's hospital in Louisville.

After another blood draw, a nurse asked me to bend my arm to hold the little cotton ball in place. A few minutes later when I straightened my arm, there was a lemon-sized swelling of blood under my skin. My mom gasped. My younger brother, Brian, his eyes wide, grabbed Dad's arm and asked, "Is he going to die?"

Everyone went silent.

That's when *I* got scared. I didn't understand why this was happening to me just a few hours after I had committed my life to serving God. The timing seemed significant, though, so I decided to pay close attention.

The following days were filled with tests and tension. Even so, I enjoyed having the attention of all the doctors and their entourages of residents and students. Aside from the ache in my ankle and the pain of a bone marrow biopsy from my hip to rule out leukemia, I never really felt sick. This allowed me to follow along as the doctors methodically solved the mystery at work inside my body. The whole process fascinated me. They said I needed a series of transfusions to treat a condition called idiopathic thrombocytopenic purpura (ITP), and I was almost guaranteed a full recovery.

The timing of my illness felt like more than a mere coincidence, and I decided right then and there that God was calling me to become a doctor.

My admiration for Ryan White only deepened after my medical scare. He'd spent his entire life dealing with the threat of painful bleeding joints and internal bleeding. I'd spent a weekend. He contracted HIV from a transfusion and faced terrible discrimination. My transfusion occurred a few years later when the blood supply was safe. He'd spent much of his life trying to convince everyone he was just a normal teenage kid. But he wasn't. He changed the way people think and made the world a better place. Several months after Ryan died at eighteen in 1990, George H. W. Bush signed the Ryan White CARE Act, establishing the national HIV health-care system and guaranteeing access to compassionate treatment for anyone living with HIV.

Later in that same decade, an unprecedented opioid epidemic began to churn beneath the surface. Much like the hidden existence of HIV in the national blood supply, the seriousness of the opioid crisis would take years to detect. Then, just as in Ryan's day, shared blood would again become the mechanism of misery.

Almost thirty years from the day Ryan was diagnosed with HIV, I was there when these two great epidemics collided—as fate would have it, in Indiana.

* * * * * * * * *

As I neared the end of high school, I knew my calling. But the road leading me there was harder than I ever expected.

Education hadn't been a given in either my mom's or dad's families. My mom was only a few generations removed from squatters who'd migrated from Appalachia to the southern Indiana banks of the Ohio River. They had followed the Hillbilly Highway north to southern Indiana.

Like generations before her, she ended up dropping out of school to get married at sixteen. In a desperate effort to escape the misery surrounding them, my dad voluntarily enlisted in the Air Force during the Vietnam War. Unfortunately, his job prospects were no better afterward. But when a stranger encouraged my mom to become a nurse, she decided to go back to school and, at the age of twenty-four, became the first person in her family to graduate high school.

That's when my dad's military service helped by enabling her to get her nursing degree at Indiana University Southeast (IUS) near our home. My dad decided to join her at IUS, pursuing a degree in art and psychology. I remember spending years of my childhood roaming the college campus.

The beauty and inspiration I felt there stood in stark contrast to the darkness and desperation I'd witnessed in the homes of some of my extended family members, who were still trapped in squalor. At that impressionable age, I already sensed a chasm separating people living with hope from those stuck in despair. These abstract feelings were etched on my mind through some of the monkeys my dad was studying in the psychology research lab.[6]

On the weekends, when it was his turn to care for the animals, he took me with him and let me help. I loved holding and feeding the monkeys. But I felt uncomfortable every time we entered the area where some of the baby monkeys were kept in isolation. Dad showed me that the students had set up fake mother figures to replace their real moms. Each baby monkey could choose a cold, hard, wire frame with a bottle of milk attached to it, or a warm, soft cloth without a bottle. All of the baby monkeys preferred the cloth surrogate—choosing to visit the wire frame only to feed. The study they were doing with the baby monkeys demonstrated a basic need for connection that existed separately from the need for food.[7]

My dad told me the baby monkeys put in a test room without their cloth would just huddle in a corner and whimper. The babies that had their cloth would playfully explore the area, periodically returning to their cloth to cuddle. However, the baby monkeys were still missing something fundamental to becoming healthy by missing the nurture of their real mom. Dad told me these baby monkeys that bonded with the inanimate surrogates remained neurotic and had difficulty socializing with other monkeys. Once I began practicing medicine, I thought often of those monkeys when meeting a patient who seemed stuck in despair and unable to avoid making one disastrous decision after another. To what lengths will people go to get a sense of belonging and gratification when they were denied those most basic human needs from a very young age?

· · · · · · · · · ·

Despite my parents' example, I knew college would be no easy task. I'd grown up with one foot in a world inherited from generations of Appalachian poverty and one foot in the strange new world of possibilities my parents introduced me to while they attended college. Frankly, I didn't feel like I fit into either.

After high school, the combination of a Pell Grant (awarded to low-income students), a music scholarship, and the financial assistance I received as the dependent of a veteran allowed me to enroll in college. Even though I attended the same university I had explored as a child, Indiana University Southeast, I felt out of place among the students from wealthier families.

I went to my classes but didn't understand how to take notes or prepare for exams, so I struggled for the first two years. I joined study groups and learned as much as I could from my classmates raised in a higher socioeconomic class, and in time, my grades improved.

When I first applied to medical school, however, I was turned down. Undeterred, I moved to Indianapolis with my new wife,

Leah, to improve my chances by completing a master's program in biology. After several more failed attempts to get into medical school, I began to question the calling I had felt at fifteen. But having watched my parents overcome even greater obstacles, I refused to give up. Leah and I moved overseas, where I was able to complete the first two years of medical school. When I scored near the top nationally on the medical licensing exam, the seemingly impossible happened and I was accepted to Indiana University School of Medicine as a third-year transfer student.

Even though I had accepted a loan that stipulated I provide primary care to an underserved community in Indiana, my professors kept trying to recruit me into specialty fields like cardiology and surgery.

One day as we were finishing up rounds, our surgery attending physician said, "Cooke, I'd like to talk to you."

My anxiety soared, and a couple of my classmates glanced my way with pity. Surgeons are notorious for making med students do grunt work.

"I understand you're planning to go into primary care?" he said, cocking his head slightly.

"Yes, sir," I answered.

"Why on earth would you do that?" he blurted out.

I paused for a second and then explained. "I believe it's my calling. I really want to make a difference in an underserved community."

"You need to reconsider," he urged. "You've got a lot of potential. It would be a shame for you to throw all that away in primary care."

I was shocked to hear him say that, but I held my tongue.

"Look," he said, pointing out a large window that overlooked the campus. A gentle snow was falling, though the grass was still green. Beyond the snowflakes there was another dance of white—students, residents, and attendings wearing lab coats of varying lengths, which signified their level of training—moving along the sidewalks as far as I could see.

"This institution is the heart and soul of medicine. Every single patient here is being taken care of by a specialist. All primary care docs do is hand us their patients."

He turned to face me again. "The only way you will ever make a difference is if you specialize. Otherwise, you'll spend your career as nothing more than a gatekeeper"— he pointed out the window again—"for them." He paused to let that sink in, then added more sincerely, "And that would be a shame."

While I didn't doubt my commitment to practice primary care medicine in an underserved community, the conversation with the surgeon left me feeling discouraged as I headed home. By this time, Leah and I had a two-year-old son, Eli. After dinner I got Eli ready for bed and carried him over to his bedroom window. The moon was big and bright. Its silver light reflected off the white snow that now covered everything.

"Where's the moon?" I asked. Eli pointed up with wonder in his eyes.

"That's right," I said.

I kissed his cheek and lay next to him in bed. I stroked his head and sang to him until he was asleep. As his breathing slowed, I felt my exhausted body relax.

But once I softly closed his door behind me and made my way down the hall, I felt a familiar tension rise within me. Things with my wife had not been going well. Our time together had been cut up into tiny pieces around my training, and we fought a lot.

In April 2001, only a month before I graduated with honors from IU School of Medicine, Leah gave birth to our second child, a daughter, whom we named Moirah. Leah and I hoped the end of medical school and the birth of Moirah would mark a new beginning for us. And although I'd been concerned about dividing my love between two children, I discovered love has a funny sort of math that allows the heart to somehow love each without that love being diminished or diluted.

· · · · · · · · ·

During my residency, I spent time caring for patients in resource-poor areas of Ecuador. I also made sure my training included C-sections and significant experience in the emergency department. By the time I completed my residency, I felt fully prepared to move to a rural area and offer a broad range of services to the community.

Shortly before I finished my training, I began searching for the place God would be able to use me most. I was struck by how much deprivation I found all across Appalachia and the Midwest. I could practically throw a dart at a map and land on a community in need. But because I had signed a commitment to practice in a rural area of Indiana, I decided to narrow my search to rural areas within driving distance of my parents, who still lived in my hometown of New Albany. I liked the idea of my kids growing up near their grandparents.

After exploring several options and spending a lot of time in prayerful contemplation, I signed a recruitment agreement with Scott Memorial Hospital in Scottsburg to establish and maintain an independent primary care clinic in Austin for at least five years. In exchange, they agreed to offset any shortages in my overhead for eighteen months. I named the clinic Foundations Family Medicine, based on my belief that good health is the foundation of a full and purposeful life; a healthy individual is the foundation of a healthy family; and a healthy family is the foundation of a healthy community. I drew a tree with deep roots as my logo to represent my personal commitment to the community, and as a Christian, I adopted Jesus' explanation about why He came to earth: "that they may have life, and that they may have it more abundantly."[8]

Of course, there was a lot more to opening a practice than I imagined. While my new building just a mile from Main Street was under construction, I had to pick out and purchase an electronic medical record system, computers, office equipment, furniture, desks, phone system, internet provider, malpractice insurance, business insurance, and health insurance for my employees; set up retirement plans, payroll, and bank accounts; get enrolled in all the insurance plans; get credentialed at the hospital; order supplies; make arrangements for medical waste disposal, garbage disposal, janitorial services, landscaping, advertising; and set up inspections for the state and fire marshal . . . It's no wonder fewer than one in five doctors operates a solo practice, let alone one in a poverty-stricken, resource-poor place in the middle of rural Indiana.

I brought my two kids to the worksite a few times a week to watch as the building went up. Once completed, the facility would be roughly fifteen hundred square feet with three exam rooms, a procedure room, and a small waiting room. Attached to it, duplex-style, would be a mirror set of offices and exam rooms I hoped would attract visiting services to help me meet the needs of the community.

The sounds of hammers and men calling to each other, mixed with the nostalgic smell of freshly cut lumber, transported me back to my childhood, when my dad took me with him when he helped my grandpa Lames, a carpenter, on jobsites. Grandpa's parents had moved to New Albany from Owsley County, Kentucky, one of the nation's poorest counties. Grandpa Lames was a stern man who'd inherited generations of toxic family drama and poverty. With only an elementary school education, he relied on his carpentry skills to get by. But he also turned to alcohol and opioids to cope with the difficulties of life. When intoxicated, he would fly into fits of rage, so my mom's earliest memories are of crawling under her bed to hide from her own dad. Though all her siblings drank from stray beer bottles left around the house when they were young, Mom realized that heavy drinking would keep her from improving her own life.

Thanks to some positive outside influences and stubborn persistence, my parents were able to escape the generations of trauma and dysfunction around them. Yet they didn't turn their backs on where they'd come from, teaching my brother and me that everyone deserves to be treated with dignity and respect. That included family members, like my grandpa Lames, who were hardest to love.

Watching Eli and Moirah play hide-and-seek at the construction site of my new office made me thankful my brother and I had been raised in a stable, loving home. I quietly prayed not only that I'd be able to provide them the same blessing, but that this new building would be a place where I could help families in Austin do the same.

By September 2004, everything was in place to start seeing patients. While I would have preferred to have a staff of four or five, I could afford to hire only a biller/receptionist and a nurse— far from ideal, but still more than the people of Austin had had access to in decades.

As the opening of the clinic neared, the idea of practicing medicine by myself in such a poverty-stricken and resource-poor area was intimidating. On the other hand, I was captivated by the way Austin reflected the quintessential American town Norman Rockwell captured in his art, some of which I hung on my clinic walls. I was also confident that God had called me here and that I could truly make a difference in this community. Of course, it helped that Scott Memorial Hospital had pledged eighteen months of financial support.

. . . .

The day I opened my practice was terrifying. After feeling God's call to become a doctor at fifteen, I had spent the next eighteen years preparing for this one moment. I unlocked the doors and called my two employees, Elizabeth and Amy, to the center of the waiting room, where we held hands and prayed, thanking God for allowing us to serve Him and asking for His guidance.

We had no idea if anyone would even show up that day. But a few minutes later, my receptionist/biller welcomed our first patient, and we were off. Some of the people we took care of had never seen a doctor before.

One sixtysomething man had a tumor on his tongue so large that he carried a handkerchief with him to catch the saliva that dripped from the corner of his mouth. It was difficult to imagine why he'd waited so long to visit a doctor while living with a disfigurement that so severely disrupted his quality of life and social interactions. The following year, however, I ran across a study from the National Institute of Health reporting that if someone from a rural area simply had a driver's license, they were at least twice as likely to visit a doctor as someone without one.[9] Since my patient lacked both transportation and insurance, walking to my office was the first opportunity he'd had to see a health-care provider in years.

In just the first few months, I diagnosed patient after patient with late-stage manifestations of chronic diseases. Some were diabetics who had never been diagnosed, let alone treated, and who were already experiencing loss of feeling in their feet and partial blindness. They had been left out of advances in medical screening and treatment because of where they lived and how they were viewed.

Perhaps the most heartrending cases, however, were the young women I diagnosed with late-stage cervical cancer. Week after week, women of all ages would come to see me, never having had a Pap smear because they'd lacked access to medical care.

Most of them turned out to be treatable, but even one pointless death is too many. I'm still haunted by the memory of the first time I had to tell a family that their thirty-eight-year-old, otherwise healthy loved one was dying of advanced cervical cancer, a disease that should have been prevented. And I had to deliver this awful news to more than one woman who had thought she was healthy. Each time it became more difficult because of the inconsolable reactions, pointless suffering, and untimely deaths I'd already witnessed.

Cervical cancer was the leading cause of death among women in the early 1900s. But this was the twenty-first century, when simple access to modern screening and prevention could virtually eliminate the risk of anyone dying of cervical cancer. Nonetheless, a flawed system had harmed the people of Austin and needlessly shortened lives.

I marveled how conditions here in the heart of the richest country on earth rivaled those I saw on mission trips to developing countries. When I shared my concerns with otherwise compassionate people within the community, their reactions shocked me. They dismissed the harms inflicted on my patients as natural consequences of their personal failings. The consensus was that my patients were paying the penalty for their laziness, promiscuity, bad choices, and ignorance. But that didn't sit well with me—after all, these people hadn't created their circumstances; their circumstances had created them.

I was reminded of the prevailing attitude in the Baptist church in which I grew up. Our preacher, a native of eastern Kentucky, preached a fire-and-brimstone gospel transplanted from Appalachia. Our small congregation was close-knit and felt like family. Yet we were implicitly taught that sickness and suffering were the consequences of refusing to live by the right morals or rules. When I was a teenager, my dad was even chided for bringing friends of mine to church dressed in T-shirts and shorts, the only clothes they had. My dad didn't mince words, telling his fellow deacons to get over it. "Christ wouldn't be trying to keep those kids out of church. They need to feel safe here, so stop being judgmental." The matter was quickly dropped, but I never forgot my dad's willingness to stand up for my friends. I wanted to show that same care to the people in my new town.

Witnessing the tragedy of innocent people being blamed for dying young caused me to question the prevailing emphasis of my upbringing and medical training on personal responsibility. Harshly judging people whose fate had been sealed in childhood, before they made any of their own choices, reminded me of Ryan White's experience. Inspired by his example and my dad's insights into Christ's love for and acceptance of others, I began to contemplate society's moral obligation to ensure all people have equal access to health, opportunity, and above all, life.

The work in Haiti of one of my personal heroes, Dr. Paul Farmer, encouraged me that a doctor could impact the health of individuals by partnering with the community to ensure that a person's social status never denied them access to the benefits of scientific and social progress. A system that harms people in this way, he said, inflicts *structural violence*—violent because it harms people; structural because it is embedded into our cultural, political, and economic systems.[10]

I realized the biggest obstacle to prevent the poor in Austin from achieving their full potential—physically, mentally, and spiritually—was their lack of such basics as nutrition, shelter, safety, and connection. For that reason, I couldn't focus only on bringing basic services like prenatal care, immunizations, and cancer screenings while ignoring the social structures that determined a person's health. The thing that nagged at my heart most was the realization that by allowing these disparities to continue, we were defining whose lives mattered and whose did not.

Although I suspected multigenerational structural violence had turned Austin into a breeding ground of disability, disease, and death, I didn't discover how destructive the deprivation was to families right away. Somehow, in all my interactions with city and county officials, not one person had warned me of the rampant drug abuse, homelessness, sex work, teen pregnancy, childhood abuse, and neglect that had plagued the community for decades. And no one could have predicted the utter mayhem that lay ahead.

. . . .

As I explored ways to address the pervasive unmet social determinants of health plaguing Austin's struggling families, I was introduced to Carolyn King at a meeting of the Scott County Partnership, a group devoted to developing services for the disadvantaged in our community. As I got to know her, she told me that she had arrived in Scott County in the late 1970s when she became director of early childhood development programs for New Hope Services. This social services agency, founded to serve the needs of people with developmental disabilities, was based in Jeffersonville, about thirty-five miles south of Austin.

King may conduct herself with all the culture and stateliness of a New England socialite, but she's as gritty as they come. Early on, she secured a van to ensure that kids from Austin could also receive New Hope's services. She often visited area families, sometimes finding homes without electricity or running water. Once she met a mom who was so overwhelmed and distraught that she tossed a loaf of bread on the floor as a meal for her kids. In the 1980s, Carolyn began collaborating with Jean Robbins, director of Scott County's Women, Infants, and Children (WIC) program, kindling a collaborative spirit in the community that would become vital in the years ahead. Frustrated that low-income families had to travel between multiple sites across the county to receive services for their children, they helped mobilize the community to open a facility to house all children and family services called Kids Place.

The first Kids Place opened in Scottsburg in 1988; another opened in Austin about eight years later. Unfortunately, the county soon discovered it could only support one site. So the Austin Kids Place closed after a few years to become one of the many abandoned buildings scattered across town.

Nonetheless, the Scottsburg Kids Place received national awards for demonstrating the effectiveness of community collaboration. The *New York Times* even quoted King: "We wanted [Kids Place] to be a nice place for people to come to. We wanted to have a place that really showed children that they're valued . . . a place people could be proud to come to and not feel like they were second-rate."[11]

In 1997, Scottsburg's mayor asked King to develop a county-wide coalition to unite workforce development, education, and human services, the way she had for childhood development. A year later, the Scott County Partnership was incorporated, and King became the first executive director.

Later that year the Austin Rural Enterprise Community (AREC) was formed after the community received a $22 million grant from the federal housing and urban development agency. At that time, Austin still had open sewers, and many areas lacked running water. AREC expanded and modernized the water and sewer system, bringing the town into the twentieth century. But the goal, Carolyn told me, was to eventually open facilities patterned after those in Scottsburg that offered education and job training. Given the interest I had in improving the health and lives of Austin's residents, Carolyn helped me partner with AREC. Since God had called me to Austin, I remained confident that He was slowly showing me Austin's unseen people while connecting me with the right people to help.

CHAPTER 3

TOO CLOSE
TO HOME

· · · · · · · · · ·

There is this difference between the growth of some human beings
and that of others: In the one case, it is a continuous dying,
in the other, a continuous resurrection.

GEORGE MACDONALD

IN MY OFFICE, I relished doing what I had been trained to do and knew I could do well: preventative care, chronic disease management, prenatal care, and well child checks. It was my new partnership with the Austin Rural Enterprise Community (AREC), however, that gave me the most hope that we could improve people's lives by increasing local access to health services and their awareness of the social determinants of health, such as basic needs for food and shelter, safety, social support, and employment.

My reluctance to turn anyone away from our clinic made it hard to cover our overhead, so month after month, I needed the hospital's help to keep the doors open. Eventually, my practice adviser told me that I needed to stop seeing Medicaid patients and people without insurance. But I couldn't imagine why God would bring me to a place like this only for me to refuse to see the people who needed me the most.

When I sought advice from a prominent member of the community, he told me that some doctors were able to make it financially by writing a lot of prescriptions for pain pills. He said he knew a few doctors who could see ten to fifteen patients an hour that way.

"There's plenty of folks who'd line up for that 'round here!" he assured me.

My stomach turned as I thought about my grandpa Lames and my mom's younger sister Sally. My mom told me Grandpa frequently called Aunt Sally his favorite, freely sharing his addiction with her. We have a few pictures of Sally as a child, obviously drunk. Later she began abusing prescription drugs as well. As if returning a "favor," she taught my grandpa how to melt down their pain pills to inject. They became a father-daughter team, finding health-care providers who would supply their habit, selling their extra pills for profit, and eventually succumbing to a similar tragic fate.

No, from what I had seen in my first few months of practice, the people of Austin had enough problems without me willingly introducing another one to the mix.

Little did I know . . . the problem was already there.

. . . .

Slowly I started picking up on a pattern. Patients from all walks of life were coming into the clinic requesting narcotic pain pills, anxiety medicines, and strong muscle relaxers—often together. The combination that troubled me most was OxyContin (extended-release oxycodone), Xanax (alprazolam), and Soma (carisoprodol). I saw so many people hooked on that dangerous combination, I named it the devil's triad. That's when I began a "do not prescribe" list for my practice with those three drugs at the top.

One day, a young woman named Samantha came in to see me. In her midtwenties, petite, with long brown hair, Samantha was friendly with a calm, pleasant demeanor. She had undergone surgery to address a pinched nerve in her lower back and, several months later, was still suffering chronic pain.

"I thought I was doing better," she explained, "but now the pain has come back even worse than before."

She appeared to be in genuine discomfort. I had requested her medical records and saw that she had been prescribed Lortab, a narcotic painkiller that is a combination of hydrocodone and acetaminophen.

"That's a pretty powerful pain reliever," I said.

"It seems to work." She shrugged. "I was starting to run out, and you're so much closer than my other doctor that I figured it would be easier to come to you."

"That makes sense," I said. "Are you taking any other medications?"

"Nope," she replied, shaking her head.

"Okay," I said. "We'll just need to run a urine drug screen first. As long as the results confirm you're just taking the Lortab and nothing else, we'll be good to go."

"Cool." She smiled.

As part of my protocol, I always insisted on seeing a patient's medical records. That was sometimes challenging back then because we had to rely on doctors either faxing or mailing the physical records to us. However, that was the only way to track patients' prescriptions since there was no universal drug database at the time. I also confirmed what my patients were taking by giving them a basic drug screen before prescribing any narcotics.

When Samantha's tests came back showing only Lortab in her system, I had her come back in so I could make sure she understood the expectations.

"Now, just so we're clear," I explained, "the goal of the Lortab is to improve function, *not* to relieve all of your pain."

"Got it," she said, nodding politely from her perch on the edge of my exam table.

"I'd like you to come in next week for a follow-up, so I can make sure you're taking this correctly and see how it's working."

She nodded again. "Okay."

Then I handed her a sheet of paper. "This is a contract that I need you to sign. It's standard procedure. It basically states that you agree not to share or sell your medication, that you will not take any other medications in conjunction with the Lortab, and that you agree to submit to random drug screens and pill counts to ensure that the medication is being used properly."

"Wow," she said, scanning the document. "That's some serious stuff."

I made sure to catch her eye and then confirmed, "Yes, it is. Lortab is highly addictive, and if you mix it with other medications—especially other narcotics—it can be deadly."

She flipped the sheet over to finish reading the consent form, took a deep breath, and looking up at me, asked, "Where do I sign?"

After she signed the agreement, we talked a little more about other things she could do to help ease the pain in her back, like stretching exercises, different sleeping positions, and hot and cold compresses. She was polite, agreeable, and seemed relieved to finally have a practicing physician in her hometown.

I saw Samantha four or five more times over the next several months to check on her progress with physical therapy and to ensure she was compliant with her medication. I was pleased that she was following the protocol and seemed to be managing her pain well.

About four months after her first visit, a random drug screen came back showing traces of two other narcotics in her system. I was shocked. I was also disappointed—not only in Samantha, but in myself. I thought for sure growing up with stories of how my aunt Sally and grandpa Lames scammed doctors into feeding their addictions, I would see it coming. But Samantha's congenial nature completely blindsided me. I had wanted to practice close to my hometown, but considering my grandpa and aunt Sally's history with prescription drugs, this hit just a little *too* close to home.

As I sat at my desk reviewing the results of the screen, I realized there was only one thing to do. Throughout my four years of medical school and three years of residency training, we had been taught to dismiss any patients who abused drugs. They simply were not worth dealing with. "They can't be helped until they hit rock bottom," we were told. "All addicts quit using—one way or the other" was the morbid motto.

So I sent Samantha a letter in the mail informing her that, because she had broken her contract with me, I was unable to continue to see her as a patient. It upset me greatly to do it. I genuinely liked Samantha. But dark memories of the way addiction had caused my family to suffer still haunted me. I didn't want to have anything to do with that world, so I simply washed my hands of the whole affair. If that was the way Samantha wanted to ruin her life, she would have to do it without my help.

· · · · · · · · · ·

A few days later, a professional fiftysomething man named Robert came to see me asking for Percocet and Xanax.

"That can be a deadly combination," I cautioned him.

"Well," he countered, "just the Percocet will do."

I gave him a quick once-over. He seemed to be in good shape. Medium build, clean-shaven, suit and tie. I asked him why he needed a prescription pain pill.

He said, "It's not for pain. I travel back and forth to Asia quite frequently for business, and—" he paused for a second, then cleared his throat—"my . . . wife is leaving me," he confessed somewhat sheepishly. "It helps me deal with the stress."

I smiled sympathetically. If anyone could relate to a demanding work schedule putting strain on a marriage, it was me. Leah and I were still struggling to find our emotional center. It wasn't unusual for weeks to go by with us barely saying a word to each other. In fact, I had recently moved out of our bedroom into a spare room in the basement. Still . . .

"That's not what Percocet is for," I countered. "If you'd like, we can get you set up with a therapist and do a trial of an anti-depressant."

"Why?" he shot back. "I know the Percocet works. Plus, I don't have time to go to a know-it-all therapist."

"Sir, I sincerely want to help you," I said reassuringly. "But I can't just prescribe Percocet without there being a legitimate medical reason."

He cocked his head and asked, "Like what?" I could see his wheels turning.

"Basically, for pain that's not relieved by other, more conservative options," I explained.

He shifted a bit, reached down, grabbed his left hip, and grimaced slightly—nothing showy—and said, "Sometimes this old war injury really gets me down on those long transpacific flights."

I thought back to the stories I'd heard of my grandpa using a walker my aunt Sally bought for him at a yard sale to trick doctors into prescribing him pain pills. This well-dressed, well-mannered man wasn't quite so dramatic, but there was no doubt in my mind that it was the same trick.

Pretty brazen of him to switch tactics during the same office visit, I thought. Clearly, this guy was used to getting what he wanted.

"That's not the way it works," I said flatly, fully realizing this was *exactly* the way it worked—far too often.

Then he switched tactics yet again.

"Look, Doc, if you don't prescribe it to me, I'll just go buy some off a buddy of mine." Before I could even respond, he put his hands up in mock protest and said, "I'm just being up front and honest with you because I want to do the right thing."

"Are you doing that now?" I asked, catching him off guard. He didn't answer.

"If I ran a drug screen on you right now, it would be positive, right?"

He nodded.

I looked him directly in the eye. "We need to get you help. What you're doing now won't lead anywhere good. Trust me. I've seen it."

His posture stiffened and he opened his mouth as if to put up an argument, but then he paused, sat back a bit, and reluctantly nodded. We talked through things for the next thirty minutes or so, and after some convincing on my end, he finally agreed to see a therapist.

As he was leaving, he paused at the door. He turned back, but not quite far enough to look me in the eyes, and said, "Doctors usually just prescribe those meds to me." After another pause, he looked down at his feet and added, "I've known I need help for a long time, but this is the first time anyone has ever taken the time to listen." Then he looked at me with tears in his eyes and said, "Thank you."

Twice in the past week, I had been caught by surprise—first with Samantha and now with Robert. I had always thought I'd be able to pinpoint someone with substance use disorder right away. I knew what they looked like because I'd grown up with them. But neither Samantha nor Robert fit the typical profile.

One question nagged at me: *Why had I treated them differently? Why had I spent so much time listening to Robert and coaxing him into counseling while never even asking Samantha to tell me her story?*

· · · · · · · · · ·

"Hello?" a female's voice called out angrily. "I need to talk to Dr. Cooke! Hello?" The woman began banging on the reception window, which Elizabeth had pulled closed for lunch.

I came out of the exam room in time to see Elizabeth hurrying back to her desk. I followed her partway and saw the silhouette of a woman through the frosted glass.

"What's going on?" I asked. "Who is that?"

Elizabeth pulled the window open a few inches. It was Samantha.

"Dr. Cooke cut me off!" she hollered, throwing my torn-up letter at Elizabeth and spewing a string of profanities.

"Please don't curse, ma'am," Elizabeth said calmly, but with a nervous edge to her voice. "Let me check."

She turned to me, her eyes wide with fright. Behind her, I could see Samantha pacing frantically around the waiting room. She was running her fingers through her hair with one hand and nervously chewing the nails on the other. She looked disheveled, and she was muttering something to herself that I couldn't quite make out.

I took a second to collect my thoughts.

"Dr. Cooke?" Elizabeth asked warily. "What should we do?"

"She broke the contract she signed with me," I said as calmly as I could. "She was just using us to feed her habit. I'm not willing to be a part of that." Elizabeth continued to stare at me. "Please tell her there's nothing I can do."

Elizabeth took a deep breath, went back to her desk, and slid the window open a little further. Samantha stopped dead in her tracks and zeroed in on her, her eyes wide and expectant.

"I'm sorry," Elizabeth began. "Dr. Cooke said there is nothing he can do since you broke your contract with him."

Suddenly, there was an explosion of profanity and commotion. Samantha started ripping pictures off the wall, knocking over furniture, and throwing things. Elizabeth locked the window and backed away from the desk. Samantha pounded on the locked door to the exam room area and the reception window. I prayed the glass would hold. During all my previous interactions with Samantha, she had been such a kind, soft-spoken woman. This out-of-control creature in my waiting room showed no hint of that person.

As Elizabeth and I stared in disbelief, we heard Amy quickly usher the last patient out the back door. When she returned, she picked up the phone and called 911 while Samantha continued to wreak havoc in the waiting room.

"What do we do?" Elizabeth looked at me frantically.

"Stay back here," I said to both of them. "And wait for the police to get here."

Samantha continued to unleash her fury, throwing things, screaming, and cursing like a madwoman.

Thank God nobody else was here, I thought.

The police responded within minutes. We stayed in the back until they placed Samantha in handcuffs. She continued to rant as one of the officers led her to the patrol car. We opened the door to the waiting room to let the other officer in. The waiting room was destroyed. Chairs were scattered, tables smashed, and posters ripped apart.

The officer told us that they knew her well, which shocked me. It turned out that she had been arrested several times for drug possession and destruction of property, but every time she was released, she would return to her old lifestyle.

I went to the window and looked out. Samantha was sitting in the back seat of the patrol car, head hanging down, arms still locked behind her, hair covering her face. In that instant, I thought of my aunt Sally. Though my parents hadn't allowed me to spend much time around her, I remember her best when she was about Samantha's age. She'd only lived another fifteen years. I wondered if, like Sally, Samantha had grown up with dysfunction and trauma. Did she have anyone who would love, support, and inspire her like my mom had? If not . . .

"What kind of help will she get?" I asked.

The police officer just shrugged.

I would come to find out that there were hundreds of people

living the same revolving-door life as Samantha with recurring stays in the local jail. They'd be locked up for a few weeks or months, go through withdrawal, and then get released only to resume the same dysfunctional life. It all seemed so hopeless—so heartless. *Almost as heartless*, I lamented, *as sending a form letter to someone in crisis.*

CHAPTER 4

SHARKS
IN THE WATER

· · · · · · · · · ·

The world is indeed full of peril, and in it there are many dark places;
but still there is much that is fair, and though in all lands love is
now mingled with grief, it grows perhaps the greater.

J. R. R. TOLKIEN

AROUND THIS SAME TIME, I met a young girl named Tammy. She was seventeen when she first came to see me. When I asked what brought her in, she told me she thought she might be pregnant. A simple urine test confirmed that she was. But her urine also confirmed that she was using the narcotic OxyContin.

As she sat alone, nervously picking at her cuticles, I was struck by how small and frail—and terrified—she looked. She was only a child. I thought of my own daughter, Moirah, then five, and my heart ached.

Where are this girl's parents?

I sat down, wheeled my chair over to the table, rested the test results in my lap, and leaned forward.

"Tammy," I said gently, "the test shows that you *are* pregnant."

Her eyes left mine and focused on the floor.

"The tests also show that you're taking OxyContin."

Her entire body stiffened, and she clutched the edge of the table so tightly, her knuckles turned white.

"Is . . . my baby okay?" Her voice was barely a whisper.

"I can't tell that without running some other tests." Medically speaking, the OxyContin did put her baby at risk of poor growth, preterm delivery, and withdrawal after birth. But the risk of taking Tammy off the OxyContin put the baby at even greater risk, as studies have shown that withdrawal significantly increases the risk of miscarriage.

"Did you come here by yourself?"

She nodded.

"Tammy, where are your parents?" She lifted her head and gazed as if she could see something beyond the blinds covering the window. Her eyes brimmed with tears.

"Do you live with your mom and dad?"

She shook her head no and wiped the tears that had begun to fall.

"Would you like to talk about it?" I sat back and let the silence sit between us. "It's okay," I assured her.

"Mom died four years ago," she said quietly. Then with a touch of bitterness in her voice, added, "She was an alcoholic and an addict. She OD'd when I was thirteen."

"I'm so sorry." What is one supposed to say at times like these? Even the sincerest of sentiments always seemed to come out sounding trite and banal.

"That's not something anyone should have to deal with," I said, "especially at thirteen. Losing your mom that way isn't a normal experience and honestly shouldn't feel normal. So you shouldn't feel ashamed of feeling angry or lost. You have every right to feel losing your mom that way was unfair because it very much was."

She looked at me as if no one had ever told her that before and wondered whether I was being sincere.

"What happened after that?" I asked.

"Dad raised me," she continued, the tears still flowing freely.

"But Mom's death really hit him hard, and he started using and selling drugs himself. Then he got arrested and ended up going to prison."

"Who took care of you?" I asked.

"I got put in foster care," she said, looking down again. The memory spread a pained expression across her face.

"Is that where you're living now?"

She shook her head. "I'm living with my boyfriend."

I had already been shocked to learn from other young women like her that "boyfriend" sometimes meant an older man who'd give them a place to stay in exchange for sex or even pimped them out in exchange for something of value to him, like drugs.

I steadied myself as I asked about her boyfriend. Any negative reaction from me could spook her, and she was being so brave by telling me her story. It turned out he was also a seventeen-year-old kid who was just as scared about their future. Without family members helping them, they'd likely be homeless.

Tammy reassured me. "Shawn's a good guy. He's trying to find a job to support us. But we're both hooked on the Oxys."

"Where do you get the drugs?"

She shrugged and smirked wryly, almost as if I had asked where she got the air she breathed. "I've been taking them since I was fourteen. They weren't hard to get. Someone gave me a pain pill they said would make me feel better." She paused, then glanced at me matter-of-factly. "At fourteen, I didn't know what it was. I just knew it helped."

"Helped what?" I asked.

She ran her fingers through her hair and sighed. Staring at the window blinds, she said, "Take the pain away. When I took that pill, I felt like I could function and almost be whatever normal is. I've been using ever since."

In Austin, there were many descriptive words that should never go together: *young, alone, addicted, poor, desperate,* and in some cases, *pregnant.* In the space of a few quiet moments, I discovered that Tammy was all of them. By this time, I was used to seeing teenage girls needing prenatal care. Still, this sweet, soft-spoken teenager broke my heart.

I couldn't help but contemplate the randomness of our start in life. We can't control where or how we are raised. Yet often we give all the credit for successes and all the blame for failures to an individual's character, work ethic, or intelligence. How can we be so blind to the obvious?

"Who we are cannot be separated from where we're from," writes bestselling author Malcolm Gladwell.[1] All the wonderful traits we ascribe to successful people—qualities like intelligence, hard work, ingenuity, and integrity—pay off and absolutely matter. But many of these attributes are developed through the investments made by parents, teachers, and mentors, and, even then, only in the right environment with the right opportunities. Every seed carries a potential that sprouts only in the right soil, while being protected and nourished. Who was there to mentor, protect, and nourish Tammy when she needed someone most?

Instead of being moved by compassion to help the hurting or even work to change a system that restricts access to safety, wellness, and opportunity, too many good, God-fearing people fall for rationales that prevent them from acting on their moral obligation to help the hurting:

"We" are mentally, biologically, or spiritually better than "they" are.
Helping "them" enables bad people to do bad things.
We must protect ourselves from desperate people because they are dangerous.
We worked hard for what we have and must protect what we have from "them."

As much as I hate to admit it, for far too long I embraced similar attitudes toward people like Tammy who abused drugs. Americans often get caught up in the concept of rugged individualism. I was realizing that this concept is a gross oversimplification of success and, in truth, little more than a myth. We all require community. Gladwell puts it like this: "We look at the young Bill Gates and marvel that our world allowed that thirteen-year-old to become a fabulously successful entrepreneur. But that's the wrong lesson. Our world only allowed one thirteen-year-old unlimited access to a time-sharing terminal in 1968."[2]

Yes, Gates had the talent and drive to take advantage of the unprecedented opportunities he was given at thirteen. But what about a young girl born into a poverty-stricken region of rural Indiana with virtually no access to upward mobility, one whose mom was high or drunk throughout her childhood and ended up dying of an overdose, resulting in her dad turning to those same drugs to cope with his loss?

Tammy's life at thirteen looked starkly different from the life Gates was handed. At fourteen, she found a pill that took all that pain away and allowed her to feel normal. If we are willing to venture through the unfamiliar landscape of another person's situation and heart, we convert that stranger into a person with whom we can empathize.

I met with Tammy frequently over the next several months, mentoring and encouraging her. By getting her access to a form of medication-assisted treatment called methadone, we helped her control her addiction to OxyContin without putting her through withdrawal during her pregnancy. She eventually delivered a healthy baby girl.

· · · · · · · · · ·

When I had come to Austin, I believed that America truly was the land of opportunity and that those who worked hard and made good choices could do anything they wanted. After all, I'd seen my parents' incredible perseverance and determination as they completed college and gained entrance into the respectable middle class. My mom even became a physician after several years in the nursing field.

Some people would look at my mom and conclude that she succeeded because she took personal responsibility and "pulled herself up by her bootstraps." Likewise, they might view my aunt Sally as a weak woman who just didn't try hard enough to beat her substance use disorder. In all honesty, that is how I once looked at their situations.

But as I met patients like Samantha and Tammy, I recognized that there had been a critical difference between my mom's childhood and Sally's. Along the way, my mom had met people who took her under their wing, providing her with a sense of safety and self-confidence. My aunt, on the other hand, had seen nothing but dysfunction and abuse. She first became pregnant at thirteen but lost that baby—and more of her hope. Married five times, she never found the love and validation she craved.

I've come to believe that the outcome of people born into poverty can often be determined by the answer to a single question: Was there one person he or she could count on for protection, encouragement, and inspiration? Children who have someone like that learn a very different lesson about life than those who don't. Their world is filled with either light, love, and life or darkness, despair, and death.

Paraphrasing C. S. Lewis, I believe in love as I believe in sunlight: not because I see *it*, but because by it, I see *everything else*.[3] How is someone to find their way when they are lost without sunlight? People who have never experienced the light of love, trapped in a world of darkness, grow sick and fearful. They've never felt safe or known beauty in the world. Then if others come rushing in too suddenly to light up their world, they will naturally hide their sensitive eyes and hearts and even fight back against those who could offer help.

. . . .

Something didn't add up. I wondered how a town without medical access had so much access to prescription drugs. So I decided to do a little digging. I was astonished to discover that Austin had led the state in prescription drug abuse for years.[4] A public health expert I talked to estimated that around 20 percent of Austin was hooked on prescription drugs.

One longtime resident named Phil told me he smoked his first joint when he was thirteen. Leaving the mines of Appalachia, his dad had moved the family to Austin. "To the eyes of a ten-year-old country boy raised in Big Rock Holler, Austin was like a big city. But kids had nothing much to do in Austin," he told me matter-of-factly, "except maybe hang out at the local pool hall."

He said the Austin kids hated the "preppy" kids from nearby Scottsburg. "They had more money there, and there was more to do. It was like a whole different world just five miles down the road.

"When I was sixteen," he continued, "a buddy and I skipped school and tried cocaine. After that, I started popping pills, selling cocaine at school, and then I tried meth.

"After high school, I trafficked meth, pills, and weed from Austin to California to Kentucky, and while I was traveling, I'd get prescriptions for painkillers from ERs, urgent cares, and dentists."

"How did you convince them to write you a prescription?" I asked.

He just shrugged. "I'd tell them my teeth hurt and they'd just write 'em out, write 'em out."

I remembered what the local official told me about doctors who would indiscriminately write prescriptions just to make extra cash. That meant pretty much anyone could get their hands on powerful, potentially deadly narcotics and then use some and resell the rest.

I also spoke with a woman named Deborah who grew up in Austin in the sixties and seventies, a time when the town was still steeped in Norman Rockwell charm.

"Back then, weed was all I ever heard of," she told me. "But after I came home from college, the city slowly devolved. I started to hear stories about people abusing Lortab." That was the same drug that Samantha had gotten hooked on.

"Where'd they get it?" I asked.

"A lot of people got prescriptions from dentists," she explained. "Others got them by traveling to pain clinics up north or down south. They could get enough to sell some here to cover their cost."

Then in the 1970s the economy collapsed.[5] As people began to suffer, they increasingly turned to the drugs pouring into town. In the midnineties, OxyContin showed up. "It was as if a bomb exploded," she said. "My hometown—including many of my friends and family—was left shattered and broken."

When I researched what happened following the FDA approval of OxyContin in 1996, I discovered that drug reps shifted their attention from pain specialists to primary care physicians.[6] They encouraged frontline doctors to prescribe pills once reserved to treat pain from cancer, surgery, and serious injuries for common problems like chronic back pain. This represented a yet-untapped lucrative market of at least 25 million Americans who could take their drug the way others took medication for blood pressure or cholesterol. Reps even provided "starter coupons" allowing patients to try OxyContin for free.[7]

Pharmaceutical companies such as Purdue Pharma targeted vulnerable places like Appalachia, awash in chronic pain from hard labor in fields and coal mines.[8] Purdue drug reps told doctors OxyContin could relieve pain without creating highs like the other opioid painkillers, so people were not likely to get hooked on it.

Drug reps generously handed out thousands of copies of promotional videos to patients and physicians. With titles such as "From One Pain Patient to Another: Advice from Patients Who Have Found Relief" and "I Got My Life Back: Patients in Pain Tell Their Story," the videos featured experts assuring viewers that these painkillers cause addiction in much less than one percent of patients, erroneously citing as scientific evidence a five-sentence letter published in the *New England Journal of Medicine*.[9]

With the help of this massive marketing push, OxyContin prescriptions for noncancer pain shot up tenfold between 1997 and 2002, when sales exceeded $1.5 billion. OxyContin was a huge hit for Purdue Pharma, accounting for 90 percent of its total prescription sales by 2001.[10]

Like sharks in the water, Purdue Pharma responded by doubling the number of sales reps calling on busy doctors' offices, spending $200 million on marketing OxyContin in 2001 alone.[11] The FDA had already cited these unprecedented, aggressive tactics twice, including ads without warnings about potentially fatal risks. Purdue Pharma was told to stop running these misleading ads but instead chose to add a black box warning as part of a risk management plan.[12]

During OxyContin's first five years on the market, Purdue Pharma gave over five thousand health-care professionals all-inclusive trips to resort areas such as Boca Raton, Florida, and Scottsdale, Arizona, in exchange for being in their speakers' bureau. Once trained, these professionals shared the message with colleagues at medical conferences and grand rounds presentations in hospitals. Purdue Pharma ended up funding over twenty thousand educational programs from 1996 to mid-2002.[13]

Meanwhile, the drumbeat about the need to treat pain continued. The Federation of Medical Boards even suggested punishing doctors who undertreated pain. In 1999, the *New York Times* reported how state medical boards were following this recommendation. When doctors failed to fall in line with this new "standard of care," health-care systems would discipline them by sending them to re-education programs (often with material developed by pharmaceutical companies). The *New York Times* said this "underscores the medical community's changing attitudes about how doctors should help patients deal with severe and chronic pain."[14]

Juries began to find doctors guilty of negligence, awarding

millions of dollars to "undertreated" pain patients and their families.[15] In 2001, the *Journal of Law, Medicine & Ethics* published a piece entitled "Relieving Unnecessary, Treatable Pain for the Sake of Human Dignity." It said, in part:

> A physician who refuses either to treat the pain in conformity with current guidelines or to refer the patient is acting unethically. One could even argue that refusal to treat a pain patient is analogous to refusing to treat HIV-positive patients. . . . Pain management obligations should be shouldered by physicians, with continuous feedback and attention to the level and quality of such management by the hospital. A failure to provide training and feedback and to detect physician reluctance to use proper techniques provides an argument of corporate negligence.[16]

The Joint Commission on Accreditation of Healthcare Organizations, the main health-care accreditation body in America, followed that year with the requirement to treat pain more aggressively. Their report included the example of treating pain as the fifth vital sign as advised by the American Pain Society. This placed a patient's reported experience of pain on the same level as the four signs of life measurable by an examiner: heart rate, blood pressure, breathing, and temperature.

They also repeated the erroneous claim that addiction was rare, stating, "In general, patients in pain do not become addicted to opioids. Although the actual risk of addiction is unknown, it is thought to be quite low."[17]

I was in residency when this shift occurred and remember being trained to start asking patients to rate their pain on a 0–10 scale. My colleagues and I quickly began to suspect patients were seeking drugs if they reported their pain level was above ten. We'd cringe inside when patients who had been calmly answering our questions and whose other vital signs were normal told us, "My pain's a 15, Doc. It's killing me." We were required to treat their pain just as aggressively as if we were trying to reduce a patient's life-threatening elevated blood pressure.

This intense pressure on the medical community simultaneously contributed to a dramatic increase in prescriptions for other controlled medications, like Xanax. What predictably followed was an explosion of prescription drug misuse and abuse. In 1999, around four million Americans were abusing prescription drugs. By the time I established my practice in Austin in 2004, that number had grown to 6.4 million—representing 2.6 percent of all adults.[18] Even more startling, more than one in ten high school seniors reported using pain pills nonmedically.[19]

Pills began to flow freely from the notorious Florida pill mills to Chicago. And to get there, they would pass along the busy interstate that ran right through Austin. The pills then found their way into the hands of people like Samantha, Tammy, Phil, and countless others living in the shadows, blocked from the healing light of love by a world too busy to notice.

CHAPTER 5

FORSAKEN

· · · · · · · · ·

Expecting life to treat you well because you are a good person
is like expecting an angry bull not to charge
because you are a vegetarian.

SHARI R. BARR

OPENING A CLINIC with very little support in a forsaken place like Austin had not been a good business decision. But since this was where I believed God wanted me to serve Him, I had no doubt He would provide. Still, as the Austin Rural Enterprise Community (AREC) executive director and I explored ways to help struggling families, we felt overwhelmed by the seemingly endless horde of mangled lives churned out by the socioeconomic system deeply entrenched in Austin. I was struggling to keep my clinic open to anyone in need while keeping my heart closed to the feelings of doubt and futility clawing for a way in. I began to feel stalked by the same darkness haunting my patients, and I knew fear for the well-being of my family and me had already followed me home.

Around that time, I met Rick, a young minister whose church was known as a supportive community for people in seemingly hopeless circumstances. Since my marriage was increasingly becoming a desperate situation, I had begun attending his church.

Pastor Rick and I would go out walking to pray for and meet with the people of Austin. One day we went to the trailer park on the west side of town to visit with people and see what the church could do for them. We found whole families living in RV-sized trailers, with broken windows covered by plastic secured with duct tape. The children wore dirty clothes, and their parents looked lost, enveloped in smoke, clutter, and despair.

I thought of Mom telling me that her earliest memories were of hiding under her bed to escape the chaos unfolding around her. Often squatting with their four children in nothing more than a shack, her parents were either intoxicated, fighting, or both. Loud noises still startle my mom. To protect her kids from Grandpa's drunken fits, my grandma Lames would sometimes seek refuge with her kids somewhere safer than home. But my mom also remembers Grandma seeking refuge for herself in the company of one of her many "boyfriends," leaving my mom and her siblings to fend for themselves. That description mirrored the hopelessness I was seeing now.

Rick and I were there to tell these families about the love of God and invite them to church, but we had no way to provide for their basic needs—clothes, transportation, food, or a way to escape their precarious way of life. Rick remained optimistic, assuring me that at least their eternal salvation would be secure. But I struggled with the thought of them being doomed to hell on earth first.

As some of the town's poorer residents became brave enough to see me, I learned of patients living on the streets and in cars, and of families of ten to fifteen people squatting in abandoned derelict shacks with no running water or electricity, burning garbage and what few possessions they had to stay warm. Some hadn't eaten for days; they had no clean clothes and nowhere to bathe.

One young woman told me she frequently traded sex for diapers, food for her children, or a safe place to stay for the night. Her confession seemed too unthinkable to be true until one day, while out exploring the north side of town, I stumbled upon an abandoned shack with broken windows and no electricity. Looking through the cracked glass into the filthy house filled with trash and shadows, I noticed a pile of blankets in a far corner that had been cleaned out. A pile of diapers bore witness to the fact that some young mother had been living there alone, in destitute conditions, with an infant.

Tears filled my eyes, and I took a few steps back in horror. This was not a nightmare to wake from in a cold sweat; this was someone's reality that I had stumbled into. I was the one the county had brought in to change things. But how do you help someone living in the shadows, unseen by the rest of society?

I searched several blocks around the house for the young mother, not really knowing what I'd do if I found her.

I drove home in complete silence, walked in the door, and hugged my wife.

"Are you okay?" she asked.

"No, I don't think I am." I didn't know what else to say but managed, "I'm so sorry. I don't know what I've gotten us into."

· · · · · · · · · ·

I began to feel like a hostage forced to watch an invisible force wreak havoc on the innocent people I was called to protect.

When I reached out for help, there was none to be found. Churches generally didn't want to deal with the drug abuse, sex work, and homelessness. The local hospital was unable to commit resources beyond what they had already invested in helping me to establish my primary care clinic in Austin. Other hospitals declined to help since there wouldn't be a return on their investment. The behavioral health center, which had a clinic in Scottsburg, told me they already provided services for all residents in Scott County. I tried to explain the desperation in Austin and how many residents lacked transportation to Scottsburg. I even offered them access to my clinic space. But in the end, they told me they didn't have the funding or resources to expand into such a small market as Austin when they already had a clinic nearby.

My patients weren't the only ones in dire need of outside help. Once the hospital had fulfilled its financial commitment to my clinic, I realized I wouldn't generate enough income to cover expenses and pay my staff. So I started picking up shifts in the emergency department at Scott Memorial Hospital to help make ends meet.

Still, month after month we were barely able to keep the clinic doors open. It was challenging trying to balance seeing patients in the office during the week, making rounds at the hospital, delivering babies, moonlighting in the ER on weekends, *and* remaining available to my family. Leah and I had added two daughters, Mirial and Elissa, to our family since arriving in Austin, so we both found ourselves stretched.

I felt increasingly stressed by these mounting tensions, along with the vicarious trauma and despair I was experiencing through the lives of patients. As the pressure built, I met with Ron Murphy, the administrator of Scott County's health department. He listened quietly as I described the extreme conditions I saw in the lives of my patients in Austin.

"Things are even worse than I thought," he said when I'd finished.

"So what can we do?" I asked.

"We're already underfunded and understaffed," he said, looking pained. "We barely get enough from the state to hire one community health nurse to cover the entire county. We don't even receive enough funding to offer basic HIV or STD testing."

"Isn't there anything you can do to help?" I pleaded.

"I can get you in touch with the people at the Indiana State Department of Health if you'd like," he offered.

After I'd left a few messages with the department of health, Patrick Durkin, head of the department's primary care division, called me back and I repeated my pitch. I felt like a broken record.

He asked if anyone was helping me. I assured him that I was at a dead end. I detailed the financial challenges my practice faced in caring for many of the town's poor, uninsured, and underinsured. "If I don't find some sort of help, I don't see how I can keep the clinic open," I said.

"There's really not a lot we can do from the state either." He paused, then said, "Have you looked into the Rural Health Clinic program?"

"No, what is that?"

"It allows clinics in underserved areas to receive higher reimbursement for those covered by Medicare and Medicaid."

Getting paid a little more for the work I was already doing would at least keep my practice afloat. Patrick agreed to look into our situation. He called me back a few weeks later.

I felt my spirit sag as he told me, "Well, I don't have the best news, I'm afraid." He said that since our local department of health was so underfunded, no one had completed the paperwork required for Scott County to obtain the necessary underserved status. Without that, I couldn't even apply to become a Rural Health Clinic (RHC).

"Can *we* get the documentation done so I can apply?" I asked. "I'm not sure how else I'll make it."

Patrick told me that my best bet would be to hire a consultant to help.

Now I was really disappointed. How would I ever afford *that*?

Reading into my silence, Patrick suggested he connect me with his predecessor, Ray Guest, who might be willing to help me. Ray, a soft-spoken and friendly older man, offered to partner with me and the executive director of the AREC, who'd also agreed to help.

It took the three of us several years to survey Scott County and the surrounding counties, and then an additional year to fill out the necessary paperwork, but we finally got the federal underserved designation we needed to apply for RHC status.

* * * * * * * * * *

Though I'd chosen to moonlight at the hospital for financial reasons, I loved the unpredictability of the emergency room: I never knew who would walk through the door next. With just twenty-five beds, Scott Memorial was busy enough to constantly have something going on but rarely busy enough to justify having more than one doctor on a shift. In other words, if you had a patient that required all your time and attention, everyone else in the ER would have to wait.

One night, after seeing a steady stream of patients with chest or abdominal pains, coughs, or minor injuries, an agitated young lady rushed up to the registration window, eyes wide in panic and screaming hysterically.

"My sister needs help! She's too weak to get out of my car!"

Both of my nurses immediately rushed out and pulled a very frail twentysomething female from the car. When we moved her from the wheelchair to the stretcher, she began groaning loudly and frantically flailing her arms around. We had no idea what was wrong with her, but based on the track marks we saw running up and down both arms, we had our suspicions. The nurses began hooking her up to the monitors and searching her arms for IV access.

"What's her name?" I asked, checking the young woman's vitals.

A quivering voice in the corner of the room said, "Amber. She's my sister."

I called her name loudly and asked, "Can you hear me? Amber? What's going on?"

"Stop it!" she replied as she slapped at the nurses trying to help her.

I leaned in and turned her head to look her in the face. "Amber, look at me. You're at the hospital and we're trying to help you. We need to know what's going on. Are you in pain?"

"Everywhere," she nodded and groaned.

Exasperated, one of the nurses looked at me and said, "She's used up all her veins. I'm not getting anything."

"Her blood pressure is 64/30 and her pulse is thready," said the other.

I put my stethoscope on her chest and listened to her racing heart and rapid breathing.

"She needs fluids now," I instructed.

"We can't get an IV, doc. She's blown out all her veins," the first nurse repeated.

I thought for a second. This young woman was critically ill, and we had to have IV access to save her life. Amber's sister still stood quietly in the corner, looking frantically from one face to the next.

"I've been wanting to try the new IO device," I blurted out. "Now's as good a time as any. Let's break it out."

An intraosseous infusion (IO) is an efficient way to rapidly give a patient fluids and medications without IV access by essentially drilling a needle directly into the leg bone and forcing fluids into the marrow. It's used only in emergency situations like this one because it's extremely painful. I'd undergone a bone marrow biopsy myself when I was fifteen, and even with a local anesthetic, it was excruciating.

The nurse handed me a small electric drill similar to what I used on weekend projects around the house, and I attached a large needle to it. Holding the drill in my right hand, I felt for the bony landmarks just below Amber's left knee with my left hand. Satisfied I had the correct place, I forced the needle through her skin down to the bone and pulled the trigger.

Amber unleashed a bloodcurdling scream as the nurses strained to hold her still.

Her sister cried out in horror, her hands covering her nose and mouth.

We quickly began pushing fluids into her. It's what her body needed, but that didn't stop her from fighting back against the pain. The nurses held her down as she thrashed about moaning as the fluid pushed its way into her bone marrow, sending waves of pain throughout her body. Unfazed, I ordered two full liters to be administered as rapidly as possible.

"Is something wrong?" her sister pleaded from the corner. "Why is she in so much pain?"

"Bone is exquisitely sensitive," I quickly answered without turning to look at her. I was too busy monitoring Amber's vital signs flashing ominously on the monitor and processing my next steps. Based on everything I was seeing, she was severely dehydrated and likely septic—probably, I concluded, a consequence of reusing needles while injecting drugs.

"She shouldn't have used up all of her veins," one of the nurses murmured knowingly to the other nurse.

As the fluids continued to flow in, Amber's heart rate and blood pressure started to improve. I began pressing below her right collarbone, searching for a landmark where I could place a central line. This meant inserting a very large, several-inch-long needle, about the size of a cooking thermometer, into her chest to pierce one of the largest veins in her emaciated body. This would allow more reliable intravenous access for the fluids, antibiotics, and other medications she needed.

Amber winced and groaned as I sterilized and prepared the area around her collarbone. Then just as I was about to insert the needle, a voice broke my concentration.

"Don't you even care that you're hurting her?"

I had forgotten that Amber's sister was still there. I turned to face her.

"What?"

"You're hurting her, and you don't even seem to care." She wiped away the tears streaming down her face. "I heard you say that you were looking forward to using that drill on her."

I was dumbfounded. I was doing everything possible to save her sister's life.

"I'm sorry," I said flatly, trying to keep the spot I had identified on Amber's collarbone sterile. "We're doing everything we can to stabilize her."

"Yeah, but that's my sister," she shot back, tears flowing. "You're not treating her like a person."

That comment hit me like a bucket of water. I looked into Amber's eyes. Her sister was right. Amber was not just a drug addict suffering the consequences of irrational behavior. She was not a test dummy on which we were practicing our treatment algorithms. Amber was a person who was obviously cherished. She was this tearful young woman's sister.

Reality's veil was lifted ever so slightly, and for a brief moment, Amber became my aunt Sally, and her sister, my mom. One day while I was in college, my mom had raced to the hospital after being told her sister had been taken there after overdosing. My mom was met by Dr. Graves, a physician with whom she worked. With sorrow in his eyes, he told my mom that despite his best efforts, my aunt had died. "I had to call it," the doctor told her.

To "call it" sounded so cold given what had really happened. Mom had worked enough codes to know. They had stripped her sister naked to expose any injuries and to allow unimpeded access to her body; they shoved a tube down her throat to breathe for her. They performed chest compressions, which if done correctly broke ribs. This was a violent, undignified way to die, just as drilling into Amber's leg bone was a brutal way to try stabilizing her. Yet neither Dr. Graves nor I had any choice.

My breath choked on a wave of emotion that washed over me as I imagined my mom pleading with me to treat her sister like a person. This young woman had every right to hold me accountable for my lack of compassion.

Composing myself, I tried to explain, "Your sister desperately needs fluid and this—" I pointed to the IO sticking out of Amber's leg—"is our only option right now."

"Can't you help her be more comfortable?" she asked.

"Of course," I said, making sure I was speaking gently.

I turned back to the nurses. "Go ahead and give her 50 cc of fentanyl."

Then I looked at Amber's sister and said, "That will help ease some of the pain."

Amber almost immediately relaxed, and I went back to inserting the central line. But her sister's admonition continued to echo in my head—and my heart.

· · · · · · · · · ·

The Rural Health Center designation helped, but it was the hope I felt working with the AREC executive director on ways to improve the socioeconomic hardships of families that kept me going. After years of dead ends and roadblocks, we finally experienced a breakthrough by teaming up with Scott Memorial Hospital and the Scott County Family YMCA to repurpose the abandoned Kids Place building on the north side of Austin into a family enrichment center. We planned to call it Sarah's House after the wife of John Morgan, the current CEO of Morgan Foods, because of her heart for children. Since the AREC still had access to millions of federal grant dollars, we planned to use some of that money to renovate, staff, and outfit the center.

Once completed, the center would include meeting rooms, a study lounge with internet access, and a resource library for parents and students. More importantly, the center would offer supplemental programs in the arts, academics, and wellness to enrich people's lives and encourage civic and cultural awareness. Sarah's House would be a beacon of hope for families lost in a landscape darkened by hopelessness and despair.

Then, in late 2007 the unthinkable happened. All the money in the AREC account suddenly disappeared, as did the organization's executive director. The other members of the AREC and I were devastated. And just like that, the fragile hope we had rekindled in Austin faded. Even worse, the scandal tainted Austin's chances of securing future grants.

A few weeks later the worst economic downturn since the Great Depression began casting its shadow over the country. Officially lasting from December 2007 through June 2009, the Great Recession devastated places like Austin. Living conditions, food insecurity, homelessness, and prescription drug use worsened just as those kids raised with the toxic stresses of Austin in the eighties and nineties came into late adolescence and young adulthood.

Frantically tending to the dying embers of hope, I felt frustrated, confused, and powerless. I began to question God about my purpose as a physician and why He'd called me to a place that now seemed forsaken even by Him. With no relief in sight, I began to contemplate quitting my work in Austin.

Worse yet, the shadows darkening the streets of Austin followed me home. Years of marital strife intensified and led us to separate. After so many years of counseling and conflict, I gave up hope and filed for divorce in the spring of 2008. The decision was extremely painful and not one I had ever imagined I would make. I had married believing I was making a lifetime commitment, but our problems seemed unsurmountable and I saw no other option.

We spent the rest of 2008 finalizing the divorce, during which time I grieved the loss of my marriage, my hope in Austin, my purpose as a physician, and my presence as a father. What followed was a monotony of misery, and as the following year seemed to drone on with no relief in sight, I felt progressively more and more exhausted, alone, and forsaken.

I had come to Austin believing that by opening a practice to bring hope and health to the community, I was following God's "perfect plan" for my life. Now that plan—I was no longer sure if it was God's or my own—had shattered into a million jagged pieces, piercing my sense of identity and purpose.

I was miserable and depressed, but it was difficult for me to admit I was not okay. I related to C. S. Lewis's observation during his own depression that "the frequent attempt to conceal mental pain increases the burden: It is easier to say 'My tooth is aching' than to say 'My heart is broken.'"[1]

When I finally did reach out to my friends and my church for help, I felt dismissed, much like when I had asked the church to help my underserved patients. Most of my friends and fellow church members appeared uncomfortable and made clear that it wasn't okay to share my burdens with them. Others bluntly said my pain was a natural consequence of my poor life choices, echoing the claim charged against my patients.

I desperately wanted someone to hear me or understand what I was going through. But it seemed as though my depression was viewed as weakness and evidence that there was something wrong with me. I began to better understand why it was so hard for people like Samantha to ask for help.

The phrases I came to dread the most were "Just get better" or "Get over it." The truth was, I didn't want to get over this pain. It was all I had left of the story I wanted my life to tell. To move past the pain would be to admit that I had failed.

Even at work, I couldn't shake the oppressive weight of despair constantly pressing down on me. Every thought and action took extreme effort. My strength faltered, and I began to struggle to get through the seemingly endless cycle of each day.

My parents were the exception among those to whom I turned in my grief. When I told them I was not doing well, they just listened. No advice, no condemnation. In their gentle, reassuring presence, it felt safe to stop hurting for a little while. Their acceptance of my pain was beautiful, real, and solid. It meant everything.

Fred Rogers once pointed out, "People have said, 'Don't cry' to other people for years and years, and all it has ever meant is, 'I'm too uncomfortable when you show your feelings: don't cry.' I'd rather have them say, 'Go ahead and cry. I'm here to be with you.'"[2]

My parents' willingness to listen patiently and with such acceptance taught me the importance of becoming comfortable with others' pain, of allowing people to be vulnerable, to be not okay, to be sad, to feel broken, and to even fail. Even with my parents' support, I struggled. One day, I came home from work and collapsed on the floor, utterly spent. I felt as if I were submerged in a sea of pain that coursed through me and spread out infinitely around me. After fighting it for nearly two years, I had resigned myself to its heaviness. Though I hadn't been praying or pleading, I slowly became aware of a presence I can only describe as God. Like the constant hum of some background noise we normally block out and don't even notice, I realized He had always been right there beside me, even when I couldn't hear or feel Him.

A moment before, I'd been panicked, drowning under the weight of pain. Now I felt relaxed as my pain separated from me, existing as a sensation I was only submerged within, like the water in a swimming pool. The presence of God continued to grow more and more solid, like the bottom of the pool. There was a firm realness to His presence that gave me sweet relief.

I stood up and, in that moment, felt as if I could breathe for the first time in a very long time. Looking over the ruins of my life, I decided I couldn't continue to work in Austin. Although I had no idea what to do next, I knew I was done trying so hard.

Seeking solitude and space, I ran as far away from Austin as I could.

CHAPTER 6

SURRENDER IN THE AMAZON

· · · · · · · · · ·

Affliction is able to drown out every earthly voice . . . but the voice of
eternity within a man it cannot drown. . . . When by the aid
of affliction all irrelevant voices are brought to silence,
it can be heard, this voice within.

SØREN KIERKEGAARD

IN OCTOBER 2009, I flew to Manaus, deep in the heart of the
Brazilian Amazon, to assist with a medical mission project and to
escape my calling in Austin. Manaus was a much larger city, but
because it had no roads connecting it with the rest of Brazil, it
conjured up images of people back home living in isolation.

On my first day there, two of the local mission leaders proudly
showed me the community center they'd recently built. It housed
programs similar to the ones we had planned to offer at Sarah's
House.

As we stood near a well-kept soccer field watching kids being
coached through drills, one of the leaders, Earl, pointed up and
down the street to apartments and small rundown houses. "This is
an area that has struggled with a lot of poverty. But this center and
our community work have really made a difference."

I pulled my hat down a little to block the glare of the sun so

I could see his face better. He was obviously proud of the change that he could see and I could only imagine. "In what ways?" I asked.

He spread his arms and turned around as he answered, "This whole area was overrun with drug use, crime, and sex workers." He paused, brought his hands to his lips, and closed his eyes. I waited. "Praise Jesus," he said after a few awkward seconds. The man next to him wiped his eyes with a handkerchief and whispered, "Praise Jesus."

It was clear to me that what had happened here had affected these two men, changed them, humbled them.

"But now things are different. People have found hope, community, and purpose." Earl's voice cracked a little with emotion as he spoke.

I was touched by their heartfelt response, but my mind was somewhere else. It grieved me deeply that we had been unable to build in the middle of America what they had somehow managed to create here, in the middle of the Amazon.

"How did you do it?"

Earl's eyes twinkled, and the deep, weathered wrinkles around them crinkled as he smiled. "We decided this land should be used for a community center about thirty years ago—" he put his hand on the other man's shoulder affectionately—"but we had no way of putting it all together."

The other man continued, "So we just started trying to help people in the area one day at a time."

"Amen, brother," Earl interjected. "Our work continued without any progress for twenty-five years." He turned and looked in my eyes with a stern expression as if delivering an urgent message I needed to hear. "It took twenty-five years of faithfully serving without much progress before the man who owned this land unexpectedly approached us about building this community center."

Twenty-five years.

With those words, I suddenly understood how self-important

my sense of burden and urgency was. I had moved to Austin with idealistic confidence that simply opening the doors of my clinic would ensure that God would somehow use me to change the town. I now realized that the man I *thought* God *wanted* me to be was not who God *needed* me to be. The glaring truth became brighter than the Amazon sun bearing down on me: I had failed.

The next day, I boarded a medical riverboat to head east on the Negro River, where its dark tea-like waters merge with the lighter, muddy waters of the Solimões River. The clear visual demarcation between the two rivers—called the Meeting of the Waters—was breathtaking. Just beyond that point, the two surrender their separate identities to become part of one river so massive it contains one-fifth of all the fresh water on earth. In fact, it would take the next six largest rivers combined to match the volume of the Amazon River.[1]

Several days passed, taking us deep into the expansive waters of the Amazon and taking me far from the heartache back home. The shore was lined with rain forests so thick I couldn't see through them, and parts of the river were so wide I couldn't see the other shore. A few times I heard the continuous roar of what sounded like highway traffic back home. Then I remembered there were no roads to or from this place. The roar turned out to be hundreds of howler monkeys lurking somewhere deep in dense forest.

During the day, we'd dock at the base of paths that had been carved through the jungle to remote villages. People would come to the boat, where I'd examine and treat them one at a time. After examining a sixteen-year-old girl who was weak and sweating with a high fever, I had our crew rush her back upriver by speedboat for a malaria test, which came back positive.

Each village was similar, with bungalows around an open central clearing. Some villages had electricity and a few gas-powered vehicles that must have been delivered by a river transport. Dinner was always a community event followed by a huge soccer match played by the entire village. I enjoyed joining these pickup games, running and playing alongside men and women, boys and girls. We didn't need to speak the same language to have fun and to feel as if we blended into one community.

At night, I'd return to the boat, where I'd meditate and then sleep in a hammock on the deck of the boat. The utter blackness of nights in the middle of the Amazon River made the sky shimmer with more stars than I could have ever imagined.

One night, I sat alone on the back of the boat. The dark night's air was cool, filled with the constant buzz and chirps of unseen creatures. The river waves lapped rhythmically against the hull of the boat, causing it to gently rock. A misty feeling of something forgotten quietly stirred within my heart, hinting at something just outside of what I knew but on the verge of breaking through.

I looked up just in time to see the brightest shooting star I'd ever seen. Then another, and another. I gasped as silver bursts continued to randomly trail across the pitch-black sky of the Amazon.

I tried to pray but had no words left. When my entire world came apart, my mind's plans and my heart's wishes were silenced. I asked for nothing and instead just listened.

I discovered the subtle lie that had been hiding in my heart: Life will always turn out well for those who walk within God's purpose. I'd often heard Romans 8:28 quoted as a promise: "All things work together for good to those who love God." But I had ignored the rest of the verse that states this "good" is "according to His purpose," not ours. That night on the Amazon, it hit me that God's purpose is ultimately good, but that doesn't mean it is *immediately* good—or even safe. After all, God's perfect purpose in Christ's life led to a brutal death on the cross.

My mind drifted to Ecclesiastes 3:11: *He has made everything beautiful in its time. He has also set eternity in the human heart; yet no one can fathom what God has done from beginning to end.*[2]

The timelessness of eternity echoed in my heart, calling me to surrender my past, present, and future to something beyond myself. I had indeed failed, and that truth set fire to the identities

I had crafted in a vain attempt to be—or appear to be—what I thought my God, my church, and my culture expected. Now I surrendered myself so that God could burn away these false identities, which had formed into a mask that I wore like a child pretending to be some sort of superhero. Fear, shame, and pride had held that mask up, and I'd clung to it in desperate fear of being found out as a fake.

It began to dawn on me that, if I could accept my true identity, the one God had given me, I could better help my patients live freely as the unique eternal selves that God had created them to be.

It was becoming clear that my ideas of how I should fulfill my calling as a community doctor conflicted with the reality of Austin. The people of Austin didn't need a hero to swoop in and save the day. No outside force or influence was going to "fix" Austin. Change would have to be organically developed from within the community, by the community.

In ancient India, a key virtue was ahimsa (do no harm), which recognizes that focusing on "I, me, and mine" creates conflict with anything that is not "I, me, or mine." The only way to resolve this conflict is to give up one's personal story and unite with a bigger one.[3] I had to kill the notion that changing Austin was a part of *my* story and instead, be faithful in my work as a part of *Austin's* story—to be fully present, and to intentionally act with kindness, integrity, and purpose toward my patients, my employees, my family, myself, and my God.

Like the tree I had drawn for my clinic's sign, I needed to stop fighting the howling winds and learn to adapt, grow, and sink roots into the broken world God had called me to live in. I needed to become a refuge for others, accept the places where I had failed, and extend that same grace to others.

As I left Brazil, I felt my depression start to lift. Trying to maintain control had led me to a place of brokenness. I determined that, from that day forward, God would guide my journey, and I would simply follow Him.

. . . .

Not long after I returned from the Amazon, a man in his midfifties came to see me. Mr. Evans had a muscular build, and his face had the wrinkled, leathery look of a smoker. He said he drove a truck for a living and had never been very sick. His blood pressure was high, but he felt he was otherwise in good health.

He personified the image we all have of a good person: honest, genuine, hardworking, positive. I leaned back a little and observed him, trying to see past the exterior we show people—who we want to be, wish we were, and hope others fall for.

I learned he had come from a particularly rough home and had to work hard for everything. Consequently, he drank too much earlier in life until he'd had a spiritual epiphany and embraced the Christian faith. He and his first wife had two girls, and they both made him incredibly proud. He told me he didn't feel he could give them much or teach them much, but he felt that, somehow, they'd done well anyway.

"One is a teacher, and the other is a nurse," he said, a proud smile crossing his face.

His first wife had passed after a long bout with diabetes, and he had since remarried. He clearly treasured his second wife too.

I listened intently.

That's not something medical school spends much time teaching. It seems that, at some point, the *art* of medicine was left behind for an overreliance on scientific data—much of which is rather useless to the average patient.

I discovered something mysterious often happened when the door of the exam room closed. Alone with a patient in what feels like a sacred space, I found total strangers willingly exposed their souls to me, entrusting me with knowledge they'd sometimes even hidden from themselves. This journey into the unfamiliar and sometimes frightening world of another person's heart required me to lay aside my own views and values to operate without prejudice on a deeper level than the physical body alone. In the most intimate moments, we approach that abstract part of what makes them a unique person. But modern medicine tends to ignore the most important part of a patient's well-being, choosing to leave purpose and meaning shrouded in mystery, lurking in the shadows of our exam rooms.

"It must be tough to be away from home so much," I said.

He nodded. "Yeah, I try to make the most of my time when I'm home. But it's not bad, really. A lot of people have it worse than I do. No sense complainin'." He paused, shifting his weight on the exam table. I waited.

Silence is one of the most powerful tools to open patients' souls. It lets them know they have my attention. I am not trying to compress our interaction into the smallest possible space so I can quickly move on to the next "disease" or "problem" crowded in my waiting room or sitting naked under thin sheets in empty rooms. Silence says, "You are important." Silence says, "Be yourself. It's okay here."

He broke the quiet, "Yeah, being on the road, there's a lot of time to think about life and all. I've even come up with a slogan for funeral homes, like 'The Hoosier funeral home where we can bury you deeper, cheaper. That's a deal you can't walk away from.'"

We both laughed. Then he added, "No, I think we've done all right."

Sadly, I would end up a pallbearer at Mr. Evans's funeral less than a year later. He died of lung cancer, which I suspected while listening to his chest one day. The breath sounds on one side were abnormal; further testing confirmed this diagnosis. I spent a lot of time with him and his wife over the next few months, watching him get sicker and eventually die.

His death brought with it an epiphany. No amount of scientific knowledge could have saved Mr. Evans. This is ultimately true for all my patients. If my success as a healer was defined by keeping my patients from their inevitable appointment with the grave, I would always be a failure. Although Mr. Evans's life was cut short, he lived with the type of abundance of life I wanted for every person in Austin. Meditating on the Scripture I'd founded my practice upon—Jesus' promise that He'd come to offer abundant life—I recommitted myself to Austin. I'd surrender my story to at least hold the line with a faith in God's plan, a hope for the future, and a love that sees intrinsic value in every soul. I truly believed that change would come to Austin—but in God's time, and through God's will, not mine. And I committed myself to being there to help when that day came.

CHAPTER 7

LESSONS NOT LEARNED

· · · · · · · · · ·

Our lives are fashioned by our choices.
First we make our choices.
Then our choices make us.

ANNE FRANK

LESS THAN A YEAR AFTER I returned from the Amazon, another drug began to tighten its grip on the town of Austin—Opana (oxymorphone). A highly addictive pain-relieving narcotic, Opana had been replacing OxyContin as the drug of choice in Austin since its FDA approval in 2006. Endo Pharmaceuticals had developed it, despite the troubling history of its active ingredient, oxymorphone.

Oxymorphone was first marketed in 1959 as an injectable or a suppository pain reliever. In the mid-1960s, doctors began prescribing a pill form under the name Numorphan. People quickly discovered it could be used to provide a more intense high, better than any other drug—including heroin. Widespread abuse quickly followed, and in 1982, it was pulled from the market.

Once again, these instructive events became lost among the faded memories of lessons not learned.[1] Opana's usage quickly spread from prescription pads to the streets. The most common way to abuse Opana was to crush the pills and snort the powder, which resulted in a rapidly induced euphoria. In response, Endo Pharmaceuticals introduced a reformulated pill in 2012 that was harder to crush and snort.[2] But people who were still physically dependent and psychologically addicted quickly discovered they could melt the pill's hard shell over a flame or in the oven, dissolve what remained in water, and inject it directly into their bloodstream.

As powerful as Opana was, the effects of injecting it wore off quickly, resulting in severe withdrawal, including body aches, restlessness, abdominal cramps, vomiting, diarrhea, a sense of dread, anxiety, and insomnia. People would use it as often as every two hours, even leaving a prepared syringe by their bed to inject when they woke up because they knew how sick they'd feel.

Under Indiana law,[3] the sale or distribution of sterile syringes was limited to patients with a prescription. It was illegal to be in possession of a syringe with the intent to use it to inject drugs, so people taking Opana resorted to reusing and even sharing old needles. In fact, it became common for entire families spanning several generations to share needles while injecting Opana together.

The reused syringes became so battered, they seemed to reflect the traumatized lives of their owners. When needles became too dull to pierce the skin, they'd sharpen them on any rough surface. Over time, these needles would get filed down until they no longer matched any standard length of syringe.

Some people would try to be responsible and not share by keeping track of their own needle. They'd accomplish this by color-coding their needle with fingernail polish or a permanent marker. But that syringe—contaminated with bacteria after the very first use—would be dangerously reused hundreds of times. They'd try to keep it with them but would chuck the needle in a ditch if they saw a police car coming down the street to avoid getting arrested. So even the people who color-coded their syringe would resort to sharing if they didn't have their personal syringe with them when there was an opportunity to use. This behavior reflects the dark power of addiction. When people are in the throes of it, they don't think about anything beyond that moment. If a used needle is what's available, they'll use it and worry about the consequences later.

And the consequences were dire. By 2010, medical communities across the country had begun to see a dramatic rise in the number of people contracting hepatitis C, soft tissue infections (abscesses), and heart valve infections (endocarditis). Scott County was no exception.

During my shifts in the emergency department, I began to see at least one abscess in every ten to fifteen patients. Until this time, I'd rarely encountered a patient with endocarditis. But suddenly we were diagnosing a case every few weeks.

What shook us most in Scott County, though, was the dramatic surge in accidental overdose deaths. Previously, overdose deaths in Scott County accounted for about 20 percent of coroner cases and sadly were predominantly suicides. In 2011, that percentage shot up to nearly half—most reported as accidental Opana overdoses.[4]

So many people dying—*to feel better.*

But even in the darkest of times, there were pockets of light.

In 2011 a smart, tenderhearted woman named Melissa, who had slowly become my most trusted friend, agreed to marry me. After so many years of experiencing hardship, loneliness, and tragedy, I was surprised to rediscover love and happiness. She had a son named Max who was the same age as my son and a daughter, Rowan, who fit in well with my daughters. Our kids had already become close friends, making the transition to six children— although challenging—a little easier. I was surprised by how naturally it was for me to feel as if Max and Rowan were my own.

Melissa brought me new hope; the sheer goodness of her heart inspired me to endure the bleakest of days. Suddenly, I felt less alone. Her caring, reassuring influence protected me from the poisons of toxic situations and people.

Another bright spot was that the Rural Health Clinic (RHC)

designation had taken some of the financial pressure off my clinic. This proved to be a bit of a double-edged sword. On the upside, the slightly better Medicaid and Medicare reimbursements made it possible for me to provide much-needed medical services to a larger population of Austin's underserved community. Because rural health clinics are required by law to employ advanced practice clinicians (i.e., nurse practitioners and/or physician assistants), I was finally able to hire a larger staff. Although ensuring compliance with these RHC mandates and hiring advanced practice clinicians were challenging, the trade-off of being able to expand health services in Austin was worth it.

To accommodate our growing practice, I moved my clinic to a larger building on Main Street in Austin in 2012. It included workstations for each of my providers and microclinics within the larger clinic. Each of my providers and I would offer primary care plus a specialty focus. If we couldn't get specialists to come to Austin, we'd simply develop our own solutions.

A few months after settling into our new building, I stumbled across a Reuters article drawing attention to how badly rural America was being ravaged by Opana, and I was stunned to see that they had cited Austin as the prime example. The fact that prescription drug use had become more deadly "in the United States than heroin and cocaine combined" and that rural residents were "nearly twice as likely to overdose on pills than people in big cities"[5] isn't what surprised me. I'd had a front-row seat to that horror show for years now. In fact, in response to the increased overdose deaths in Scott County, I had added Opana to the growing list of medications on my "do not prescribe" list to ensure none of my providers would inadvertently contribute to this tragedy.

What amazed me was that someone finally seemed to be sounding the alarm that we desperately needed help in Austin. Even though the article was truly tragic, it brought me hope that help was on its way. God knows, we needed it. Yet the article seemed to be quickly forgotten, as were the suffering people of Austin.

· · · · · · · · ·

About ten hours into one of my twelve-hour shifts at the ER, one of the nurses came to me and said, "Dr. Cooke, the lady in 8 wants pain meds."

"I've not made it into her room yet," I replied while scrolling through another patient's chart. "What's going on with her?"

"She's constipated." She shrugged, then walked away.

It's easy to get jaded responding to the demands of the emergency department. The word *emergency* in the department name holds a great deal of weight for the staff. But it often seems lost on the many people who use it as their primary care.

While constipation didn't strike me as an emergency, I fought my inner cynic and headed over to room 8. Before I made it there, the other nurse called out, "Dr. Cooke, don't go too far. EMS is pulling in with another overdose."

I shook my head in frustration and knocked as I opened the door to room 8. A young woman who looked to be in her early thirties was curled up in the fetal position on the bed, her hair obscuring her face, which was flush with perspiration. As I came in, she looked up, and I froze. It was Samantha, the young woman who'd ransacked my waiting room six years before after I'd refused to prescribe her Lortab. The last time I'd seen her, she was sitting in the back of a police car. The look on her face told me she remembered our last encounter as well.

Before I could speak, a very concerned-looking man sitting next to her bed stood and said, "Dr. Cooke, she's really hurting. Can you help her?"

"I'll do my best," I assured him. As I made my way over to the bed, I smiled gently and said, "It's been a while, Samantha." For some reason, it felt like acknowledging that I remembered her would make things less awkward. It didn't.

"What's going on?" I asked.

Samantha grimaced. "It's my stomach," she said, curling into herself even tighter. "It's killin' me."

Knowing I would be interrupted at any second to tend to the incoming overdose patient, I quickly continued. "How long has it been going on?"

"I've been constipated for a few weeks," she moaned, "but now I can't go at all."

When I pressed on her abdomen, she grabbed my arm and cried out in pain. Her friend looked at me pleadingly. "Can you give her something to stop the pain?"

"Yes," I assured him, "but we also need to figure out what's causing it."

Turning back to Samantha, I said, "Tell me more about the pain."

"It's been coming and going, off and on, for a while now," Samantha began. "But this time," she said, gritting her teeth, "instead of going away on its own, it just keeps getting worse."

I needed to ask about her drug use, but I felt uncomfortable. I could hear the ambulance sirens approaching though—my overdose patient would be here soon. I fought through my discomfort and asked, "Are you still using pain pills?"

She nodded but didn't look at me.

I didn't ask where she got them. I'd been in Austin long enough to know they weren't hard to find.

"That can cause severe constipation," I told them both. "It may be contributing to what's going on."

Samantha didn't respond. I looked up and saw the nurse at the door, signaling that they needed me. My overdose patient had arrived.

"Samantha, I need to go take care of another patient. But I'm going to order something to help ease your pain while we run some blood work and get a scan of your belly. Once I get the results, we can talk through them and make some decisions together, okay?"

"Okay," she whimpered. Then she looked up and met my eyes. "Thank you, Dr. Cooke."

I put my hand on her shoulder. "You're welcome, Samantha. I'm going to do everything I can to help you. I promise."

As I turned to head into the hall, a wave of guilt coursed through my veins, and I felt my face go red. Samantha needed my help six years before and I coldly sent her away without asking anything about her circumstances or trying to help her. She needed compassion, understanding, and an empathetic ear. Instead, she got a form letter telling her never to come back. Where else was she supposed to go in a place like Austin after I cut her off from my office? *Lord, forgive me.*

I placed a few quick orders with the nurse to give Samantha something non-narcotic to help ease her pain and to begin her workup. Then I hurried to the trauma room where the paramedics were moving my next patient off their stretcher and onto a hospital bed.

I put on my surgical gown and gloves as the nurses began hooking up a man in his twenties to the monitors. He was awake but short of breath, sweating, and pale. Track marks ran up both arms, and an abscess several centimeters in diameter bulged from his left forearm.

"What do you know?" I asked the medics.

"We were called out for an overdose, but he was gasping for air and writhing around when we got there. His sats were low," one of the medics said, referring to his oxygen saturation, which should be near 100 percent. "It was only 76 percent but came up to the low 90s on two liters of oxygen."

I leaned over the man and asked him directly, "What are you taking?"

He continued to writhe on the bed, his eyes closed, so I asked again. "Sir, what are you taking? What are you on?"

Finally the response came: "Opana."

I put my stethoscope to his chest. "I need you to take a deep

breath for me." He flinched in pain. "I know it hurts," I said, leaning in closer. "Another deep breath, the best you can."

His breath sounds were coarse, but it was his heart sounds that
sent a chill through me. There was a harsh murmur, and his heart
raced about twice as fast as normal.

"His temp is 103, Doc," one of the nurses said.

I knew instantly what was wrong. I'd been diagnosing it far
too often over the past six months—endocarditis. This very rare,
life-threatening condition occurs when bacteria is introduced into
the bloodstream, travels to the heart, and starts growing on one of
the valves. Even when caught and treated, this catastrophic infection can lead to heart failure, and pieces of the clumpy growth
of bacteria can break off, showering the rest of the body with the
fragments and damaging other organs, most often the lungs.

I ordered two liters of intravenous fluids to be given rapidly
along with antibiotics. He'd likely need open-heart surgery to
remove the infected heart valve.

I turned to the patient and told him, "I'm concerned that you
may have an infection in your heart."

"What? How?" he asked hoarsely.

"Probably from injecting with dirty needles," I said.

He cursed.

"I'm going to send you for a CT scan to get a better look
at what we're dealing with." I looked up at the nurse. "Can you
please page radiology?" She nodded and stepped out of the room.
As soon as the rad tech wheeled him away, I began taking care of
the other patients.

A few minutes later I heard a near-hysterical woman at the
reception window. "I'm looking for my son."

I shook my head. *What a terrible place to have to look for your son.*

She gave his name and added, "I heard an ambulance brought
him here."

"Yes, ma'am," the receptionist said.

"Is he okay? Can I see him?" she pleaded.

The receptionist answered in a reassuring tone, "Let me check with the doctor."

I had them bring her to his room and quickly surveyed the tracking board. I was waiting on test results for several patients, including Samantha, and the other patients listed all had minor complaints, so I headed over to update this frantic mom about her son.

She was nervously pacing as I entered the room. "I'm Dr. Cooke," I said, shaking her hand. "Your son is stable enough for me to have sent him to radiology for a quick scan of his chest. We're running several tests to help us determine how best to help him. He should be back down in a few minutes."

Her eyes were like saucers. "He's alive?" she half stated, half begged.

"Yes, ma'am," I assured her. "But he's in very serious condition. We're doing everything we can to help him." I ushered her over to a chair and she all but collapsed into it.

"We've been trying to get him help for so long," she said, wiping a tear from her eye.

I genuinely felt for this woman. There is nothing more devastating to a parent than seeing your child suffering and not being able to help. I'd seen far too many overdose cases in my short time in Austin and far too many families torn apart by substance use disorder.

I put a hand on her shoulder. "I'll be back as soon as I have more information," I assured her. Fearing that her son would get worse or even code, I went back to busily trying to help the other patients before another emergency situation presented itself.

After I finished a few cases, one of the nurses let me know his scans were back. I pulled the results up on the computer and dropped my head. They reinforced my diagnosis of endocarditis, revealing multiple septic emboli—clumps of bacterial growth—scattered throughout his lungs.

Lord, this guy is really sick. Please be with him and his family . . . and be with me as I try to help him.

I returned to the young man's room. His vital signs had improved, and he was breathing a little more comfortably. Seeing him had apparently helped his mother calm down as well. When I shared the results with them, they held hands and cried.

The young man closed his eyes, forcing tears to run furiously down his face. He clenched his fists and cursed again, the frustration evident on his face and in his voice. He took a labored, staccato breath and began coughing.

Once he caught his breath, he said, "I was trying so hard to do better."

I pulled a chair up to the bed and sat down. "What happened?"

"I'd been snorting Opanas, but then the stupid pills changed so we couldn't crush 'em anymore. I swore I was gonna quit," he paused and put his hand on his chest as a pained expression swept across his face. "But the withdrawals were so bad." He stared straight up at the ceiling and shook his head. "I seriously thought I was gonna die."

His mom, still crying, leaned forward and brushed her hand through his hair affectionately. His breathing slowed. As he gazed at something beyond the ceiling, his eyes filled, and he said, "I couldn't sleep or get comfortable. I threw up. My head buzzed and spun. It was the worst thing I've ever felt. Even worse than this." He took a few more shallow breaths and cleared his throat. "That's when someone hit me with the needle."

He looked over at me as if he was trying to convince me of something deeply sacred to him. "I couldn't stick that needle in my arm, Doc. I refused." He closed his eyes. "But my friend . . ." His jaws clenched. Then he shook his head, chuckled to himself, and sighed. "Some friend, huh?"

I glanced across the bed at his mother. Her eyes met mine briefly, then turned to the floor, the tears cascading down her cheeks.

Her son continued. "It worked like magic. All the pain just melted away. It was the most amazing thing I've ever experienced." His expression shifted for just a moment and he appeared relaxed.

"I've been injecting ever since . . . not even to get high, really. But I gotta inject every few hours or else that sickness comes back." He closed his eyes and laughed sardonically. "Maybe this will get me back on track—if I even make it."

"We'll do everything we can," I assured them both.

I made arrangements to transfer him to a larger hospital in Louisville where I expected him to remain for several weeks. *After that* . . . I shook the worst-case scenarios from my mind and went back down the hall to check on Samantha.

When I got there, she was asleep. The man who had come in with her quietly rose from his chair and with an expectant look on his face, motioned me into the hall.

"What can I do for you?" I asked.

"Here's the thing, Doc," he whispered, then glanced back over his shoulder to make sure Samantha was still sleeping. "Sam hasn't been doing well." He pulled a crumpled envelope from his back pocket. "She's been carrying this around in her purse for a little over a year. It's addressed to you, but she couldn't bring herself to send it. I think you should read it."

I didn't know what to say or do. I reflexively took the envelope. It had "Dr. William Cooke" written on the front along with my office address.

I thanked him, though I wasn't sure why, and we shook hands.

Once I got back to my desk, I opened the handwritten letter. Samantha began by apologizing and explaining how she got hooked on opiates. When she was fifteen, her dentist prescribed them. She discovered that, not only did they take away her physical pain, they also made her feel safe for the first time in her life.

I sighed. Once again, a patient reported beginning to abuse drugs because they provided the security they should have gotten from loved ones.

Samantha said she began sneaking pills from family members and then figured out how to get doctors and dentists to prescribe them to her. A boyfriend also showed her how to get a more intense rush by crushing and snorting the pills, feeding her drive for pills even more.

She was able to get a legitimate prescription after back surgery, and by the time she came to see me, she had resolved to wean herself off them. But after connecting with the wrong people again, she relapsed. "I was terrified that you'd find out," she wrote. "I should have just told you. But I didn't and you found out anyway."

When she received the letter from me, she freaked out and snapped, trashing my waiting room. She ended her letter this way: "Would you be willing to take me back as your patient? I don't want pain pills anymore. I just want help. Will you help me? Please?"

I folded the letter and sat in silence. My heart broke for Samantha. I wasn't sure what I could do to help, but nothing would stand in my way of trying. I'd let her know that I'd take her back when I went over her test result with her. I was confident a laxative and less opioid use would help her.

After tending to a few other patients, I sat back down at my desk. My shift was almost over. It had been quite an evening. I glanced over at Samantha's letter and allowed myself to relax a little with the thought that I'd have a second chance to show her the care I didn't the first time. Just then, the nurse poked her head around the corner.

"Dr. Cooke? The patient in 8's scans are back. I thought you might want to look at them before you leave."

I smiled. "Thanks," I told her as I pulled the results up on my computer.

No, God. This can't be right.

I leaned in to take a closer look, but it wasn't necessary. The scan clearly showed a massive tumor beginning in Samantha's cervix that had eaten all the way through her rectum, completely obstructing it.

The report was long but the words that jumped off the screen at me were *metastatic cervical cancer*.

I felt sick. Given the size of the tumor, odds were, it had been silently growing there for years. If she had been receiving regular medical care, a routine Pap smear could have identified it early enough to spare her suffering. She could have gotten treatment and she would have been okay. Now . . . she probably had only six months, maybe nine at most.

What made things even worse was knowing I had participated in shortening Samantha's life by cutting her off from preventative care. How was that any different from a structurally violent system that limited lifesaving and life-affirming care for the most vulnerable?

If only I hadn't dismissed her so callously. If only I had followed up with her after her arrest. If only I had learned the lessons Austin was teaching me sooner.

If . . . If . . . If . . .

I fell back in my chair aching—physically and emotionally—as I searched for the right words to say to Samantha. I wanted so desperately to walk into that room and tell her there was nothing to worry about—that I could fix what was wrong with her. But I couldn't. Nothing I could do would undo the damage generations of toxic stress, unemployment, poverty, lack of access to medical care, and rampant drug abuse had done to Samantha, to my endocarditis patient, or to countless others just like them living in the shadows in Austin.

Dozens of people sharing bacteria-infected needles.

Accidental overdoses.

Endocarditis.

Hepatitis C.

I gently massaged my temples in a feeble attempt to fend off my impending headache. As bad as the current situation was, I couldn't shake the sickening feeling that the worst was yet to come. But I never expected to be broadsided by the news while mindlessly clearing my email in-box as I drank my morning coffee.

CHAPTER 8

SCARLET LETTERS

· · · · · · · · ·

The opposite of addiction isn't sobriety. It's connection.

JOHANN HARI

"HIV OUTBREAK TIED TO PAINKILLER, DIRTY NEEDLES."

On the cold morning of February 26, 2015, I discovered HIV had come to my small community the way everyone else in town found out—by reading about it in the morning paper. A friend had forwarded me a link to the article. As I sat alone at my desk in Austin reading the article on my laptop, my mind struggled to take in the words: "Indiana state health officials said Wednesday that they have confirmed 26 cases, and four more preliminary cases, since mid-December, most linked to Opana injection," representing "the largest HIV outbreak the state has ever experienced in one region."[1] All of the cases would end up being connected to Austin.

I was stunned but not really surprised. The opioid epidemic continued to rage, with many of those struggling with substance use disorder still sharing needles. What we didn't know until later was that a person who had been living with HIV since 2004 had moved to Austin in 2011.[2] At some point after that, cases of HIV began to silently proliferate through our community.

On November 16, 2014, Scott Memorial Hospital diagnosed the first case of HIV the county had seen in more than ten years. One week later, a pregnant woman who had come in for routine prenatal care tested positive for both hepatitis C and HIV. Two cases in two weeks in a county that had reported only five cases in the previous decade.[3]

Instead of that information traveling forty-five steps across the parking lot to the Scott County Health Department, it went thirty miles south to the Clark County Health Department, which collected HIV data from nineteen counties across southern Indiana.[4] Disease Intervention Specialist Jessie Shields immediately notified the Indiana State Department of Health (ISDH), hoping to enlist more resources. Although she didn't hear back from the state, she got to work behind the scenes, feverishly investigating each new case of HIV, interviewing patients to find links to other people they may have exposed to HIV who needed to be tested.

By January 2015, Jessie had notified the ISDH of at least fourteen HIV cases in Scott County. But the state still hadn't committed any additional resources to the outbreak or let us know about it locally.

We later discovered HIV cases were being tracked separately from all other infectious diseases in Indiana. So ISDH's director of epidemiology didn't even know about the mounting numbers of HIV cases in Scott County. Finally, sometime around January 23, a concerned ISDH worker pulled the director of epidemiology aside to show her the reports. Shocked, she immediately presented those findings to state health commissioner and future US Surgeon General Dr. Jerome Adams, and deputy health commissioner Dr. Jennifer Walthall. Together they began planning how to inform Mike Pence, the governor and future vice president, and then the local health department about the public health disaster.

By February 7, nineteen people had tested positive for HIV. By Valentine's Day, the number had risen to twenty-eight. Privately, the Clark County Health Department's medical director was trading emails and phone calls with state officials. Even then, there was no public warning or local involvement.

More weeks passed before anyone told local officials. Ron Murphy, who had led the Scott County Health Department for forty-two years, said, "I didn't hear about it until [state officials] called and told us [on February 23] we had a problem." He continued, "I've lived here all my life. These are our people. I think knowing about it would be very helpful."[5]

A few days later ISDH prepared a press release to notify the public. Sources in the newspaper article I was reading quickly connected the dots between opioid abuse and HIV, pointing out that "when you have injectable drugs like prescription pills and other narcotics being abused as much as they have been, (Hepatitis) C and HIV are soon to follow." Dr. Adams added that "because prescription drug abuse is at the heart of this outbreak, [Indiana State health officials] are not only working to identify, contact and test individuals who may have been exposed, but also to connect community members to resources for substance abuse treatment and recovery."[6]

But we don't have those resources in our community, I thought.

The article warned readers to take measures to stay safe by not injecting drugs, sharing or reusing needles, engaging in unprotected sex, or having sex with commercial sex workers.

I closed my laptop and gazed out the window. *This town has been through so much.* For years, I couldn't get anyone to pay attention to the desperate need in Austin. But now that the scarlet letters *H-I-V* had captured everyone's attention . . . *Please, Lord, now—help them see the need.*

· · · · · · · · ·

As news and fears began to send shock waves out from the epicenter of the rapidly evolving HIV outbreak, our clinic saw a frenzied surge of activity. Since HIV was unheard of in places like Scott

County, people generally had very little understanding of how it was and was not transmitted. Frightened and confused, some expressed fears of touching grocery carts, using public restrooms, and even shaking hands.

People flocked to my office for information and testing. Among them was Deborah, whom I had gotten to know fairly well over the years. Although her family originally hailed from Appalachia, she had been born and raised in Austin when life was easier. She had witnessed firsthand the decline of the hometown she loved, and after moving away for college and work, she had returned after a divorce, determined to carve out a life here.

As soon as I entered the exam room, I could tell something wasn't right. I quietly shut the door. "Hey, Deb," I said and sat down near her.

She didn't answer.

"What's going on?" I asked gently.

She looked up, and I could see she'd been crying. I reached over and grabbed the box of tissues off the counter, handed it to her to pull a few from the box, and waited.

After wiping her eyes, she said, "It's Jude. We just found out he's using Opana again."

Jude was her twenty-year-old son. He'd begun using prescription painkillers after injuring his knee playing football at sixteen. Like countless other Austin kids, once Jude got a taste of Opana, it inadvertently unlocked something lying dormant deep within him. That insatiable drive to use combined with unbearable withdrawal symptoms proved too overwhelming for him to quit.

"Are you sure?" I asked her.

She nodded, her face a crumpled mask of despair.

"I mean," she said, an ironic grin on her face, "his dad's a cop. I'm an addiction counselor. And our son's an addict!" She dropped her head. "I don't know what else to do. We've tried everything. We sent him to a treatment clinic a while back and he seemed to be doing better. Then . . ." Her voice trailed off.

"I know it's hard," I said, placing my hand on her shoulder. "I'm not sure if this helps much, but you're not alone. There are so many families dealing with this."

She wiped the tears from her eyes. "I know. I see them at the treatment center." Her voice broke. "Jeff arrests people like Jude. We feel like such . . . hypocrites."

"It's not your fault, Deb," I reassured her.

"And now there's all this talk about HIV." I could read the fear on her face. "I'm just so terrified he's going to . . ." Her voice broke again, and she dropped her head, weeping.

I leaned in and made eye contact with her. "Listen, I'm here for you anytime. You know that."

She looked up and nodded resolutely.

"In the meantime, please know that I'm praying for Jude. If he wants to come in and get help or be tested, we can do that."

"Thank you, Dr. Cooke," she managed. "I'll talk to Jude. He's heard about the outbreak. I think he's just scared."

"Of course he is." I handed her another tissue. "All you can do is be there for him, okay? When he's ready, we are here to help. Just do your best to make sure he's safe."

Deb nodded, blew her nose, and began preparing to leave. As she stepped into the hall, she turned to me, and with tears still falling down her cheeks, said, "He's a good boy, Dr. Cooke. I know he wants to quit. He really does. But when he's on opioids something about my kid's soul is dead."

"I know." I felt a knot forming in the pit of my stomach. I had heard far too many stories like Jude's—"good" kids who got caught up in something more powerful than their bodies and brains could possibly control.

When I was in med school, I studied how scientists offered rats isolated in cages a choice between water and morphine-laced water. Predictably, the rats preferred the morphine-laced water. In fact, the drive for the morphine was so strong, some rats even died from neglecting to eat.[7] Since coming to Austin, I'd seen the same basic behavior play out in countless people who'd become addicted to Lortab, OxyContin, and Opana—including young women who had become so dependent on drugs they'd trade their own bodies to get them. The psychological drive to cope with unmet needs for safety, security, and love, combined with the chemical pull of addiction, is just that strong.

However, exposure to opioids alone didn't seem to explain what I was seeing. Some people appeared to be able to walk away from them when they wanted. Did that mean it was as simple as choosing to stop? That had not been my experience working with frustrated families and patients. More than 90 percent of people graduating from rehabilitation facilities were relapsing.[8]

Interestingly, my research showed that of the nearly 260 million prescriptions for opioids written by dentists and physicians to 91.8 million Americans (enough for every adult in the US to have their own bottle of pills), 25 million misused opioids, and only 3 million of them were actually addicted.[9] Something else must explain why only a small percentage of people exposed to opioids actually developed a substance use disorder.

After meeting with Deborah, I spent more time digging and discovered that I had not been given the whole picture regarding the rat studies in medical school. A Canadian psychologist named Bruce Alexander wondered how keeping the rats in isolated confinement where their basic social needs were unmet affected the rats' choice to use opioids. He repeated the study by comparing a group of rats allowed to live in a large, open-topped container with cedar shavings to dig in and things to crawl through, hide, and nest versus being isolated in cages.

The results showed that the rats in isolation drank nineteen times as much morphine water as those in a more communal setting dubbed "Rat Park."[10] Then when the isolated rats hooked on morphine were introduced into the rat park, they spontaneously cut back dramatically on their consumption of the morphine water. Social isolation and purposeless existence seemed to be what caused addiction in these rats, not simply access to opioids alone. Conversely, socialization and purposeful activity seemed protective. Addiction then could be described as a form of adaptation to toxic stress, such as social isolation, mental illness, and trauma.

Since most people could take opioids intermittently without developing an addiction, access to opioids plus some sort of toxic stress or genetic predisposition was generally required for addiction to develop.

As far as I knew, Jude hadn't been abused. But Deborah and her husband had moved around a lot while he was young, and when they divorced, he went to live with Deborah's sister. Perhaps he never felt as if he fit in anywhere. That made me think of an experiment I'd learned about as a boy tagging along with my dad, who at the time was majoring in psychology at the local college. As part of his coursework, he studied the toxic effects of social isolation on monkeys in the psychology lab. I decided to call him on my way home that evening.

"You know," he said, "the Vietnam War seemed to confirm what that Rat Park study explained about the reason certain people struggle so much with addiction."

"Really?" I asked, my interest piqued.

"Yeah," he continued, "it all started when a couple of congressmen visited Vietnam in 1971." My dad explained that, when they returned home, the two men announced that 15 percent of US servicepeople were addicted to heroin.[11] "That scared a lot of people," he added.

"I'm sure it did," I said.

"So the government hired a sociologist to follow what happened to us when we returned home."

Curious, I asked, "Did you know anyone who tried heroin while you served?"

"No, but we were stationed in the Philippines, out of harm's way. In Vietnam, the trauma of killing people and watching friends die really messed people up. As you know, it wasn't long after the war that post-traumatic stress disorder was officially classified as a mental health condition."

"Right," I said, remembering studying that in school. "Before then the behaviors of people suffering from toxic stress were just thought to be psychotic."

"Hard to believe now, right?" he said. "The sociologist found that 85 percent of servicepeople in Vietnam were offered heroin, 35 percent tried it, and nearly 20 percent became addicted."[12]

"Oh, yeah," I said excitedly, "I remember this. The veterans stopped using when they came home, right?"

"Nearly all," Dad answered. "One year after coming home, more than 90 percent of those previously addicted to heroin spontaneously recovered."[13]

Versus as few as 10 percent of people who graduate from rehab centers, I thought.

"The conclusion," he continued, "was that the toxic stress of war and isolation from family in a foreign land made soldiers vulnerable to addiction."

"That makes so much sense," I said. "Why would they need to keep using to cope after coming home to a safe, healthy environment surrounded by supportive family and friends?"

We hung up and I remembered watching Deborah leave my office earlier looking defeated. We tell people to "just say no," as if becoming addicted to drugs is a conscious decision. And if you can't quit, the prevailing view is that you must not be trying hard enough. But no matter how strong-willed people are, without help, they become completely exhausted battling their own hijacked brain and subconscious unmet needs.

It's just like the fact that no matter how strong we are, we can't simply will ourselves to walk with a broken leg. Sure, with effort, we may manage a step or two. But we will eventually fall. We are not weak for falling, for needing someone to help us up, for asking a doctor to treat us, or for giving ourselves time to heal. A brain broken by exposure to drugs, a heart broken by unmet basic needs, or a mind broken by mental illness is no different.

One evening, as Melissa and I got ready for bed, Deb's impassioned plea for me to believe that her son was a "good person" continued to ring in my head. The prevailing assumption has long been that people who use drugs are deranged, dangerous, and morally bankrupt. I remembered feeling that same judgment while suffering the mental anguish of depression following my divorce.

I shared some of what I'd been thinking with Melissa.

"I heard about an interesting study on the radio that might be related," she said.

I smiled while getting into bed and said, "Tell me more."

"Well," she said, "apparently, they placed two groups of people in a room set up to smell like fresh-baked chocolate cookies."[14]

"You're making me hungry," I joked.

"Stop interrupting," she said teasingly.

I laughed and said, "Sorry, please continue."

"The researchers then brought in plates of chocolate cookies along with bowls of radishes. They let the first group eat the cookies and made the second group eat the radishes."

"How sadistic!" I whispered.

Melissa rolled her eyes at my dramatic response but continued, "After both groups had finished eating, they were given a persistence test, and the radish eaters ended up giving up in half the time it took the cookie eaters."

"Does that mean the Cookie Monster is more persistent than Oscar the Grouch?" I asked.

"Stop!" She smacked my arm. "Do you want to hear this or not?"

"I'll stop, I'll stop!"

"Okay, but you're really wearing down my persistence in telling you this story," she warned.

"What did they conclude?" I asked. "Obviously, the radish eaters weren't just a bunch of randomly selected lazy people, right?"

"Nope, they had simply used up their willpower," she answered and let the significance linger.

I propped myself up on one elbow and looked at her. "The radish eaters were so mentally and emotionally exhausted from resisting the cookies and forcing themselves to eat the radishes, they just gave up early. That explains why I can't stick to a diet."

Melissa shook her head at me. "But it could also explain why so many people who try hard to quit using drugs eventually give up and relapse."

"They aren't bad or weak or sinful," I said. "They're just exhausted." I let myself collapse back into the bed. "Thank you, darling. That was a great bedtime story."

"You're welcome," she said as she rolled over and turned out the light. "Goodnight, love."

As I drifted off to sleep, I thought, *Of course Jude's afraid to come in. Samantha was afraid too. She carried that letter with her asking for my help for over a year. And by then it was too late. Please, Lord, help us provide hope in a way that feels safe to people like Jude.*

CHAPTER 9

LOVE VERSUS FEAR

· · · · · · · · ·

When we choose to love, we choose to move against fear—
against alienation and separation. The choice to love is a choice
to connect—to find ourselves in the other.

BELL HOOKS

THE NEXT DAY, I spent a few hours researching statewide HIV statistics and treatment plans to find out what resources might be available to us. What I discovered put numbers to what I had seen leading up to the HIV outbreak. It turned out that Scott County had posted the highest rates of hepatitis C in the state for three years straight—more than *twice* the state average.[1] During this time, Indiana public health spending had dropped from a dismal thirty-fifth nationwide in 2012 to forty-fifth in 2015.[2] By 2013, the Indiana State Department of Health (ISDH) explained that "it is clear that the lack of funding for prevention programming translates into more positive cases [of HIV] and, therefore, more people needing services in Indiana."[3]

In response to these findings, the ISDH issued a Statewide Comprehensive Plan that stated, "The illicit and stigmatizing nature of injection drug use . . . can compromise the efforts of public health professionals to accurately identify and locate persons at high risk [for HIV]," and recommended "targeting the testing service to known or assumed substance users."[4]

The report went on to warn that the lack of "access to clean needles and other sterile injection equipment . . . remains a barrier to increased disease prevention." It was another line in the report that really stood out to me: "Research has proven that syringe exchange programs decrease disease transmission."[5]

When I noticed the report's release date—April 2013—my heart sank. Two years before the outbreak. *For two years, public health officials had been sounding the alarm about the connection between intravenous opioid use and HIV, and no one listened.*

I sat back in my chair. I'd never really given much thought to syringe exchange programs. Since I had witnessed firsthand in the ER the tragic repercussions of sharing needles, the ISDH's recommendation seemed logical enough to me. But syringe exchange programs were illegal in Indiana. *How do you address a public health crisis when part of the solution is against the law?*

I soon discovered I wasn't the only one in Indiana asking that question. Since news of the outbreak had hit, public health experts from across the country had begun to pressure then-Governor Pence to immediately lift the syringe exchange ban to prevent further transmission of HIV and hepatitis C. Places where syringe services programs (SSPs) were allowed, like New York City, had dramatically reduced HIV and hepatitis C transmission years before, and the message from the CDC, the Rural Center for AIDS/STD Prevention, and public health experts from coast to coast was that a similar program here would help stem our own outbreak.

"Do you think the governor will lift the ban?" Melissa asked me when I told her.

"I'm not sure," I confessed. "On the one hand, it makes sense. There's no question that sharing needles leads to the transmission of HIV—not to mention hepatitis C, endocarditis, and a host of other potentially life-threatening infections. I see it every day at the

ER." I thought back to an article I had read the previous evening. "The World Health Organization has been saying for over thirty years that syringe services programs are effective at dramatically *decreasing* the transmission of HIV and hepatitis C." I paused for a second before stating what suddenly seemed obvious. "Frankly, as a doctor, it's hard to argue with thirty-plus years of proven, consistent medical findings."

Melissa sat quietly for a moment and then asked, "So what's the downside?"

"Well," I said, collecting my thoughts, "a lot of people would argue that handing out free syringes just enables drug use. They'd say that using drugs is illegal, so why make it easier by supplying the needles?"

Melissa nodded and smiled knowingly, "At taxpayers' expense, no less."

"Exactly," I agreed. "And of course, morally, there's the question of whether supplying free needles implies that you are *condoning* drug use. Kind of like when they started passing out free condoms in high schools back in the eighties. On the one hand, there's the argument that 'teens are doing it anyway; why not make sure they're at least safe?' But on the other hand—"

"Aren't you just encouraging kids to have premarital sex?" Melissa finished. "That *is* a conundrum." Then she looked at me, cocked her head off to one side, and asked, "Didn't they prove that giving condoms to teens didn't change their sexual behaviors?" She paused, but I could tell she wasn't finished with that thought.

"Yeah," I said.

"So *does* giving people access to syringes increase drug use?"

I shook my head. I'd only been researching the matter for a few days, but so far, I had yet to find anything that definitively proved needle exchanges increased drug use among current users *or* that they served as a gateway for people using drugs for the first time.

"No." I sighed. "All the research I've found points solely to needle exchanges lowering the transmission of hep C and HIV.

The evidence I've seen points to either no change or even a decrease in drug use."

"So . . . why don't you sound more confident?" Melissa pressed. We hadn't been married long, but already she could read me like a book. She was right. I wasn't optimistic. Even though all the medical and scientific research supported the immediate implementation of syringe exchange programs to halt the transmission of HIV through shared needles, history was not on our side.

To my surprise, I'd discovered that the debate over needle exchanges dated all the way back to 1988, when Senator Jesse Helms persuaded Congress to ban the use of federal money for such efforts—and Governor Pence supported the ban during his six terms in the House.

In 2013, right around the time the ISDH was sounding the alarm about sharing needles and the transmission of HIV and was calling for more funding for testing, Pence not only maintained the ban on syringe exchange programs but also closed the only free HIV testing center in Scott County, the local Planned Parenthood facility, which did not perform abortions.[6]

So no. I wasn't confident.

* * * * * * * * * *

On March 9, I was wrapping up a staff meeting in anticipation of another hectic day at the clinic when my phone rang.

"Is this Dr. William Cooke?"

I didn't recognize the voice. "Yes," I said, tentatively.

"Dr. Cooke, my name is Dr. Joan Duwve. I'm the chief medical officer at the Indiana State Department of Health. Do you have a few moments?"

I signaled to my team that I needed to take this call and ducked into my office.

"Yes, of course, Dr. Duwve," I said, closing the door behind me. "How can I help you?"

She wanted to hear about my experiences working with the people of Austin.

Finally.

After I filled her in, she said, "Frankly, I'm stunned by the level of need you're describing." Then, after a brief pause, "How can we help?"

I was speechless.

"Dr. Cooke?"

"Sorry," I responded. "In all the time I've struggled to do this work, I've never had anyone ask me that question."

"That must have been hard."

"At times," I said, "but what I've gone through can't compare to the horrors the people here face every day."

"They're fortunate to have you," she insisted. "It could be much worse."

I paused for a moment to consider her offer of help. Over the past week, I had heard ideas being discussed, such as bussing patients eighty miles north to Indianapolis or forty miles south to Louisville for treatment. But that contradicted the whole reason I had established a clinic in Austin in the first place.

"I'd like to build on what I've started here," I told her. "My goal is to develop a local, patient-centered, sustainable, full-spectrum, primary care–based response at my office. And I believe that with a little extra training and support, my clinic can meet the needs of our community."

"What kind of support are you looking for?" she asked.

"Well," I began, "what we really need is help growing local resources and finding community partners willing to help address the underlying socioeconomic and addiction issues."

While she agreed with my proposed solution, we both knew that reversing decades of structural harm and generations of substance use disorder, trauma, and poverty was a seemingly impossible task that, at best, would take years. Meanwhile, HIV diagnoses were rapidly multiplying.

"Let's start with something practical," she countered. "I'm going to send you a refrigerator and some free vaccines."

We spoke for a few more minutes. I thanked her for her willingness to help, and we agreed to keep in touch.

I fell back in my chair and smiled. *A fridge and some free vaccines.* It sounded so trivial when we faced such a mountain of need. But to climb a mountain, you need the right gear. And even then, you've got to start with a single step.

· · · · · · · · · ·

Three days later, a group of state health officials and local community leaders convened at Scott Memorial Hospital, where the state's director of epidemiology brought us up to speed on what was happening.

When she finished, Dr. Jennifer Walthall, the state's deputy health commissioner, delivered some sobering news.

"This is an unprecedented health-care disaster," she began. "We are not so bold as to claim to have all the answers. Today is meant to begin a conversation so we can develop a plan together that works for your community."

With that, she turned it over to the room for suggestions. What she got was stunned silence. She was right. This outbreak was unprecedented. There was no established protocol in place for us to follow. We had been seeing and testing people at the clinic in droves since the news broke. The problem was, the people who really needed to be tested weren't coming in. Therein lay the challenge.

Decades of research confirms the single greatest way to prevent the transmission of HIV is through treatment. In fact, today's treatment is so effective that people who maintain an undetectable viral load on treatment for at least six months cannot transmit the virus sexually. We call this U=U (Undetectable=Untransmittable), and in practical terms, it eliminates the risk of transmitting HIV.[7]

But people can't be treated unless they know they have HIV. Without this knowledge, they continue to transmit the virus.

I raised my hand. "My name is Dr. William Cooke. I run Foundations Family Medicine in Austin." I took a quick breath as all eyes settled on me. "My staff and I have been seeing patients regularly since news of the outbreak. The challenge is, the people who are most likely to be transmitting the disease are also the least likely to come in. Finding them isn't going to be easy." There was a low rumble in the room.

"Why is that?" came a voice from the back.

"We're talking about desperate people, often doing whatever they can to survive," I explained. "Hundreds of people are sharing needles, many without stable housing. They've been living off the grid for years, hiding from authorities, squatting in abandoned houses, doing whatever it takes to make it. Most of them don't have a mailing address, driver's license, health insurance, or paperwork of any kind. We simply don't have any record of who they are or where to find them. In fact, there's a good chance some don't even know there *is* an outbreak."

More mumbling followed. The room was a sea of concerned faces, shaking heads, and almost palpable frustration. I hated that Austin had become the center of such a tragic story. And yet I was glad the plight of the hurting people here was finally being recognized.

I leaned back in my chair and sighed. If only we'd done something to connect with and help these people before now. *If we had found and treated people earlier*, I lamented silently, *we could have avoided this whole mess.*

In the days that followed, Dr. Janet Arno, an infectious disease specialist for IU Health who was based in Indianapolis, joined Dr. Walthall and Dr. Duwve in helping us develop a local response.

Needless to say, getting everyone needing to be tested in and around Austin was a primary concern. This included marginalized people who injected drugs or engaged in sex work. But what scared us was not knowing how far beyond these groups the virus had already been transmitted. When ISDH told us only five certified HIV testers were available from agencies across Indiana, I sent a few of my nurses to be trained. We needed to make sure we found everyone who had contracted HIV—and we needed to do it quickly.

The law prohibiting drug and syringe possession made most people who use drugs very wary of people in authority. So we asked a few of the people we knew with a history of using drugs to help connect us with people who needed to be tested for HIV. Tyler, an outgoing twenty-six-year-old with a muscular build, was one of the first to offer his help.

"I *gotta* get tested so these other people can know it's okay," he told me. When we drew his blood, he tested positive for hepatitis C, but the HIV results came back negative. When I told him, his relief was palpable.

"Thanks, Doc." He exhaled deeply.

Tyler was a lifelong Austin resident who had gained the strange reputation of being able to hit a vein in anyone having trouble finding a usable vein to inject drugs. As a result, he knew most of the people in town who injected. One by one, he began bringing them by the office to be tested. Since most people were too scared to come into town, he often arranged for them to meet a tester at a particular house in north Austin.

Over those first few weeks, Tyler was frequently seen walking around the clinic introducing my staff to someone who needed to be tested. "Man, Doc, you should get me a name badge and let me join your staff," he joked to me one day.

"Ya know, Tyler, you *could* get legit with that whole vein whisperer routine and make an honest living," I half-teased him. "Phlebotomists make a pretty penny these days."

"No, thanks, doc," he shot right back. "Nobody could afford these beautiful hands."

Tyler was an easygoing, likable guy. I couldn't put my finger on it, but something about him reminded me of my family, and we hit it off from the very beginning and naturally began to call each other "brother."

I'd met him about a year before the outbreak when he first came to see me at the clinic. He asked me to prescribe pain pills and sleeping pills for him. A couple of his friends had been busted for using drugs, and he worried he'd be arrested next.

"Tyler, you know I can't prescribe those for you," I told him then.

"Figured it wouldn't hurt to try, Dr. C," he said with a big grin. "But I really do need something to help with aches and pains. It's one of the reasons I inject Opana."

"What can we do to help you not use?" I asked.

"Brother, weren't you listening to me?" he joked. "If I didn't hurt so much, I think I'd be able to quit."

"All right," I said, changing tactics, "what have you tried?"

"Well, Tylenol and ibuprofen didn't do nothing. So it's gotta be stronger than that."

"How about Neurontin?" I asked.

"Gabapentin?" he asked, laughing as he referred to the drug by its generic name. "That's just like you doctors to give an addict somethin' like that."

I was confused. Gabapentin was not a narcotic but was effective in treating pain. "What do you mean?" I asked.

He shook his head and said, "We use those to make the Opana high last longer."

Tyler eventually admitted that prescription strength anti-inflammatories did help, and I finally got him to understand that the pain pills he used only made things worse. After all, withdrawals were what caused most of his pain.

"Can I help get you into rehab?" I asked him.

"Nah, man. I ain't ready for that," he said, looking down at his worn shoes.

I put my hand on his shoulder. "If that changes, let me know. Until then, I'll do anything I can for you."

He looked up with a mix of surprise, fear, and suffering. "I know, Dr. C. I appreciate that." Then after a lengthy pause, he added, "It's not like I wanna keep using, you know? It's hard. It's all I know. It was super rough when we was growing up on the north side of town. You gotta fight or lose what you got. Then the drugs . . . they were always right there."

Over time, I learned that Tyler used drugs to cover up the pain he carried from being repeatedly raped by one of his male relatives as he was growing up.

Tyler explained that he used to get prescriptions for painkillers from area dentists, telling them he had dental pain, even when he didn't.

"I had a hard time dosing up enough to get the effect I craved," he told me. "I basically gave up everything just to chase that moment or two of not feeling."

His life became increasingly chaotic until he found himself homeless, staggering down the railroad tracks that run past my office. At that point, he said he didn't even see the point of trying anymore. That's when he let a friend "hit" him with a needle to inject Opana. Within an instant, his cravings disappeared into a euphoric high.

"Any time after that, anything that could go in that needle, I'd do it," he told me. "I'd just as soon slobber on myself as be a normal person in society. You do Opana one time," he told me holding up his finger adamantly, "and you'll just be crippled . . . crippled as soon as you do it. Brother, it got to where I needed a 'hit' to even get out moving in the morning."

His first wife left him when he went to prison for dealing. He married again, and his wife gave birth to his two kids before she died from a drug overdose in June 2013. He cried like a child when he told me that the people she was shooting up with were too afraid to call 911, so they loaded her into the back of a truck and tossed her body in the hospital parking lot.

"Can you believe that, man?" he said, wiping away a few tears.

"I don't know if she died at the drug house or if she died in the hospital parking lot, but they just left her there." He paused and looked around the room helplessly. "I got high as s— that day."

Now, months after his first visit to our office, I'd just told him he had hepatitis C and could contract HIV from shared needles too. I asked Tyler again if I could help him get into rehab. He told me he still wasn't ready. A few minutes later, he left through the side door of the clinic.

He's been through so much, I thought. *And just moments ago, I diagnosed him with hepatitis C in the middle of the worst HIV outbreak in decades.* I sighed and shook my head. *What is it going to take?*

. . . .

Meanwhile, the political debate over lifting the ban on syringe exchanges to curtail the outbreak grew more and more heated. While many encouraged Governor Pence to stand strong against syringe services programs (SSPs), those of us opposing the ban found two unlikely supporters. After years of enforcing the ban, Scott County sheriff Dan McClain changed his stance after examining the evidence with Dr. Adams over a drink. He then advised Governor Pence to allow an SSP in Scott County. Ed Clere, the Republican state representative from my hometown of New Albany, set to work drafting legislation to allow the distribution of sterile syringes throughout Indiana.

Anxious to make sure the people of Austin were well represented, I made plans to go to Indianapolis myself and testify in favor of Representative Clere's bill. Late one night after Melissa and the kids had gone to bed, I set to work drafting my own statement, coming to the issue from several angles. I began this way:

Even though I've worked in several underdeveloped countries for short periods throughout my career, I doubt anything could have prepared me for what I would experience in Austin. . . .

During this time, I've worked with, prayed with, and even wept with patients in desperate circumstances who have little to no social support and even fewer resources to make the circumstances of their lives better.

My staff and I have sincerely tried to meet people where they are in life, in a nonjudgmental, compassionate approach. Because of this, we've been accused by many of condoning or even encouraging my patients' behaviors. They say people are experiencing the negative consequences of the choices they have made. Some community leaders have even told me statements as harsh as "They've had their chance." But I would challenge that thinking with real patient encounters.

I wanted the lawmakers to better understand how desperate some of our state's citizens were—including people who weren't so different from their own children and grandchildren:

I think of the thirteen-year-old girl who was consistently on the honor roll at school. I spent years counseling her about preventative care, including abstinence and safe sex. My staff encouraged her, and we became part of her support system. She, like so many in the community, started to turn to us for advice and help. We celebrated with her when she committed to attend college and do something better with her life than what she knew in the lives of her parents and friends. This was a girl I was convinced would rise above the culture surrounding her in Austin.

So I was sad when I entered the exam room for her first prenatal visit. She seemed self-conscious and wouldn't make eye contact. I sat, and we talked. She slowly opened up and revealed how her parents couldn't afford for her to continue to live with them. So they asked a thirty-year-old man to take her in, and she fell into the lifestyle of how she was expected to live. The awful and ugly reality of Austin shattered what was otherwise a bright and beautiful future. . . .

Our local hospital recently spent three months exploring the health needs of our county. The number one concern of everyone is IV drug use. We need help.

Evidence shows needle exchange programs work to reduce the transmission of blood-borne diseases such as HIV. I'm not going to go into all the evidence supporting the effectiveness of needle exchange programs. That research is readily available. I will highlight just a couple I find interesting.

I then presented some of the statistical evidence I had found most convincing:

- Diabetic IV drug users with legal access to sterile needles had only a 9.8 percent rate of HIV compared to 24.3 percent in nondiabetic IV drug users, even though the duration and intensity of drug use was similar.[8]

- According to the National Commission on AIDS, "[Laws against] injection equipment do not reduce illicit drug use, but they do increase the sharing of injection equipment and hence the spread of HIV infection."[9]

- The authors of a study in the *Journal of Public Health Policy* showed that the states with needle exchange programs had sustained reductions in their HIV transmission rates among people who injected drugs. Conversely, states without continued to have high HIV transmission rates.[10]

I also wanted the lawmakers to know that syringe programs end up saving the government money:

These programs are also extremely cost effective and reduce the burden on taxpayers supporting public sector programs. . . .

Considering HIV-positive IV drug users are often uninsured or reliant on public-sector programs (such as Medicaid, Medicare, and Ryan White Care Act) for their care, the cost of treatment associated with new infections related to injection drug use is passed on to the taxpayers. . . .

Significantly in a 2012 study, [researchers] showed that for every dollar invested in needle exchange, there is a savings of three to seven dollars in HIV treatment costs directly related to prevention. Again, this was only looking at HIV treatment costs and doesn't even include the additional treatment cost for related conditions such as hepatitis C.[11]

When Chicago opened a syringe services program they saw 75 percent reduction in new HIV cases from 2001 to 2011, saving the state an estimated $200 million worth of medical expenses.[12] Massachusetts had a similar experience, cutting new HIV cases in more than half between 1999 and 2012, saving the state over $2 billion in medical expenses.[13]

Furthermore, needle exchange programs often serve as a bridge to treatment and recovery. Once in recovery, people can repair their lives and become productive members of society. In one study, employment increased 44.8 percent within six months among clients of needle exchange programs connected to recovery services.[14]

I closed my remarks with a plea:

Please, resist the claim that needle exchange programs
condone or encourage IV drug use. The evidence insists
needle exchange programs are effective and should
be a part of a comprehensive program to prevent the
transmission of HIV.

As I read through the speech one last time, I realized there was
so much more I wanted to say—so many people I wanted to tell
them about. I sat back and stared at the screen. It was almost 2 a.m.
In a few hours, I'd be back at the clinic. A wave of exhaustion, both
physical and emotional, washed over me. This would have to do.
I clicked Save. *From one lone voice in the howling wind to speaking
before an audience of legislators.* I smiled to myself. *It's a start.*

. . . .

On March 23, roughly a month after the *Courier Journal* article
sounded the alarm about the outbreak, the CDC visited my office.
I was ready for black helicopters and hazmat suits, but instead,
they arrived in rental cars wearing business suits.

The team of about seven people was led by Dr. Phil Peters.
Contrary to what I had imagined, he was a soft-spoken man with
a calming demeanor.

"We are just as shocked as anyone by this situation," he said.
"I can assure you, the CDC is here to help. We can assist you with
testing and data collection, and we can help link you to other
resources." Then he leaned in. "To be honest with you, Dr. Cooke,
we are concerned that this is just the beginning."

You and me both, I thought. We talked for almost an hour
about how this event was more a disease that reflected the structural violence in places like Austin than a disease of the blood.

Dr. Peters said the CDC wanted to understand the system

in Austin so they could predict and prevent outbreaks in other places.

"Up to this point, HIV outbreaks have been isolated to urban settings," he explained. "Rural settings have many challenges we've not faced, like how to even find people or get them to a clinic."

It was at once reassuring and discouraging to hear that the CDC was struggling with the same challenges I was. I told him how we had enlisted a team of current and previous people who inject drugs to help us track down people needing to be tested. He agreed that it was, at best, an imperfect solution to a seemingly unsolvable problem. We continued to discuss our options, which were limited. For my part, I offered to let the CDC use my clinic as a testing base so we could pool our resources and benefit from each other's expertise.

Later that day, we were joined by Drs. Arno and Walthall, as well as several other state and local officials. Together we talked through the situation.

"We believe there are currently three pregnant patients in need of HIV services," Dr. Arno began.

That's two more pregnant patients than we knew of three weeks ago, I thought.

"One has started treatment, but she has to travel to Louisville for it," Dr. Peters broke in, "and only ten of the people who have tested positive have even had labs drawn."

"That means most have not started treatment," Dr. Arno clarified.

"Correct," Dr. Peters replied, "the pregnant patient is the only one." The gravity of the difficult task ahead settled over everyone. "Fortunately, Dr. Cooke has offered the use of his office in Austin."

"I thought we could hold a weekly HIV clinic," I explained to Dr. Arno, "at least in the initial phases, followed by monthly telemedicine support after things are going smoothly."

Dr. Arno nodded in agreement and offered to come to my office the following Tuesday so we could start getting people on treatment. She then added what everyone was thinking. "The cost is going to be a problem."

There was no question about that. Most of the patients we needed to reach didn't have insurance, transportation, or even stable housing. Everything we were talking about—office space, personnel, travel expenses, and physician time—would be costly. A rough estimate of a single-year budget for an HIV clinic in Austin totaled $1.3 million, and I was barely making ends meet as it was.

"Of course, HIV care is only part of the solution," Dr. Peters interjected, gesturing toward me.

"That's right." I then explained to Dr. Arno that I had invited a group of public health, school, church, social service, health-care, and behavioral health officials along with several people in recovery to meet the following week to address the underlying addiction and psychosocial issues.

"It's part of the Get Healthy Scott County Coalition," I continued. "We started it back in 2010, after the Robert Wood Johnson Foundation (RWJF) ranked Scott County dead last among Indiana's counties for health outcomes. A small group of us have been meeting regularly to discuss how to address the ranking. We don't have any definitive answers, I'm afraid, but the more local resources we can bring together and get plugged in, the better."

Both Drs. Arno and Peters agreed that the depth and complexity of the crisis appeared hopeless unless a locally developed collaborative recovery plan could be embraced.

Once I was alone again in my office, I had strangely mixed feelings. After years of suffering in silence, the struggling and hurting people of Austin were finally getting the attention they needed—if, that was, we could find them. But as local and state officials began to descend on our tiny rural town, I worried the emergency response would focus solely on the HIV outbreak in an explosion of activity, not unlike the type set off by firefighters to steal the oxygen from a fire, thereby extinguishing the blaze.

The people already working in Austin were few, but we were

passionate about helping people. The risk of an explosion of activity from outside groups descending on Austin was that it would burn up all the resources and snuff out the good work of dedicated people already struggling to do extremely difficult work.

My goal was to convince the people bringing outside resources to Austin to connect directly with local efforts and infuse them with fuel to expand, not quench, their flames of passion. I genuinely believed this would leave our community in a stronger, more sustainable position to help every person have access to health and opportunities to thrive.

I looked up at the clock. It was almost eight. *I missed dinner again.* I grabbed my phone and texted Melissa, "Sorry it's so late. I hope you're not worried. Long day . . . heading home now. Looking forward to seeing you."

I grabbed my keys, turned out the lights, locked the back door, and made my way down Main Street. It was eerily quiet.

Please, Lord, I prayed. *I feel like I'm in a whirlwind. Help the roots You've asked me to grow here to be strong enough. I know this is what You've called me to be ready for—for such a time as this. Ready or not, I am Yours.*

CHAPTER 10

THE LAW OF LOVE

· · · · · · · · ·

It always seems impossible until it's done.

NELSON MANDELA

"LET'S GO, GIRLS!"

It was almost 10 a.m. I had hoped to be on the road by now. Since the congressional hearings on the syringe exchange coincided with spring break, I had decided to bring three of our daughters with me to Indianapolis for a few days of "daddy-daughter time." I'd been working long hours at the clinic since the outbreak started, and this seemed like a great opportunity for us to spend some quality time together. Also, there was a special exhibit at the Indianapolis children's museum I wanted them to see.

I slipped the speech I had prepared earlier in the week into my backpack and checked my watch again. At this rate, we were really going to have to hustle to make it to Indy by lunch. My son, Eli, had decided to spend his spring break on a mission trip to Guatemala, so I pulled up the church's Facebook page for a quick update while I waited. I smiled as I watched a video of him singing and clapping with little kids. My smile faded as I noticed the time.

"Girls!"

"They're coming," Melissa announced, walking down the stairs. "How about you?" she asked, smiling. "You ready?"

I took a deep breath. After years of making little to no progress in soliciting help for Austin, it was almost surreal how quickly everything was suddenly unfolding.

"Yeah, I think so." Truth be told, I felt like a little kid heading off for his first day of school—a weird mix of excitement, anticipation, and apprehension. "I wish you, Max, and Rowan could come."

"Me too," she agreed. "It's too bad their schools have different spring breaks." She paused and added, "You're going to do great."

Just then three of our daughters, Moirah, Mirial, and Elissa, came staggering down the stairs, each lugging an overnight bag. As the girls made their way to the car, Melissa looked up at me one last time, and before kissing me goodbye, said, "You're ready for this, Will."

I hoped she was right.

Just over two hours later, we checked into our hotel and headed out for lunch and to spend the rest of the day exploring Indianapolis.

The following morning as the girls were putting on their "church clothes" and I was reading over my testimony, my phone rang. I figured it was probably Melissa checking in, but the area code was from Indianapolis.

"Will?" It was Dr. Walthall.

"Yes," I replied.

"I'm calling on behalf of Governor Pence. He would like to meet with you and a few other county leaders in Scottsburg at 1 p.m. today."

"Oh." I wasn't sure what to say. "Well, I'm scheduled to testify at the syringe exchange meeting here in Indy in a few hours," I hedged.

"I know. But the governor asked me to get you there," she said matter-of-factly. "I think it is important for him to hear what you have to say, and this will give you the opportunity to address him directly."

I sat down on the bed, a little stunned.

After a few moments, she reiterated, "Dr. Adams and I feel it is important that he hears what you have to say."

"Okay, I guess I'll be there," I said, glancing over my shoulder at the girls, who had become distracted rifling through the complimentary soaps and shampoos in the bathroom.

"Thanks, Will. Are you still able to meet with Dr. Arno and me tonight?"

I dreaded dragging the girls all the way back to Scott County just to turn back around and come back to Indianapolis. But what choice did I have? "Yes, I'll still be able to meet. Eight o'clock, right?"

"Yep. See you then. Good luck today," she said.

"You too," I replied as we hung up.

I just stared at my phone in stunned silence. *A personal invitation to meet with the governor.* I sure hadn't seen that coming.

I called the girls in and told them about the change in plans, expecting them to be devastated and bracing myself for tears.

"You mean you're going to meet *the governor?*" Turns out they were thrilled. *I didn't see that coming either.* After promising them we'd head straight back to Indy for a few days after the meeting, I called Melissa to let her know the change in plans.

Thankfully, the girls and I were already dressed for the hearing, so we were able to get out the door and back on the road quickly.

Once in the car, I got the girls interested in an audiobook we'd been listening to and then called my office manager. She agreed to drive up and read my testimony to the legislative committee in my place. Luckily, I'd emailed it to her the night before to get her feedback. Although it was frustrating not to be able to make the speech myself, it was hard to be too disappointed given the circumstances. *If I can just help Governor Pence get a glimpse of the structural violence that exists in parts of Austin and the importance of lifting the ban . . .*

As we made the long drive back home, I started thinking

through everything I wanted to say. I assumed he would want to see Austin, the epidemic's hot spot, for himself. *Maybe I can even give him a tour of the clinic; give him a chance to see how understaffed and under-resourced we really are down here.* With each passing mile, I grew more and more excited. *I can't believe the governor is actually going to come to our community!*

Or so I thought. As soon as I arrived, I learned that the entire meeting would be taking place at the Mid-America Science Park in Scottsburg. Governor Pence had no time to visit Austin. It was incredibly deflating to think that the girls and I had just traveled two hundred miles round trip—with another eighty miles to go before we were back in Indianapolis—to meet with the governor, yet he was not going to be able to make the five-mile journey from Scottsburg to Austin. *How can I help him understand the needs of the people if he can't even see them?* Shaking off the frustration, I steeled myself for the meeting. *If the governor won't come to Austin, I'll just have to bring Austin to the governor.*

The meeting with Governor Pence was closed to the press, but a few photographers took pictures before we started. *Anything that increases the exposure*, I thought optimistically. After the governor posed with Health Commissioner Adams and our sheriff for a few staged shots, we were quickly whisked away to a conference room.

As people filtered into the room, I made my way over to the governor and introduced myself.

"Governor Pence, it's nice to meet you, sir," I said, extending my hand. "I'm Dr. Will Cooke. I run the Foundations Family Medicine clinic in Austin."

"Yes, Dr. Cooke," he said, shaking my hand. "It's nice to meet you."

"I used to listen to your radio show during my residency up in Muncie," I said. "I still remember your tagline, 'Like Rush Limbaugh on decaf.'"

"So *you* were the one," he quipped, and we both shared a laugh. *Well, this is off to a good start*, I mused.

His aides then ushered us to a table where a small group representing law enforcement, local government, health-care institutions, faith-based organizations, our county coalition, and both the Scott and Clark County Health Departments had all gathered. I was shown to a seat with a placard with my name on it near Governor Pence. Once everyone was seated, the meeting started, and one of his aides reintroduced me and gave me a chance to address the governor directly. Since it was still fresh in my mind, I began to share the speech I had prepared for the syringe exchange hearing. As I launched into my presentation, it occurred to me that, at that very moment, my office manager was probably making the exact same speech on my behalf in Indianapolis. *Well, that's okay,* I thought. *The more people who hear about what's happening in Austin, the better.*

Governor Pence listened intently, holding my gaze the entire time. When I got to the part about the needle exchange, he interrupted me. "How long have you been there?"

"A little over a decade," I answered. He nodded. *Did he interrupt me to stop me from talking about the needle exchange?*

I continued cautiously, "We honestly don't need a lot of temporary, outside activity. Austin will be distrustful of that. What we need is your help to strengthen and expand our local capacity. Everything we do has to have roots in the community, allowing it to be sustainable."

Realizing this would likely be my only chance to speak directly to him, I added, "One of the *most critical* pieces of this response—the one that will allow health-care professionals direct access to this hard-to-reach demographic—*must* be a syringe exchange."

"Thank you, Dr. Cooke," he said. "I think we'll move on now." Before I could say another word, the governor shifted his attention to Scottsburg mayor Bill Graham, seated directly to my left, and after introductions were made, Mayor Graham launched into his own speech.

It wasn't the response I had hoped for, but I had said what I needed to say. I took some solace in the fact that Sheriff McClain was seated just to the governor's left. Other syringe services program (SSP) supporters, like Indiana Health Commissioner Jerome Adams, were also present and had Governor Pence's ear. With Sheriff McClain, Dr. Adams, and the CDC all encouraging Governor Pence to lift the ban, I felt hopeful that if the only doctor in Austin echoed their sentiments, the governor would follow their recommendation.

I sat back in my chair and listened as the conversation continued. After about an hour, Governor Pence thanked us all for coming and told us he'd reveal his plan soon. When one of the health-care officials from Scott County pressed him for a more solid answer to the syringe exchange question, Governor Pence looked at him and said, "I'll pray about it."

As a Christian, I appreciated that. At the same time, given the stakes, I wasn't sure what there was left to pray about. I've always believed that the time to pray, study, and thoughtfully reflect is *before* a crisis hits. Decisions are best made during moments of clarity, not crisis. As far as I was concerned, the science, the statistics, and the needs were clear. Any further delay would only make the situation worse and hurt even more people.

Meanwhile, about eighty miles to the north, these same sentiments were being echoed at the legislative committee hearing by Democratic representative Charlie Brown. "It is Scott County today, but it could be Lake County tomorrow. It could be St. Joe County the next day," Brown warned the deputy health commissioner. "So why can't we get out in front of this and . . . be proactive, as opposed to reactive?"[1]

· · · · · · · · ·

After the meeting with Governor Pence, the girls and I drove back up to Indianapolis. That night, after I finished reading a story to the girls and made sure my two youngest were settled in bed, I told Moirah, "I need to go meet with a few doctors downstairs. Keep the door locked until I get back. Text or call me if you need anything, okay?"

"No problem, Dad," she answered. She smiled and gave me a hug.

I walked down to the lobby where I met up with Dr. Walthall, Dr. Arno, and IU Health infectious disease specialist Dr. Diane Janowicz to come up with a plan.

"The governor will probably sign the executive order tomorrow," Dr. Walthall began. "He is currently considering several versions, and two include a syringe exchange."

We all agreed that sounded promising. Since the emergency order would finally unlock the state resources we needed, we started discussing what we needed to do. I reaffirmed my willingness to build the HIV clinic around my office and staff, and Drs. Arno and Janowicz agreed to come to my office every Tuesday to help establish treatment plans and train us.

"Meanwhile," I said, "my staff will remain available to care for patients the rest of the week."

Dr. Walthall also promised to bring state resources so that people could get birth certificates and picture IDs, which would enable them to register for the health insurance offered by the state to low-income residents. "And care coordination can help track down some of the people who've tested positive and bring them to the clinic for us to help."

I agreed to arrange for the county community mental health center to be on site to offer services. Dr. Janowicz added, "Midwest AIDS Training and Education Center will help patients navigate the services and provide education."

Dr. Walthall wrote furiously as the four of us threw out ideas.

I sent Moirah a quick text asking how things were going. She replied, "Just fine. Girls are asleep and I'm reading."

"Thanks for being awesome!!" I quickly typed.

I then shifted my attention back to the meeting and thought

about what we'd done so far. We weren't just planning a clinic; we were planning a way to break down the structural barriers people faced to access care every day. Realizing how important that was, I turned to Dr. Arno and said, "You know what? Why don't we open this event up to the entire community? Allowing everyone to access these services will help provide the HIV patients with some anonymity and decrease some of the stigma HIV and drug use carries. The last thing we need," I added, "is for people living with HIV to have a separate clinic or to enter by a separate door with flashing lights reading, 'People who use drugs or have HIV enter here.'"

They liked that idea, so we agreed to surround the first clinic with an event for everyone in our community.

"Well," Dr. Walthall said, pushing back her chair. "We all have a lot to do. It takes me six months to plan a bike fair, and here we are planning a historic emergency response in a few days." We laughed in agreement. Then she looked at me and said, "You've been waiting a long time for this, Will. Take a deep breath because here we go."

"A deep breath sounds great," I conceded. "I sort of feel like I'm drowning right now."

"That feeling is what makes things work," said Dr. Arno. "Don't forget how you sign your emails." I smiled as I realized she was referring to Galatians 6:9: "And let us not grow weary of doing good, for in due season we will reap, if we do not give up."[2]

The next morning, I took my girls to the Indianapolis children's museum. We started by walking through the dinosaur exhibit in the basement, then we made our way to the fourth floor, where we rode the carousel. After riding for a while, we took the central spiraling ramp down to the third floor, where I led my kids to *The Power of Children* exhibit. It honored an inspirational young man I had thought about a great deal lately, Ryan White.

Ryan's mom, Jeanne, had kept his room exactly the way it was the day he died of complications related to AIDS in 1990. Ten years later, she contacted the museum, and they meticulously re-created the room as part of the exhibit.

The idea was to honor children who stood for change in the face of hatred. The two other children featured were Ruby Bridges, who endured racism in the South, and Anne Frank, who faced genocide in Nazi Germany. These young people had, as the museum states, "transcended their time, becoming symbols of courage in the face of the ignorance, bigotry, and hatred they faced."[3] I wanted my girls to know about them.

It was surreal to stand with my girls in Ryan White's bedroom during a time when HIV and all the stigma attached to it had resurfaced. It gave me the opportunity to talk with them about how the HIV epidemic had circled back to Indiana, as well as the importance of showing compassion to those in need.

I'd grown up in a church that preached that we were called by God to "come out from among them and be separate"[4] yet been raised by a father who drilled into me the danger of placing rules above an individual's need for Christ's compassion. I'd had to rec-oncile what felt like a moral disconnect between what the church taught about suffering people and what I had seen and experienced through the lives of such people.

I strongly resonated with a saying attributed to St. Augustine about the need to temper our interpretation of the law with com-passion. He said, "Scripture teaches nothing but [love], and we must not leave an interpretation of Scripture until we have found a compassionate interpretation of it." I also agreed with Martin Luther, who wrote that, "all law, divine and human, treating of outward conduct, should not bind any further than love goes. Love is to be the interpreter of law."[5]

To that end, I told my girls about how Christ socialized with adulterers, lepers, and tax collectors—considered at that time to be the lowest of the low—and how He healed the sick on the Sabbath, disregarding the way Old Testament law was interpreted at that time. In this way, He demonstrated that people matter more than rules.[6]

I shared with them one of my favorite passages, in which Jesus answers a challenge for Him to name the greatest law. He answered, "'Love the Lord your God with all your heart and with all your soul and with all your mind.' This is the first and greatest commandment. And the second is like it: 'Love your neighbor as yourself.'"[7]

That, more than anything, was the truth I wanted to impart to my daughters that day—that we are literally commanded by God to love and care for each other—especially "the least of these" (Matthew 25:40). We must approach each other as human beings, first and foremost, regardless of race, religion, political party, or socioeconomic status. God, I reminded my girls as we anxiously awaited the governor's decision, is neither Republican nor Democrat. He is simply love.

· · · · · · · · · ·

The next day, as the number of known HIV cases swelled to seventy-nine, Governor Pence signed a thirty-day executive order declaring a public health emergency in Scott County and allowing our health department to run an SSP under state supervision "only to the extent medically necessary to suppress the HIV epidemic [there] and only for the duration of this order."

"I do not support needle exchange as anti-drug policy," Governor Pence said at a news conference announcing the order, conceding, "but this is a public health emergency."[8] He then went on to say, "It is the sharing of needles that has caused this epidemic to take place."[9]

As relieved as I was that the ban had been lifted—albeit temporarily—I was nonetheless discouraged by those comments. Sharing needles may have been the vehicle for the outbreak, but they were not the root cause. Adverse social determinants of health like poverty, social isolation, and generational trauma had left many people vulnerable. This order focused solely on the behavior or personal responsibility of people (needle sharing) as opposed to ways to end the underlying structural violence that was wreaking havoc on the people of Austin.

"This whole disaster," I lamented that night to Melissa, "could have been prevented by proactively investing in the community and in public health."

Melissa finished my thought. "Instead of blaming and further isolating people in need."

"I get the tendency to focus on personal responsibility," I continued. "But seeing what has happened in Austin has convinced me social responsibility is at least as important. We need to focus more on how to help people than on how to control them."

Later that same day, Governor Pence quietly signed additional legislation, set to go into effect as soon as the thirty-day executive order expired, upgrading the possession of a syringe from a misdemeanor to a felony charge, subject to imprisonment for up to two and a half years.[10]

In getting the ban temporarily lifted, we had won a small battle. But we were still a long way from winning the war, and I believed that adding increased criminal penalties to syringe possession once the order expired had no public health benefits. I feared that before it was all over, Austin would not be the only town suffering casualties. I had little doubt that other places were experiencing all the same structural harms we were. Austin was the sentinel event, the canary in the coal mine to warn the rest of the nation to pay attention and make changes. The only ingredient missing elsewhere was a crisis like our HIV outbreak—and as decades of experience suggested, it was just a matter of time.

CHAPTER 11

VOICES

· · · · · · · · · ·

You can't stay in your corner of the forest waiting for others
to come to you. You have to go to them sometimes.

A. A. MILNE

GOVERNOR PENCE'S TEMPORARY APPROVAL of a targeted
syringe services program (SSP) met just one of our urgent needs.
The truth is, no one was prepared for this unprecedented health-
care disaster, which had left our rural community with one of the
highest HIV rates in the world. The Indiana State Department of
Health (ISDH) wasn't. The CDC wasn't. Scott County's health
department wasn't. I wasn't either.

The biggest obstacle remained finding the people in need. If
we failed to get people tested and treated, they would eventually
develop AIDS or end-stage liver disease from hepatitis C. Or they
would overdose and die.

Meanwhile, the growing number of county, state, and national
agencies that had gotten involved was quickly becoming overwhelming. We needed someone to help make certain our messag-
ing to the public was correct and consistent and to ensure that

local resources and efforts didn't get trampled on or drowned out by the larger government entities—and I knew exactly the person to do it. Carolyn King.

As the founder of the Scott County Partnership nearly two decades prior, Carolyn had given me hope years earlier that my team and I could improve access to health care in Austin. Her spirit inspired me to invest in bringing cutting-edge, evidence-based health care to the poorest among us. We both believed that the isolated and disadvantaged of our community did not deserve less than others; if anything, they deserved more from the rest of us.

Carolyn knew the challenges we faced, and she knew many of the key stakeholders personally. If anyone could coordinate such a massive operation, it was she. I wrote to Indiana Health Commissioner Jerome Adams and asked him if he would please consider running everything through her.

Dr. Adams agreed and quickly reached out to King who, tragically, had lost a granddaughter to an accidental drug overdose just ten days earlier. Because Scott County was dear to her heart and the HIV outbreak was related directly to the opioid epidemic, she agreed to accept the position in honor of her granddaughter. This gave many of us at the local level confidence and hope.

With Carolyn on board, I could sense the momentum building behind a coordinated, joint response between the state and local forces. Later that day, I wrote a public Facebook post[1] thanking the governor for approving the syringe services program and letting people know how committed we were to getting the outbreak under control.

I stressed that the HIV clinic would be permanent, that it would use an integrated approach to address all the needs of people living with HIV, and that it would help patients gain access to addiction counseling and the SSP. In addition, I assured people that we would develop mobile units for testing and linkage to care, and that we would assist people who needed to secure insurance.

"This is a rapidly evolving situation," I wrote, "and we are acting now to do all that we can to start making Austin better. I'll not stop until this epidemic is controlled, the drug abuse has disappeared, and our community is healed. . . . So, please join me in praying earnestly for healing. Then, we will start heading to where Austin can and should be. A beautiful place where families and businesses thrive. We may not be there yet, but we are closer than we were yesterday."

Of course, not everyone agreed with what I was doing.

I had already been receiving backlash for showing compassion to "those people." One community member asked me, "Why not just let 'em die?" Another quipped, "These worthless addicts dying is nothin' more than social Darwinism. Good riddance!"

I was accused of everything from somehow trying to get rich from the outbreak to enabling "addicts" and "hookers" to continue their "debauchery." But the day after Governor Pence signed the emergency order and I posted my commitment to provide services to people living with or at risk of contracting HIV, the backlash against me and my office intensified.

As I was driving my girls back from Indianapolis, my office manager called me.

"Things are getting pretty intense here at the office, Dr. Cooke." There was a hint of fear in her voice.

"What's going on?" I asked.

"Well, a lot of people are not showing up for their appointments. Others are calling and canceling upcoming appointments. I mean, we're struggling to keep the doors open as it is. If people stop coming, what are we going to do?"

"We're doing the right thing," I reassured her. "People are reacting out of fear and misinformation right now. All this will blow over, and even if some patients leave the practice, most will come back because they know we care about them and the community."

Though I kept my voice even and calm, what she said chilled me. The only way the practice could offset expenses was by seeing patients. *If people stop coming . . .*

Her voice cut through my thoughts. "Are the hundred or so people with HIV really worth sacrificing the thousands of other patients we normally serve?"

That's a solid point.

"I understand what you're saying," I conceded. "But I will keep my office open to *everyone* or not at all. I need you and the staff to remain steadfast and faithful through the next few weeks. It might be hard, but together, we *will* make this happen."

She didn't acknowledge what I said, allowing the silence to linger. Just as I began to wonder if we'd been disconnected, she said, "There's more." She hesitated before continuing. "The phones have been ringing off the hook all day. Angry people have been harassing, yelling, and cussing at us because you promised to open our office to the people with HIV." Her initial hesitancy evaporated as she spoke, replaced by anger. "They've threatened us, saying that we're going to 'get what we deserve,' that we are going to hell for what we are doing, and that people will not stand for it." She paused before continuing more calmly, sounding concerned. "We've even received a few death threats against you, Dr. Cooke."

I remained quiet, not only because I didn't know what to say, but because I didn't want to worry my daughters. I turned up the volume on the audiobook we were listening to so they'd remain focused on it instead of the phone call.

My office manager pressed on, clearly agitated. "I don't think you realize what you've gotten us into. The staff and I are a little freaked out right now from being told off, harassed, and threatened."

"Okay, I hear you," I said and then paused to gather my thoughts. "Go ahead and send all incoming calls to voice mail. Have the front desk check the messages and only return the calls of those who need us to help them with something. Delete the rest." I lowered my voice so the girls couldn't hear me as I continued. "If anyone appears threatening when they come to the reception window, make sure the doors to the back are locked and call the police."

"Got it," she replied. "I let Chief Spicer know what's going on. He said he already added the clinic to his officers' routine patrol because he'd been hearing the same sort of threats. Our staff does such an amazing job. I hate that they are being treated this way."

"Me too," I said. "Schedule an office meeting first thing in the morning. I want to talk through all this and make sure everybody knows how to respond. We need to stay focused on why we are doing what we are doing."

We hung up, and I hit pause on the audiobook. "Did I miss anything interesting?"

· · · · · · · · · ·

Once my daughters and I arrived home and our kids were all in bed, I told Melissa about the threats.

"I thought we had moved past all that after Ryan White," she said.

"I know, right?" I replied

"What are you going to do?" she asked.

Just then my phone rang. I showed her the caller ID. We both recognized the number. It was a prominent Scott County community leader. We exchanged a concerned look, and I answered the phone. "Hello."

"Dr. Cooke?"

"Yes."

"I have some concerning news," the person said, getting right to the point.

"Okay, what's up?" I asked.

"Well, there are some people planning to burn down your building this weekend."

"What?" I blurted out as I stood up.

"I wasn't going to bother you with this, but I've heard it from a couple of reliable sources." The voice seemed far away as images of my building burning filled my mind. Melissa was close enough to hear what the caller was saying. She put her arms around me and laid her head on my chest. I held her with my free arm, and even though I thought I knew why someone would make that threat, I asked the caller anyway.

"For one, some people are saying you're legitimizing illegal and sinful behavior. Others don't want Scott County to be known for this, and they see you as the face to fight against. But there's another camp that may be the most dangerous." Silence followed.

After a few seconds, I looked down at Melissa, who was staring up at me wide-eyed.

"Go on," I prompted.

"Let's just say that this outbreak may reach far beyond people who inject drugs. There are people who pay for sex and don't want to be found out, and they're scared."

I squeezed my eyes shut and Melissa held me a little tighter. I took a breath and said as calmly as I could, "Got it. What do you think I should do?"

"Are you willing to quit speaking out and back off on your efforts to help?" the voice asked.

Melissa looked up at me again pleadingly. But I knew she was urging me to stand strong and not give in to the threats.

"No, that's not an option," I said more firmly than I intended. Melissa seemed to relax slightly.

"Does your clinic have a security system?" was the next question.

I furrowed my brow as I began to feel paranoid. "Yes, of course."

"Good. Then all you can do is pray and wait."

"Is there anything else I need to know?" I asked.

"No, that's all I called to tell you. Good luck."

"Thanks for calling. Goodbye." I ended the call and we sat back down in stunned silence. Melissa cursed and laid her head on my shoulder.

* * * * * * * * *

The next morning, a Friday, I got to the clinic early to work on what I would say to my staff. As everyone arrived and we began to gather, I thought back to the first time I'd gathered my employees—only two of them at the time—when I'd first arrived in Austin. I wondered what that naive, idealistic, younger me would think about what was going on now. I looked up to find my staff—now numbering a solid twenty—had pulled chairs into a circle to hear what I had to say. They looked worried.

"When I came here eleven years ago," I began, "I had no idea what to expect. You've each seen tragic endings to lives filled with heartache. Austin has been sick for a long time, long before I opened this practice."

A few people nodded.

"We've each felt the hopelessness of some of the people we serve. We've experienced the trauma they've lived and vowed to do all we can to make a difference."

Heads were still bowed dejectedly.

"Look at me," I said as I walked around inside the small circle they had formed.

"You each make a difference in the lives of people every single day. We have been here when no one else was willing to come and help. If we went around this room, we could spend hours sharing stories of lives being healed and futures being restored. I'm proud of each and every one of you, and I'm honored to work with such a dedicated group of people."

A few sat up a little straighter and looked around the room as if to acknowledge that others felt the same way.

"When I was in high school, I was inspired by the courage of a boy my age named Ryan White who lived right here in Indiana. Because he had HIV, people were so afraid of him that they harassed him and his family. He refused to give in to the hatred. He bravely stood for compassion and insisted that every single life mattered. He changed hearts and history. Because of him, people with HIV were able to access compassionate care. We have that same opportunity right now. The world is watching to see if we fold; to see if our conviction to defend the right of every person to have access to health and opportunity means something; to see if it's even possible to care for people the rest of the world has forsaken.

"The history of how we respond to this challenge will be written, and the world will know that the bonds of compassion are stronger than the bonds of fear; that light will always drive out darkness; that we will not turn our backs on a single sacred soul, regardless of who they are, how they live, or what the rest of the world thinks of them or of us. Let's stand strong together to prove that this sort of compassionate care is not only possible, but can change the lives of people, families, and entire communities. I'm committed to seeing this all the way through. Nothing—certainly not the fear of a handful of misguided people—will keep me from standing with those who need us the most. Are you with me?"

I saw several smiles, and the tension in the room was replaced with a quiet confidence. People nodded to each other, and a few wiped tears from their eyes.

"We just needed to hear that you're not going to bail on us, Dr. Cooke," my office manager said.

My nurse echoed her words. "We're ready to fight for this community. We were just afraid you might give up."

"Never," I said, feeling relieved. "I think this fight might just be the reason God called us here."

. . . .

I spent the weekend with my family. Even though I received a few more calls from concerned community members who warned me about rumored threats, Melissa and I refused to spend any time fretting about what-ifs that we considered unlikely. We did our best to protect the kids from knowing about those trying to intimidate me and the clinic, feeling there was no point in scaring them unnecessarily.

On Monday morning, I reassured myself that if the clinic had been burned down, someone would have called me. Still, I didn't know what I would find waiting as I headed off to work. Images of people with picket signs throwing things at me and my staff flooded my mind.

I'm ready, Lord. Ryan and others faced so much worse. Whatever is waiting for me, I know You'll be there too.

I drove all the way to work with the radio off. I needed the silence to let my spirit breathe and to feel God's reassuring presence. Rounds at the hospital went quickly. A few of the hospital staff thanked me for what I was doing for the community.

"Everyone here thinks what you're doing is great," one of the nurses said. "But be careful."

Another said, "Most people wouldn't have helped. I mean, you didn't have to." Then she voiced what I expected most of them were thinking. "Still, with the threats and all, why are you risking so much to help those people?"

Her question triggered renewed concern for my staff and my building. I needed to get up there. As I turned to leave, I offered the only answer I could. "They are the children of God who've been cut off and forsaken. God didn't call me to Austin to help only the people who already have access to health and opportunity. He called me there to ensure they are available to every person. I can't turn my back on those who need care the most."

The short drive from Scottsburg to Austin seemed longer than usual. As I pulled into the parking lot behind the clinic, I felt a little silly for worrying as much as I had. The clinic was fine, and there were no protesters in sight. *Thank You, Lord,* I prayed.

In fact, the only thing out of the norm was the number of cars and vans in the parking lot marked with TV and radio station call signs.

One step at a time.

"How long have they been here?" I said, drawing my office manager's attention to the small bevy of reporters camped out in front of the clinic.

"Since around sunup," she replied sardonically. "They've been waiting for you."

Since the historic magnitude of the Scott County HIV outbreak had been made public, the media coverage had crescendoed to a fevered pitch, with emails and phone calls coming in from all over the world requesting interviews with "the only doctor in Austin."

I had mixed emotions about the attention. Although HIV was a serious issue that merited the spotlight, the fact remained that for years, we had been ignored while much worse fates befell the men, women, and children of Austin. In a few short weeks, the world went from ignoring what I had to say to literally knocking on my door to get the inside scoop.

"They won't go away until you go out there," she chided me. "I saw one of them talking with the police earlier. They probably want to ask you about the death threats."

I sighed. *This whole situation is difficult enough already. Why can't they just let us do our jobs?* Resigned, I headed out front to talk with the press. As my office manager predicted, one of the first questions I was asked had to do with the death threats.

"No one likes negative press," I said, trying to remain as calm and reassuring as possible. "The citizens of Austin have a very good reason to be upset. It is a tragedy that this is happening in our community. The people of Austin deserve to be proud of their town, not ashamed of where they are from. So with all this negative publicity, they have a right to be angry, and I think they are voicing that in the only way they know how right now."[2]

After reaffirming my vow to continue serving the people of Austin, I told them, "I need everyone to clear out. I can't allow any identifiable media presence anywhere around the clinic."

"Why is that, Dr. Cooke?" someone asked.

"We work hard to help people feel safe accessing help here," I explained. "If they see cameras and cars marked with the call letters of TV stations, they are not likely to come in."

I turned to leave when I heard another voice ask, "Can we talk to any of the patients affected by the outbreak?"

I felt my face flush, and I pivoted to address this question. "No, that's not something I'm going to do. Listen, many of my patients have been used and abused and harassed and traumatized their entire lives. They come to me because they trust they will be safe here. That is a sacred bond we share. I'll not betray it. Please don't show up tomorrow for the HIV clinic. You'll only be asked to leave." I paused and said, "In fact, don't ever come back to my clinic looking for a patient to interview."

"I'm sure the state will provide updates," I added and turned to walk away again.

"But you're the only doctor here, and people need to hear from you."

"I'll think about it," I said. "Now, please clear out so my patients aren't scared off."

As I headed back inside, the media began loading up. But soon news crews could be seen driving around the streets of Austin, even setting up a few blocks down Main Street with cameras aimed at my office.

Our first HIV clinic was scheduled to take place the following day, and I wanted to make sure the media was kept away during that all-important day. I emailed Dr. Walthall and had my office manager call Austin's police chief, Donald Spicer. He sent a patrol car to keep the cameras out of shot of the clinic, and Dr. Walthall agreed to ensure the media was nowhere near the clinic when we started seeing patients.

Later that day, Garith Fulham of the AIDS Healthcare Foundation (AHF) contacted me. "We've seen the reports of what's happening," he began. "Frankly, the hostility, lack of understanding, and controversy is reminiscent of the AIDS crisis back in the eighties, and what people like Ryan White faced. Would it be okay for me to visit you?" he asked. "We'd like to see what we can do to help."

We agreed to meet in two days—after we had gotten through our first HIV clinic.

That night after dinner, I did a quick online search and learned that AHF was started by Michael Weinstein in 1987 to help people with AIDS, including many of his own friends, die with dignity. It was called the AIDS *Hospice* Foundation then, since there was no effective treatment yet. They had since grown into the largest provider of HIV care in the world. *Well*, I thought, *if anyone can empathize with what we're trying to do here . . .*

"Will," Melissa called, "could you please give me a hand with the dishes?"

I closed my laptop and headed toward the kitchen. I could hear the kids playing out back. I loved being home with my family. It was like an oasis amidst all the insanity.

"Something bothering you?" Melissa asked, handing me a dish towel.

"All this media attention just feels so . . . wrong," I admitted.

"I bet it does," she said, catching my eye. "How are you handling it?"

"I'm not sure. It's like some messed-up nightmare that I've lost control of and can't wake up from."

"Honey, you've been trying to get people to listen for over a decade," she prompted me.

"Yeah, but this all seems more like a freak show to them, you know? A way to boost ratings, not to help people."

"Are the journalists all like that?" she asked.

"No," I conceded. "But I'm concerned that many of them already seem to know what message they want to communicate, and they're just looking for me to give them the sound bite they want."

"What kind of stuff are they asking about?" she asked, handing me another dish to dry.

"Well, some want to bash the governor for dragging his feet on lifting the ban, and others seem interested in cracking down even harder on people who use drugs."

"Oh," Melissa interjected, "like this outbreak is all *their* fault?"

"Something like that." I shook my head. "We knew a crisis like this was coming. All the indicators were there, and no one listened."

"So the reporters are right," she suggested. "All of this could have been avoided if Governor Pence had listened to the state health department and CDC years ago."

I could feel a headache coming on. "I'm not going to say that on the news just to support their agenda." I walked over to the back window to watch our two youngest daughters race across the yard.

"I hear what you're saying, Will," Melissa said softly, following me to the window. "But don't people need to know things like this can be avoided?"

"People *do* need to know that this can happen anywhere people are marginalized," I said quietly.

After a few moments, she broke the silence with a gentle question, "What would you do if *our* kids were in danger?"

I looked over and met her eyes. "If I speak to the media, it will be for the people whose voices are not heard."

She smiled in a way that made me feel she was proud of me and took my hand. "Good."

"People may not like what I have to say," I warned.

"Who cares?" she squeezed my hand. "Indiana is where Ryan White stood his ground," she reminded me. "You can do this." She looked back out at the girls. "We'll all support you."

Then Melissa wrapped her arms around my waist, and we stood in the quiet stillness of our house, watching our children play.

Still one thought continued to pull at the corners of my mind.

God forbid that the only thing the press talks about is the HIV outbreak—and then nothing ultimately changes.

CHAPTER 12

ANY POSITIVE CHANGE

· · · · · · · · ·

I am more than my scars.
ANDREW DAVIDSON,
THE GARGOYLE

ON TUESDAY, MARCH 31, 2015—just five days after Governor Pence signed the emergency declaration but over four full months after the first HIV cases were detected—we started treating HIV patients at my office. All the government officials who had pledged their support, representing just about every division of the state government, turned up as promised. Tents had been set up in the parking lot where anyone could get vaccines and ID cards or apply for insurance. Volunteers were posted around the clinic to help steer people wherever they needed to go.

When a handful of news crews began hovering a few blocks away, Dr. Walthall sent state officials to chase them off. It was an emotional day, and the gravity of it was not lost on me. *What if none of the people with HIV show up?*

Shortly after 9 a.m., the disease investigation specialists began to show up accompanied by a few HIV patients they had managed to track down and convince to come see us. To ensure they'd not be harassed, we discretely ushered them in through a secured side door. Once within the protected space of the clinic, we reassured them we were there to help. They appeared haggard and nervous. Some were literally nodding off from being intoxicated while others were experiencing withdrawal symptoms. Most had track marks running up and down their arms—visible scars of invisible wounds.

Regardless, we let them know we cared about them. These were the modern-day lepers: People were afraid to be near them, and they felt untouchable. To combat this, I made sure to greet each person with a handshake or a hug and told them they would be all right. All the pent-up tension that had been building as the crisis had steadily worsened over the past few weeks finally broke, and we sprang into action.

"Modern medications are so effective," we assured one nervous patient after another, "that as long as you take your medicine, you'll be okay." Previously convinced they had been given a death sentence, the relief was so overwhelming, many of them wept. Drs. Walthall, Arno, Janowicz, and I shared a few tears as well. At around eleven, I stepped out front to take a breather, and two men approached me.

"Excuse me, are you Dr. Cooke?" one of them asked.

I didn't recognize them. They were dressed in casual street clothes and didn't appear to be with either the press or any of the agencies we were working with.

"Yes," I said hesitantly.

"Hi," said the older of the two, extending his hand. "I'm Dan Bigg. I'm with Chicago Recovery Alliance." *Bigg*, I mused. His name certainly fit him. He looked an inch or so over six feet and was heavyset. Because he was also balding with a tightly trimmed gray beard, a big booming voice, and a broad smile, he reminded me of the kind of guy you'd expect to see playing Santa at the mall at Christmas.

As I shook his hand, he nodded in the direction of his companion, a younger, intense-looking guy wearing a black newsboy cap. "And this is Chris Abert of Indiana Recovery Alliance."

"Nice to meet you, Dr. Cooke," Chris said, extending his own hand.

"Dr. Walthall asked us to come down today and see if we could help," Dan continued.

As if on cue, Dr. Walthall approached from across Main Street, just back from holding a press conference at Austin City Hall. "Dan," she called, waving. "I thought I recognized your van out here."

"What's up, Doc?" He smiled. "You remember Chris."

"Of course I do," she beamed, shaking Chris's hand. "I'm so glad you were both able to be here." Reading the confusion on my face, Dr. Walthall took the introductions a step further. "Will, I asked Dan and Chris to come down today to see if they could help us out. Dan is the founder of the Chicago Recovery Alliance, one of the first syringe exchanges in the country. He's been working with people with HIV for almost thirty years.

"In fact," she continued, "he was one of the very first people to identify ways to protect people who use syringes from dying or contracting diseases like HIV."

Now that piqued my interest. "Really?" I turned to Dan. "How did you do that?"

As we began to walk together, Dan just shrugged. "Basically, by listening." He paused for a second, then added, "And then responding with actionable solutions to help keep people alive."

"Some people refer to Dan as the patron saint of harm reduction," Dr. Walthall said, smiling.

I actually felt my pulse quicken. I had studied the concept of harm reduction, and I loved it. It covers everything from using a seat belt to intermittent fasting to lose weight to teaching patients the proper way to monitor and care for their diabetes.

Since the Mayo Clinic estimates only 2.7 percent of Americans follow "healthy" lifestyle recommendations[1] and over half of all deaths in the United States are a result of lifestyle choices,[2] the basic goal of harm reduction is to help people reduce the adverse consequences of their daily decisions. In this case, that meant getting people to stop reusing and sharing syringes.

"Probably the most important thing we did," Dan continued, "was to define recovery as 'any positive change.' In those three words was a revolution we're still living to this day."

Amen to that, I thought. I instantly recognized a kindred spirit, and I was anxious to learn more.

We had circled around the outside of the clinic to the parking lot in the back where we paused, surrounded by all the tents, tables, and activity.

"Thirty years," I shook my head. "And here I thought *I'd* been trying forever. How'd you get started in all this?"

"Well, I originally planned to go to medical school," Dan said, nodding at the stethoscope hanging around my neck. "I wanted to do something to make a difference in the health and happiness of people. That dream lasted until I had to care for someone with a pilonidal cyst."

He chuckled and looked at the ground as I grimaced. I'd seen my fair share of pilonidal cysts, which develop where the tailbone ends, and suffice it to say, they're not pleasant.

"Yeah," he continued, "that was enough to make me choose another profession. So I started taking night classes at the Chicago School of Professional Psychology while working at a drug treatment program during the day, and a lot of the patients at the treatment center started showing up with HIV/AIDS."

"When was that?" I asked.

"Around '85," he said. "The height of the AIDS crisis."

I just shook my head. *And thirty years later, here we are again.*

"It drove me crazy not to be able to offer people who were withering away in front of me anything except compassion," he lamented. "Then I found out that people living with HIV were being banned from attending recovery support meetings, so I formed HIVIES."

"Hivies?" I asked.

"HIV Information Exchange and Support," he explained. "You see, at that time over a third of the people who had AIDS were people who inject drugs. HIVIES allowed people with HIV who injected drugs some connection with people who cared about them. But people were still dying. So in '92, a buddy of mine named John Szyler and I started the Chicago Recovery Alliance (CRA), a place where people who were formerly or actively using drugs and people with HIV could find community and health resources. One of our first initiatives was to team up with public health researchers to develop a syringe exchange."

"Syringe exchanges were legal in Illinois?" I asked.

"Oh, no," Dan waved me off. "But CRA *could* distribute sterile syringes legitimately as part of a scientific study."

"Dan was also instrumental in getting Narcan (naloxone) distributed into communities that needed it," Chris interjected. "God knows how many lives that saved."

I had used Narcan a number of times myself on patients in the ER, and frankly, the stuff was amazing. Nicknamed the Lazarus drug, I had seen people who were basically dead sit straight up and start talking within a few seconds. The challenge was getting it to people in time. Dan told me he started collaborating with pharmacists and physicians to allow Narcan to be available in the community after John, his friend and CRA cofounder, died of an accidental overdose in 1996.

A lot of people were resistant at first, Dan explained. "They argued that addicts wouldn't use it correctly."

"But they did," Chris chimed in, "and now twenty years later, community distribution of Narcan has been replicated across the country. It's really no different than teaching people how to provide CPR or perform the Heimlich maneuver."[3]

Looking at Dan, Chris continued, "What did that DePaul prof

say? That you were light-years ahead of almost everyone in the harm reduction movement when it came to saving lives?" Dan, now red-faced, just smiled and stared at the ground.

Sensing Dan's embarrassment, I turned my attention to Chris. "So then you brought the same program to Indiana?"

"Yep," Chris said. "At first we failed miserably because we didn't have any relationship with the people who really needed our help. I mean, I'd lived in the area for twenty-five years and for a while had even been homeless and injected drugs myself. But that street cred *still* wasn't enough."

Now *that* caught my attention. Just looking at him, I never would have guessed Chris had a history of injecting drugs.

"You have to have preexisting relationships with people," he continued. "You can't just parachute in and expect to, like, save the day." He glanced around the parking lot at all the tents and people with name tags scurrying around. "So many people mean well," he added, "but they want to step in right in the middle of a crisis, and they end up ignoring or pushing aside the people who are already involved."

"So how'd *you* get around the syringe ban?" I asked. "Same way Dan did?"

Both of them laughed. "Sort of . . ."

Dan smiled. "Actually, Chris went a little more rogue than I did."

"I was like, *I'm just going to go to the local pharmacy and buy some syringes,*" Chris said matter-of-factly.

"And that worked?" I asked incredulously.

"Oh, heck no." Chris waved me off. "In fact, they flat-out refused."

"So what'd you do?" I asked.

"He called me," Dan said.

"Dan told me, 'Bring a van up to Chicago, I'll load you up with everything you need, and then you can take it back with you,'" Chris said, mimicking Dan's voice. "At first, I thought he was joking! It took me a while to realize he was serious. I mean, I never heard of that kind of compassionate generosity."

"What did you do?" I asked.

Chris laughed. "We did exactly what he told us to do!"

We all joined his laughter.

Chris put his arm around Dan and continued, "But, of course, anyone who's met Dan knows you get what we call 'Dan-napped.' You know, kidnapped—but with him, three hours later you're thinking, *Well, that's everything I never wanted to know about naloxone.*"

As the laughter settled, we resumed our short lap around my building and Chris continued, "The next day my team and I started handing out socks stuffed with Narcan and ten sterile syringes."

"What if they got caught with them?" I asked.

"As word got around, people figured out what to ask for without drawing a lot of attention to themselves," Chris explained. "Just in case, we made cards they could keep with them stating they were part of a research program and, therefore, exempt from state paraphernalia laws."

"Is that legit?" I asked, side-eyeing Dr. Walthall. I was all in favor of getting sterile syringes into the hands of people who needed them, but the law was still the law.

"Oh, completely," Dan assured me. "We collect data from everyone and report it to local and state officials so they can be better informed on what's happening out there. Since most habitual users have gone off the grid, this is the most effective way to obtain useful data."

"Anyway," Chris interjected, "a few months after Dan and I connected, we found out about the HIV crisis down here, so . . . here we are."

"We brought a few of our peer counselors with us," Dan said, gesturing toward a white van with the CRA logo painted on the side parked a few yards away. Leaning up against it were a fiftysomething heavyset guy with a gray ponytail; a small, rough-looking woman who appeared to be missing several teeth; and a tall, thin guy, perhaps in his late thirties, who wore a fedora.

My eyebrows shot up. "Interesting bunch."

"Yeah," Dan began, "they were all part of the syringe program at one point. Now they're in recovery and helping us out."

"That makes sense," I said, nodding. "We've been asking some of the locals to help us track people down to be tested too."

"Great minds . . ." Dan beamed. "The program *does* work. Those three are living proof."

"So what do you need from us?" I asked.

"Nothing, really," Dan said. "If it's okay with you, we'd just like to go out into the community and start talking to people. Let them know what's going on, ask some questions, and point them in your direction so they can get some help."

Dan's words were like music to my ears.

"That sounds perfect," I said.

We exchanged a few more pleasantries, I suggested a few spots where they might want to concentrate their efforts, and then, like a small but dedicated army, the five of them headed out to do their thing.

As their van pulled away, my heart offered a simple yet sincere benediction. *Thank You, Lord, for people like Dan and Chris and for bringing them today. We're in a race against time here. Please . . . let us find even more ways to rescue the perishing before it's too late.*

· · · · · · · · ·

As the first day of the clinic wore on, word began to spread throughout the community that we were "safe." Soon more and more people needing care for their HIV or substance use disorder showed up. After lunch, things began to slow down a little, and Dr. Arno asked if I wanted to take a walk.

It was sunny but cool, so we grabbed our jackets and headed

out the back door of the clinic. As usual, people were out walking or sitting on their porches. We waved to some and engaged others in conversation. People were curious about the HIV outbreak and what it meant for their sleepy hometown. We tried to be reassuring and encouraged them to let others know about the HIV and addiction services we were providing.

Eventually, we happened upon about a dozen or so people hanging out behind some rundown apartments on the north side of town. We noticed a CDC worker we knew named Priya was with them, so we headed over to join her. As we approached the group, I realized I had taken care of most of them over the years. There were a few more men than women, and most appeared to be in their twenties and thirties. Three or four looked like they were in their fifties, but they were probably younger—hard living takes its toll. About half of them were smoking. Their clothes were old, and even the women wore baggy jeans with either a hoodie or a jacket. Everyone except Dr. Arno, Priya, and I had tattoos.

Dr. Arno and I introduced ourselves. A few of those gathered said they hadn't used "the needle" in a while, instead taking Suboxone (buprenorphine/naloxone)—a less powerful but safer version of methadone—to dull their cravings, though most admitted they were still injecting Opana.

"I hate the needle," commented a guy with L-O-V-E tattooed on his four right-hand knuckles and H-A-T-E tattooed on his left. "I only do it cause the drug company put that formula in where you had to cook 'em."

"Yeah," a younger woman agreed. "We'd all rather snort 'em but we can't anymore."

There was suddenly a grumbling of agreement from everyone.

Priya, Dr. Arno, and I looked at each other knowingly. Endo Pharmaceuticals admitted that they changed the formulation in 2012, not for patient safety but to protect their patent on Opana against generic competition. Their chief operating officer said that if they allowed competitors to market generic versions of Opana, "annualized net sales will decrease by an amount up to $135 million."[4]

The FDA eventually denied their request in 2013 after discovering that the new formulation did not effectively deter abuse. In fact, the FDA had stated, "Reformulated Opana ER can be readily prepared for injection, despite Endo's claim."[5]

A 2014 study coauthored by Endo's medical director reported that injection abuse of Opana nearly doubled after the formulation change.[6] Yet it was still heavily marketed and sold as safe across the country.

Eventually, Priya asked, "How do you prepare the Opana to inject?"

"We basically cook it in the bottom of a pop can," an older gentleman to my left explained. "You burn it with a lighter and it kills the gel in it. Once you burn it, you smash it down and cook it some more, till it's all cooked. That's when you put some water on it and work it with your fingers till you start seeing this black stuff oozin' out. If you add the water before you cook it, the gel's not killed and it'll just gunk up your syringe."

"Even then," the younger woman added, "you have to add a lot of water 'cause it's still real thick."

The older man agreed. "It's enough water for the three or four of us sharing to take two or three shots."

Priya put her hands up. "Wait, so are you saying that three or four people each draw up from the same pop can, inject, and then put their needles back into the liquid to draw up again multiple times?"

"Yeah," the young woman said matter-of-factly. "We know it's double dippin', but we ain't gonna waste it."

"Does everyone have their own syringe?" Priya asked.

A couple of people pulled their own used syringes from their pockets and held them out for us to see. A quick glance revealed that they had seen better days.

"Not everyone's got one, though," the woman answered. "Sometimes three or four people share the same syringe."

Wow, I thought.

"How do you filter the liquid you inject?" Priya asked, knowing people usually draw their drug up through some sort of material to filter out particles and clumps before injecting. This keeps the needle from getting clogged and also decreases the risk of injection site complications like soreness, abscesses, or clotted veins.

The man with LOVE/HATE tattooed on his knuckles took a last drag on his cigarette and said, "We just use cigarette butts," as he flicked his to the ground.

I surveyed the ground littered with them and cringed. Priya shook her head and said, "Cigarette filters are filthy and have tiny glass particles in them. Please, if you're going to use something, use the cotton end of a clean Q-tip. That is much safer, okay?"

A few people raised their eyebrows, seemingly impressed by this revelation.

The thought of injecting dirty water—contaminated with bacteria, disease, other people's blood, and glass particles from a cigarette filter—directly into the bloodstream with a straight shot to the heart and lungs made me cringe. *That explains the patients presenting to the ER with chest pain, shortness of breath, and hypoxia immediately after injecting*, I thought.

Suddenly, a car came barreling up out of nowhere and stopped a few feet from our group. A young woman jumped out, waving her arms excitedly.

"Hey," she shouted. "Some guys over at the gas station are passing out clean needles!"

She went still once she noticed Dr. Arno, Priya, and me among the crowd gathering around her car. "Wait, who are you people?" she asked.

"Oh, don't mind us," Priya said with a gentle smile. "We're just here to help." The young woman looked around at the others, who nodded reassuringly.

The woman relaxed, popped her trunk, and pulled out a box of one cc syringes.

I pulled Dr. Arno to the side and asked, "Did you know Dan and Chris were doing this?"

She nodded. "Dr. Walthall mentioned it to me this morning."

As soon as the crowd had cleared the trunk of boxes, Priya started educating everyone on the proper way to use them.

"Remember," she began, holding up a sterile syringe, "always wash your hands thoroughly with soap and water before using a needle. Any bacteria or germs you have on your hands will contaminate everything you touch, so at the very least, rinse your hands with clean water, or wipe them with a moistened towelette before you even take the syringe out of the package."

The group listened with rapt attention, and Dr. Arno and I stepped aside to allow others to move closer.

"And if your materials are not brand-new," she cautioned, "make sure they're all thoroughly cleaned, and don't unwrap or uncap your syringe until you're going to use it. Make sure each person's equipment is clearly separate from yours so that accidental mix-ups don't occur."

She continued to walk them through basic safety precautions—don't lick the needle; there are bacteria in your mouth that can get on the needle; always inject yourself; take your time; rushing can lead you to make a mistake . . .

Dr. Arno leaned over, and in a slightly hushed voice, said, "This is the piece most people don't see. They think we just throw needles at people and go, which is why so many people oppose SSPs. But by bringing people who use drugs into the program, we not only get a chance to educate them on how to keep themselves safe, sometimes we can even get them into treatment, get them tested for HIV and hep C, and offer whatever other help they might need."

I had seen plenty of research to back up what Dr. Arno was saying, but this was the first time I'd seen it in action. I had to admit it made a lot of sense. Just seeing how attentive and receptive everyone was to the information the CDC worker was sharing, I felt more encouraged than I had in ages.

"But most importantly," Priya concluded, "never share used or discarded needles."

Before the group could disperse, I quickly jumped in. "Many of you know me, but for those who don't, I run Foundations Family Medicine over on Main Street. We're operating a special clinic today and every Tuesday for the foreseeable future to provide HIV testing and treatment, as well as to connect people to primary care and addiction programs—whatever you need. My staff and I are there Monday through Friday. Please come over and see us." I tried to make eye contact with each person as I spoke. "We will help you in any way we can."

"Hey, man, thanks," one man said.

I heard someone else say, "That's awesome."

The woman who had brought the syringes over asked me, "Are those guys who are passing out needles with you?"

"Yeah . . . sort of," I said. It was still so strange to think of anyone as being *with me.*

She nodded her head and said, "They're really cool. Asked me a bunch of questions about how often I use, people I'd used with. Then they told me a lot of the same stuff she said," pointing toward Priya.

"That's great." I smiled. "You should come by the clinic sometime."

She sized me up for a second before saying, "Yeah . . . I might just do that." Then she turned back around and got into her car. She rolled her window down, waved, and tossed out a quick, "Thanks, Doc."

As she drove away, I asked God to help her and every person struggling with poverty, trauma, or substance use to find their way to us. I prayed that we'd find the resources to partner with them to become healthier—physically, emotionally, and spiritually.

. . . .

Other than a few slight hiccups, the day went better than I expected. One such hiccup involved Dan and Chris's disbursement of free syringes. Even though the ban had been lifted, technically the health department was the only entity legally authorized to distribute needles. Not knowing Dr. Walthall had approved their syringe distribution, Scott County officials made Dan and Chris stop.

It was unfortunate that paraphernalia laws continued to force two groups that should be allies—law enforcement and public health—to square off on opposite sides of the SSP issue. Regardless, by the end of the day, Dan and Chris had distributed their supply of sterile syringes, and in the space of only a few hours, the town without access to sterile syringes suddenly had a surplus, finally giving us a fighting chance at lessening the transmission of HIV, hepatitis C, endocarditis, and a host of other potentially deadly infections.

Before they left, Chris and Dan stopped in to tell me what their team had learned by talking with some of the local people who inject drugs.

"We talked to over sixty people who admitted to injecting. We wanted to find out what kind of needles people preferred, the number of times they injected each day, and how much sharing occurred," Chris said. "One guy told me he can sell a dirty needle for five to ten dollars—to people who *know* he's HIV-positive." He shook his head. "Crazy."

"I'll write up a formal report right away and send it along to the Indiana State Department of Health and the local health department," Dan assured me. "But based on what we've seen here today, it's clear that people who inject drugs with and without HIV are ready and willing to collaborate with us on finding a way to stop the transmission of HIV and make some positive changes."

"By the way, we tried to communicate that to the county

officials when they came to shut us down," Chris added, with an air of frustration in his voice. "For some reason, I got the feeling they weren't interested in gathering that information."

"Why on earth not?" I asked.

"I don't know." Chris shrugged. "I kind of got the feeling they didn't want 'outsiders' telling them how to do things."

Dan nodded in agreement.

"What they didn't seem to understand," Chris continued, "was that we were getting this information from people using *in Austin.*"

The disconnect between trying to maintain control and providing emergency relief during this unprecedented health-care disaster was mind-boggling to me. Nevertheless, my staff and I were encouraged by what we *had* accomplished. By the end of the day, we had seen nearly half the people in town known to have HIV, which we considered overwhelmingly successful. Of course, that also meant many more people with HIV were out there who needed immediate medical care.

Later that evening, as I prayed for the people we had encountered that day, I meditated on words from C. S. Lewis that I had paraphrased and written in my journal:

> Let the burden of the glory You've planted deep within these tattered souls be laid squarely on my back—a load so heavy I can only bear by recognizing the frailty of my own humanity.
>
> Let me remain mindful of how my actions help these eternal beings edge closer to their final destination of becoming either a creature which, if I saw now, I may be tempted to worship, or else a horror I would only now encounter in my worst nightmare.
>
> These are not merely tattered souls with scarred flesh. They each possess the flame of their Creator's eternal glory.

Next to the Blessed Sacrament itself, they may well be the holiest of anything I will ever have the privilege to encounter here on earth.[7]

As I finished my prayer, I decided to check my in-box before heading to bed. Dan had copied me on the report he had emailed to the Indiana State Department of Health (ISDH). After sharing the information that he, Chris, and their team of counselors obtained from local people who use drugs, Dan wrote:

The most impressive and consistent finding was the joy and appreciation people shared about receiving assistance with safer injection and other ways to reduce drug-related harm in their lives. In short, Austin, like many other places, focused solely on law enforcement to lessen drug-related harm in a community. People were used to oppression and hardship in their lives as well as stigma and condemnation. For most, collaboration of any kind, not just an alliance for public health, was welcomed with open arms. Participants in our advisory outreach were respectfully engaged and excited about the improvements to come to their community.

Not a bad day, I thought. *Not perfect, but after waiting so long for change to come to Austin, it was a hopeful start.* Right then and there I decided to take up Dan Bigg's mantra of celebrating any positive change.

CHAPTER 13

THE OTHER SIDE OF HELL

· · · · · · · · · ·

*We must learn to regard people less in the light of what they do or
omit to do, and more in the light of what they suffer.*

DIETRICH BONHOEFFER

GARITH FULHAM, who'd called me the day before our first HIV
clinic with an offer of help from the AIDS Healthcare Foundation
(AHF), followed up by traveling to Austin the day after that first
clinic. My team showed him around town and introduced him to
our office and our work.

When he sat down with me later, he looked visibly shaken as
he said, "I have to tell you, Dr. Cooke, this is so much worse than
I expected."

"People have been suffering here for a long time," I replied.

"Your team is an impressive group of caring people," he said.
"We'd be honored to help. We don't have any intention to come
in here and tell you how to do things. This is your work, and we
would only come here at your invitation to support your efforts.
So how can we help?"

That caught me off guard. Several other organizations had
reached out to me since the outbreak started, but they all had

some predefined way in which they intended to help. AHF was the first organization, other than Drs. Walthall, Arno, and Duwve from the Indiana State Department of Health (ISDH), that didn't *tell* me how they could help, but rather *asked* me how they could help. It was a subtle but important difference, and it meant the world to me.

I told him we needed help hiring community health workers who could find people and offer them help outside the four walls of the clinic. Garith responded by immediately sending for a mobile medical van to be driven to Austin from California and had a few of their experienced community workers fly in to spend a week with my staff training them how to reach and care for marginalized populations.

AHF also provided us with much-needed funding to offset some of the administrative and financial burdens I'd been carrying while navigating the complexities of such a large health-care disaster, not to mention the resulting fallout. Since the state could not directly provide my team with any funding, and testing was still a major concern, I welcomed AHF's involvement.

Like an answer to a prayer, obstacles kept falling away one by one. By combining the resources of state and federal agencies with the experiences of the largest HIV care provider in the world (AHF) and the largest health-care provider in Indiana (IU Health), we had developed a strong and strategic response to the crisis.

As soon as AHF's mobile medical van arrived, I sent staff members out to look for people with the directive that we would offer the same level of respect and care for a homeless person who injected drugs as we would offer the CEO of a million-dollar corporation.

"Each person out there is a person of value and equally deserving of our best," I reminded them.

We made no demands or judgments. We simply wanted to show people that we cared and that we were available to help them when they were ready. Accordingly, AHF committed to help me hire staff to assist people in securing transportation and medications and to connect patients with community partners that could help them.

Later that week, the Scott County Health Department opened the state's first official syringe services program (SSP). To protect people's privacy, a database of participants was not kept, and each client received a card to decrease the risk of arrest for possessing the syringes. Although the collection of used syringes and the distribution of sterile ones received the most attention from the media, it was only *one* of the many services offered. Clients could also get free HIV testing, health-related education, linkage to care, care coordination, behavioral health referrals, and vaccinations. Perhaps most importantly, the invisible people of Austin became willing to be known. Some would even say these early interactions were the first time they had felt compassion in their lives.

Injecting behaviors in Scott County changed almost immediately after the SSP opened, with the CDC reporting that syringe sharing dropped from 74 percent down to 22 percent, while safe disposal of used syringes rose from 18 percent to 82 percent.[1] Just as the previous three decades of research had indicated, the SSP was working.

. . . .

On the morning of the second HIV clinic the following Tuesday, I performed a C-section at the hospital, finished my rounds, and then headed to the office. By the time I arrived, Drs. Arno and Janowicz were already seeing patients.

"How are things going?" I asked.

"More patients have come," said Dr. Arno. "This is working much better than we expected."

"It feels good to finally start some of the patients on medication," Dr. Janowicz said with a big smile.

I left Drs. Arno and Janowicz to walk around the clinic and

see how everything else was running. The pharmacist showed me the new handouts they planned to provide to patients as they educated them about the medications. The behavioral health tech was counseling a patient, and my other providers were hard at work taking care of our regular patients.

Just then, I saw Deborah and a young man in his mid-to-late twenties walking down the hall with one of the nurses. I waved at Deborah, and she nodded, but she looked concerned. She reached over and took the hand of the young man I figured must have been her son, Jude.

Thank the Lord, I thought. *Jude's coming in for help with his drug use.*

Then I noticed they were heading back to the area of the clinic where Drs. Arno and Janowicz were stationed . . . *Or are they here for another reason?*

I quickly pulled up the HIV clinic schedule and saw Jude's name.

"Do you mind if I go in with you to see this guy?" I asked Dr. Arno.

"We're your guests, Will," she said, laughing. She stepped to the side so I could lead the way.

After Dr. Arno and I entered Jude's room, I introduced her to Deborah. They greeted each other and then Dr. Arno turned to Jude and said, "You must be Jude."

We both shook Jude's hand and sat down. Then Dr. Arno turned to me and said, "Go ahead."

Up to this point, I had been shadowing Drs. Janowicz and Arno during patient visits so I could learn the latest best practices in caring for people living with HIV. There's a mantra in medical school, "See one, do one, teach one." Mentor-mentee relationships are built on the willingness of mentors to push each student out from behind them and take a position behind the student for support. I had been studying my two mentors during clinic hours and spending countless hours outside of the clinic researching HIV and hepatitis C. Apparently, the time had come to show them what I'd learned.

I leaned forward. "Jude, I'm so glad you came in today." I met his eyes reassuringly. "I know this is scary and I just want you to know that you are not alone. We are here to help you in any way we can."

I paused to make sure Jude was hearing me. He nodded. I looked over at Deborah and said, "That goes for you, too, okay?"

"I know," she replied with a cautious smile. They both looked terrified.

"The very first thing I want you both to know," I said, fixing my gaze on Jude, "is that you are going to be okay. With modern treatment, this virus can basically be put into remission and you can expect to live out a normal life expectancy." I could see he wasn't convinced.

"Finding out you have HIV must have been devastating," I continued gently. "Do you want to tell me about that?"

After several moments of silence, Deborah spoke first. "When we talked last, Doc, I told you how we thought Jude had gotten his life back together. Well, he told us what happened." She paused and took Jude's hand.

"Jude was going to get married," she began, "and they didn't want anyone to know that his fiancée was expecting." Tears started to well up in Jude's eyes. "Their son was stillborn," she continued. "Nobody knew. They just told the family she wasn't feeling well. Even I didn't know." Deborah squeezed his hand before letting it go to wipe away a few tears of her own.

Dr. Arno walked over and handed them a box of tissues. She put her hand on his shoulder softly and whispered, "I am so sorry." Jude nodded quietly. After Dr. Arno sat back down, Jude broke the silence.

"I just couldn't bear the pain, man. I mean, why would that happen?" he looked up pleadingly with tear-filled eyes.

My heart broke, and the light in the room became distorted

through my own tears. *He pulled himself through the hell of addiction only to find this waiting on the other side? Why fight? Why try? Why hope?*

Jude continued. "We didn't know what to do. We were lost and alone and scared. Man, we couldn't even look at each other. So we just split up." Then he added under his breath, "I don't even know where she is now."

"He started using again to cope with his grief." Deborah's tone was laced with resignation that Jude's relapse somehow made sense.

"Went right back to injecting Opana," Jude said, shaking his head as he let out a quiet laugh. "Here's the thing, Doc. I'm not like those other people out there getting high, sharing needles, and doing whatever." His eyes had cleared, and a fiery determination now shone in them. "I'm not a junkie. I work. I do my best. I just don't know how else to cope with the pain."

"I can't imagine how hard it must have been to lose your son and your fiancée. I'm so sorry," I replied. "Sometimes life doesn't make any sense. I get it, I do. And we only have so much we can deal with before it's all a flood of overwhelming emotions. It makes it hard to breathe, let alone think or feel anything else."

Jude nodded.

"Anyone would feel overwhelmed by all that. But Jude, we're going to make sure that you are surrounded by good, supportive people who can help you feel safe enough to start to heal."

"Okay," he whispered, dropping his head.

After a few quiet moments, I asked, "How do you think you were exposed to HIV?"

"My idiot cousin," he said.

"Apparently, my nephew showed Jude how to inject Opana," Deborah filled in.

"It seems so stupid now," Jude confessed, "but I didn't think twice about sharing a needle with him. He's family. We didn't want to get caught, and it's not like syringes are easy to come by.

So we kept this one syringe hidden. We'd take turns using it in his basement."

"Jude didn't know his cousin was sharing needles with a few other people too," Deborah clarified.

"I thought he was all right. I mean, he's an idiot and all, but I've always sort of looked up to him." He rolled his eyes.

Then Dr. Arno broke in. "We can never be sure what other people are doing when we're not around. I've known men and women who were happily married for decades only to find out they contracted HIV from their spouse who was cheating or using drugs without their knowledge. That's why we advise everyone to be tested."

"When we started hearing stories about people around Austin contracting HIV," Deborah said, "I got worried. After a few weeks of pestering him, he finally agreed to go to the health department to be tested for HIV."

"I was just trying to get her off my back," Jude said, smiling at his mom. "I didn't think I had anything to worry about." He paused for a moment and took a breath. "The CDC tester put a swab in my mouth," he said, motioning with his hands before letting them drop. "It came up positive." He paused again before continuing numbly, "He handed me a card with your clinic information on it and told me to make a follow-up appointment. That was it."

"When Jude walked out of the health department, he looked stunned," Deborah took over. "I could see it written across his face, but I waited until we got into the car to let him break the news." She paused and took his hand again. "We sat there sobbing in the parking lot together, feeling hopeless. I had horrible visions in my head of what might play out. I had horrible fears about what Jude might do for lack of hope . . ."

"But there *is* hope," I assured them, smiling gently. "What do you know about HIV?"

"It's a virus that attacks the immune system," Jude replied.

"That's right," I said. "And do you know how it is spread?"
Jude looked down, obviously uncomfortable.

"That's okay," I reassured him. "It's transmitted through sharing blood and having unprotected sex." I paused. "It's also important to know that the virus is not spread through tears, saliva, or sweat."

He glanced up at me.

"That means people can eat after you, share the same dishes . . . you can even kiss them."

Turning to face Jude's mom, I said, "And Deborah, that means Jude can't transmit the virus to you, so you can hold him if he's upset and crying." I sensed her relax a little.

I took out a piece of paper and drew three circles at the top. "There are several types of blood cells: red blood cells, platelets, and white blood cells." I labeled the third circle *WBC* for white blood cells and drew three lines from it ending in more circles. "WBCs can be broken into macrophages, neutrophils, lympho-cytes, and a few others." From *Lymphocytes* I drew two more lines with circles labeled *B-cells* and *T-cells*. Then, from the circle I had labeled *T-cells*, I drew two final lines ending in two more circles. "Finally," I said, "T-cells can be broken into CD8 and CD4 cells. These," I said, pointing to the circle labeled *CD4*, "are the cells that HIV attacks and kills. That's a problem because these cells help the body identify and fight off viruses, bacteria, other organisms, and even cancer cells." I paused to let them think about that.

"Now I want you to remember just two numbers when we are discussing your HIV treatment. The first one is your CD4 count and the second is your HIV viral load." I paused and wrote *CD4* and *VL* on the next page. "Your CD4 count is how healthy you are, and your viral load is how healthy the HIV is." I wrote *You* under *CD4* count and *HIV* under *VL*. "Does all this make sense so far?" I asked.

"It does," Jude answered. "So I want my CD4 count to be high and my viral load to be low, right?"

"Exactly," Dr. Arno and I said at the same time.

"Now think of your CD4 count as a train heading toward a cliff," I drew four boxes on the left side of the page to represent the train, and I extended a line from under the train to the right side of the page where I made a steep drop-off to represent the cliff. Then I divided the distance from the train to the cliff in half. Under the train, I wrote, *Over 500*; under the middle section I wrote, *200–500*; and past the cliff I wrote, *Less than 200/AIDS.*

"These numbers represent your CD4 count and are the distance the train is from the cliff." I pointed to each and said, "Over 500 is the green zone, 200 to 500 is the yellow zone, and less than 200 is the red zone or AIDS. We want to keep your CD4 count in the green zone and far away from AIDS."

Deborah and Jude studied my crude art and nodded.

"So the distance the train is from the cliff is your CD4 count. The speed the train is traveling toward the cliff is your viral load. The higher your viral load, the faster your CD4 count will move toward the cliff of AIDS."

"That makes sense," Jude said.

"What your medication will do is stop the train and even reverse it," I said and paused.

"Seriously?" Jude asked.

"Yes, within two to three months of starting your medicine, we should expect your viral load to be undetectable, essentially zero. You can think of it being in remission at that point. In fact, after you've had an undetectable viral load while on your medicine for at least six months, you'll no longer be able to transmit the virus sexually. We call this U=U, for 'Undetectable equals Untransmittable.'"

Jude teared up again, cleared his voice, and said, "So are you saying that I still have a chance to have a family?"

"Absolutely," I reassured him. "But keep in mind that we don't have enough data to know how this affects transmission from sharing needles."

He nodded and said, "Actually, I want help getting off the needle too."

Everyone smiled.

"I'm going to send in our social worker to get you connected to a therapist and addiction services," I told him. "They'll also make sure your insurance is lined up so you can start your HIV medicine as soon as possible. This will be a journey, but you'll not be taking it alone. We will be here with you to make sure you understand what is happening and to have what you need. Okay?"

"Yes," he said more confidently.

"Everything is going to work out," Dr. Arno said to them both.

As Dr. Arno and I were about to leave, Jude stood up and put his hand out for me to shake. "Thanks, Dr. Cooke."

"Thank *you* for being brave enough to come in, Jude," I said. "And please . . . let me know if you have any questions or if you need anything."

After the appointment, Deborah contacted me. "I need to tell you something. I came here today with Jude to protect him. I've worked in the field of addiction for a long time. My ex-husband is a police officer. I've seen the way 'addicts' are treated by professionals. Not just doctors, but addiction treatment providers, churches, and therapists. But this is my son. He hasn't always made good choices, but he's a good person. I was determined to stay by his side today because I was afraid he might be treated with disdain, disgust, or at the very least, an 'I am tolerating you because I have to' attitude. Dr. Cooke, what we experienced here today has been the exact opposite of what we've experienced in the past.

"Thank you, doctor. For listening. For helping. For everything."

CHAPTER 14

A BROKEN BALLERINA

· · · · · · · · ·

*It doesn't matter who you are or what you look like
so long as somebody loves you.*

ROALD DAHL

OVER THE NEXT SEVERAL WEEKS, the AIDS Healthcare Foundation (AHF) continued to invest in the community by opening a community advocacy center at my office to help connect people to resources; funding a community center at Church of the New Covenant to help feed and clothe people; underwriting community events in partnership with the city of Austin; and helping me hire two community health workers to extend our team's reach outside the four walls of my clinic.

Slowly but surely, the percentage of people with HIV on treatment increased. Thanks to the work Dan and Chris had started, and the Scott County Health Department had continued, most of the people who were still injecting were now using the syringe services program (SSP). This resulted in a dramatic reduction in the transmission of HIV.

For a community that staggered into March in a state of panic and despair, we headed into April with our heads held high and a host of reasons to be optimistic. At long last, hope seemed to be spreading faster than HIV.

In early April, Governor Pence established the Incident Command Center (ICC) in Austin. Almost immediately, agendas and political differences replaced our initial spirit of shared purpose. The first hints of trouble came early, as Carolyn King's position as Scott County community coordinator was quietly terminated.

Then Garith Fulham received a call from a state official notifying him he would be found in contempt of the governor's emergency order and arrested if AHF was caught dispensing syringes.

Garith was flabbergasted. "I can't make any sense of it, Dr. Cooke," he confessed to me after the call. "I'm the only AHF employee in Austin, and I haven't dispensed *any* syringes."

IU Health then raised concerns about AHF's history of litigation in other states. They made a strong stance to protect themselves by not allowing their infectious disease specialists, Drs. Arno and Janowicz, to interact with AHF while at my office. I quickly reassured Drs. Arno and Janowicz that AHF was only providing support, and together we agreed that IU Health would continue to support our weekly HIV clinic while AHF assisted with our outreach and linkage to care.

Then during a policy meeting of state and county government officials on April 5, concerns about the syringes Chris and Dan dispensed came up again. Following that meeting, the directive from the state and county government, aimed primarily at law enforcement, was to get the bulk of the needles they had handed out off the streets. Some people were even tracked down and arrested.

Still wanting to help, Dan donated many more syringes along with other supplies to Scott County. A government official called to tell him it would be best for him to take the donated supplies back.

"He said, 'We are taking care of things on our own,'" Dan told me.

Since the Indiana Recovery Alliance was only about an hour from Scott County, Dan offered the supplies to Chris. When Chris showed up to get them, however, the state police met him there to escort him all the way to the state border near Chicago and threatened to arrest him if he brought the supplies back into Indiana. Chris told me with a twinkle in his eye, "You know, it's been on my bucket list to be escorted across state lines and told to never come back."

Our well-coordinated response suddenly appeared to be unraveling. Seemingly overnight, all decisions were made at the Incident Command Center under the direction of Governor Pence's administration rather than public health officials. It was made clear that unless we attended the daily planning sessions at the Command Center, our local efforts and interests would no longer have a voice. They didn't seem to understand that Foundations Family Medicine was a busy practice with thousands of other patients or that I delivered babies, worked in the emergency department, and made hospital rounds.

My team and I couldn't abandon our other responsibilities to the community to focus exclusively on the response, nor were we willing to ignore the underlying adverse psychosocial and socioeconomic factors that led to the outbreak to begin with. Our local partners and my team grew increasingly frustrated over being left out as the gulf widened between our efforts and those of the officials at the ICC.

Even so, my team at Foundations continued to care for all the HIV patients in Austin, except for the few who opted to travel to Louisville to keep people in town from finding out they had HIV. IU Health and the Indiana State Department of Health (ISDH) continued to partner with us on Tuesdays for the HIV clinic. To bridge the disconnect, the city of Austin, AHF, and I rehired Carolyn King to serve as Austin's community liaison. She began attending the meetings at the ICC to represent our interests and keep us informed. King said the ICC's emphasis was exclusively on stopping the transmission of HIV. There were occasionally heated discussions between people with vastly different opinions about how to deal with drug use, but there was virtually no discussion of how to deal with the underlying socioeconomic factors that had led to the outbreak.

The ICC itself was isolated on a dead-end street in an old warehouse. Indiana officials moved all state-sponsored services there and branded it the Community Outreach Center. The first state-approved SSP was also at the center, at what state officials called the One-Stop Shop. Just outside was a big construction sign flashing "Needle Exchange." And since a quarter of the women who tested positive admitted to sex work, the state also placed flashing emergency signs at the truck stops nearest to Austin that read "WARNING: HIV OUTBREAK" to caution truckers and travelers who might unknowingly proposition a sex worker who had HIV.

This was exactly what we had been trying to avoid. We had worked so hard to not single out people injecting drugs or living with HIV. Yet somehow a flashing sign reading "People who use drugs enter here" had become the accepted approach. Instead of destigmatizing the disease and normalizing our town, the response had morphed into something more resembling an emergency quarantine. We were assigning a negative label to those who most needed our help.

Quite simply, I found it demoralizing.

· · · · · · · · ·

One day after work, I drove northeast of town until I came to a narrow country road. I was searching for one of Austin's earliest settlers—literally. After parking on the side of the road, I walked to an arched entrance bearing looming letters that spelled "Harrod Cemetery." A cast-iron and stone fence stood guard over the remains of lives long passed. The gate was held together by an old bungee cord. Once unhooked, it swung open on its own, as if inviting me to explore.

I stepped gently across the threshold and unexpectedly felt a change. I'm not a particularly superstitious person, but my skin sensed a new stillness. After weeks of responding to a chaotic emergency, I relaxed in the sacred silence around me.

I'd been thinking about the history of Austin a lot lately, particularly when interviewed by out-of-state media. I wanted to be sure I was representing the town accurately. Also, as I evaluated how to use my position as a physician to best help Austin's residents, I felt as if I needed to know more about our town's cultural and medical heritage. That led me to a book by Dr. Carl Bogardus, the physician whose retirement had left Austin without a doctor for several decades before my arrival. He'd written several pieces on the history of Austin, one of which goes back to its earliest days.

So on this sunny spring day, I walked slowly through the stone garden of the fallen. No one, I knew, had left an earlier or deeper mark on Austin's story than the family after which this hallowed place was named.

John and Caroline Harrod, the great-grandparents of William Harrod, one of Austin's original settlers, had sailed from England in 1722, making their home in New Jersey. Eleven years after their arrival, Caroline was brutally killed by Native Americans just before John and his sons returned with supplies from town to see their home on fire.

Although John was devastated, he eventually remarried and had four more sons and two daughters. The Harrod men became renowned for their courage as soldiers and explorers, many serving in the French and Indian War or the Revolutionary War. In 1774, John's son James led an expedition of almost forty families who built the first permanent settlement west of the Allegheny Mountains at modern-day Harrodsburg, Kentucky. The town would soon relive the horrors his own family had experienced when Native Americans, who'd been offered payment by the

British for every settler's scalp, began killing residents. George Rogers Clark captured their peril in his memoir, "No people could be in a more alarming situation. Detached at least two hundred miles from the nearest settlements of the states, surrounded by numerous nations of Indians, each one far superior to ourselves in numbers and under the influence of the British government and pointedly directed to destroy us."[1]

The Harrods, however, survived to help secure and settle what was then known as the Northwest Territory. I was mindful of this family's profound influence on early America, Kentucky, and southern Indiana as I walked to the back of the cemetery.

When I finally found William Harrod's name, I was surprised to find two graves. The first ancient-looking stone read: "Here lies the body of William Harrod who was born May the 22nd, 1779, aged 55 years and 8 months, and died January the 28th, 1835."

The other looked more modern, like a stone column, and bore his name and the dates of his birth and death.

I knew from my reading that William Harrod had left something for his town that I felt no monument could match. In 1883, his son Samuel described to the local newspaper his father's actions after hearing gunfire for several days near his home in what became Austin. "Determined to find out who it was that was doing so much shooting . . . one evening he quit work and took his rifle and followed the sound of the guns about three miles up Quick's Creek."[2]

When he arrived at the creek, William spotted two Native Americans cooking supper. When I first read this account, I thought how likely it was that William had heard stories of how Native Americans had killed so many family members, including his great-grandmother, Caroline Harrod.

Samuel reported that when William spotted the Native Americans near the creek, "his first thought was to shoot them, and he took a sight on them as they both sat on a log talking." But something stopped William. His initial flare of hatred vanished. Suddenly William no longer saw two "savages" responsible for terrorizing his family but two friends sharing a meal. Not wanting to "shed human blood," he bravely decided to "risk their friendship," so "he took down his gun and walked up to them and shook hands with them as a friend."[3]

Samuel said that because other families in the area had also experienced fearful run-ins with Native Americans, his dad knew these two men were in danger if they stayed in the area. He wrote that his dad "ate supper with them and afterward talked to them and persuaded them to leave, which they did the next day." One of the new friends William encountered that day was called "Quick," so the creek became known as Quick's Creek. Today the creek empties into a man-made reservoir known as Hardy Lake, which has become a recreational attraction for families across the region.

So what did a story more than a century old have to do with our town's history as it battled the opioid epidemic? As I moved on to other gravestones bearing the name Harrod, I thought about how William Harrod was an example of someone who was willing to see beyond the stigmatizing stories and horrifying accounts of "savages" to connect with another human being, a man named Quick.

While walking back to my car, I realized that William Harrod had something to teach everyone responding to Austin's crisis: If we lose our willingness to connect on a human level, we lose everything.

· · · · · · · · ·

As I sought additional partners to help our state navigate this crisis, I met someone who was as interested in addressing the underlying social and addiction issues that precipitated this crisis as I was. In March, I contacted Indiana's Division of Mental Health and Addiction (DMHA), which was part of the state's Family and Social Services Administration to explore the resources DMHA might be able to offer in the emergency response. Carolyn King first met with the division's deputy director and then told me the official wanted to sit down with me.

The following week, I was sitting in my office when a blonde woman who looked to be in her late twenties poked her head around my door.

"Excuse me," she said, smiling. "Are you Dr. Cooke?"

"Yes," I replied, sounding more exhausted than I intended.

She let herself in and extended her hand for me to shake. "I'm Stephanie Spoolstra, deputy director of the Division of Mental Health and Addiction."

"Mental Health and Addiction," I mused. "What kept you?"

Happily, she seemed to have a good sense of humor.

"I know, right?" she chuckled. "I would have been here earlier but I'm afraid my department wasn't looped in right away." She sat down.

"When the outbreak was first announced, we were told, 'There's not a lot going on, and it's really not that big of a deal.' Then later we were told, 'The state's department of health has it.' Luckily, I had a few trusted sources quietly chirping in my ear. They kept telling me, 'This is going to be a really big deal. You guys need to be more involved.' I had a feeling they were right.

"I told my boss, 'This is not a little thing; we need to be involved. This isn't just an outbreak of HIV, at least primarily.' I explained that this is an outbreak of adverse social determinants leading to a surge in substance use disorder. The HIV and hep C epidemics are several layers out."

I did a double take. With all the hyperfocus on HIV in recent weeks, it was shocking to hear someone outside of our core local network acknowledge the underlying cause of the outbreak.

"How did you know that?" I asked.

She just smiled at me knowingly. "Let's just say I know Scott

County better than most trying to come in here with all the answers." Then she looked out the window and added more softly, "I also know a little something about how easy it is to get hooked on opioids."

Once again I was surprised. I couldn't imagine her having a personal history with opoids. She was impeccably dressed, bright eyed, had a perfect complexion, and was . . . graceful.

"Are you from the area?" I asked.

"Nope, I'm originally from Philly," she answered more brightly. "But I spent some time here while studying at IU Bloomington."

"Did you major in psych or social services?" I asked.

She smiled as if she had a great secret.

"What?" I laughed.

She finally said, "I studied ballet."

"Really?" *How does a ballerina end up working with the DMHA?* I wondered.

"Yep," she replied, sitting up very straight and proper. "I double majored in ballet and criminal justice."

"That's an interesting combo," I said, amused.

"My parents thought so too," she said, smiling. "Anyway, I met a guy during my freshman year whose family lived in Scott County. He flunked out the first semester after we started dating, and even though our relationship had become kind of—" she searched for the right word—"unhealthy," she continued, "I stuck it out. Anyway, he had no place to live, so he moved into his cousin's basement."

I had a feeling I knew where this was going.

"I remember going to visit him on the weekends." She wrinkled her nose in disgust. "The house was positively foul. They had a toddler who was almost always unsupervised, the place reeked of marijuana, and there was almost always alcohol around."

Sounds familiar, I thought.

"I knew that they were probably using other drugs when I wasn't around and that what was going on there was not okay, but—" she sighed—"I was young. I pretended I didn't see because I didn't know I could do anything about it."

"Is that how you got exposed to pain pills?" I asked.

"No," she said. "I knew that guy was a dead end, so I eventually broke things off with him."

"Good for you," I said.

"Yeah, well . . . I was lucky. I had pretty amazing parents. They were extremely supportive. Kept telling me how much potential I had." She paused for a second, then added, "That helps, you know?"

I thought back on my mom and my aunt Sally. *Yeah*, I mused, *it does.*

"So then what happened?" I asked.

She took a deep breath. "Ballet happened," she said. "I pushed my body too hard. The pressure to maintain a social life, good grades, and the expected physicality of a ballet dancer was intense. To have enough energy I sometimes resorted to habits that damaged my instrument," she said, gesturing to her body. "By the time I graduated, I could barely walk because of the excruciating pain in my right foot.

"I didn't want to give up dancing, so I moved back home to Pennsylvania, where a specialist repaired two large tendon tears and freed up a compressed nerve." As she traced the scar along her foot and ankle, showing me where the surgery was, I couldn't help but wince.

"Unfortunately, the wound wouldn't heal," she continued. "I had to use wet-to-dry dressings for six months. There was just a huge gaping hole."

"Ouch," I shifted in my chair. "Let me guess. They prescribed Lortab for the pain."

"Oxycodone," she corrected me.

This part of the story was all too familiar to me by now. Like so many others, the pain pills didn't just soothe her physical pain.

"I was so high on pain meds at one point," she recalled, "that

I'd fallen in between my bed and the wall. I couldn't get up, and my mom had to come help me. I had crutches but couldn't stand. My mom would often watch me crawl just to get to the bathroom." She paused, then said, "Years later, my mom told me she would go into her room and just sob. Here was her daughter, this beautiful ballet dancer, who couldn't even walk."

I just shook my head. "How'd you turn it around?"

Stephanie's face lit with a huge smile. "I have an awesome mom," she replied. "She charted my pain pills and really pushed the issue when I should have just been taking Motrin or Advil or Tylenol. I also had a pretty great professor at IU who encouraged me to pursue a graduate degree in social work."

There but for the grace of God, I thought.

"Anyway, I knew I had another career in front of me . . ."

"And here you are, deputy director of DMHA," I finished for her.

"And here I am," she said, smiling.

I considered how my family still bears the scars of a different sort of story. Aunt Sally suffered and died, never experiencing that kind of healing love or encouragement from an inspiring mentor. I couldn't help thinking how tragically different things could have turned out if Stephanie had gone through her extended, emotionally traumatic time on opioids while trying to recover in the basement of that rundown house in Scott County—without her mom, surrounded by drug use and poverty.

It seemed she was thinking something similar as she continued, "Now I try to help people understand that, with the amount of opioids I was prescribed, if anything along my path had gone a little differently, I could be that person wearing khaki and maroon at Rockville Correctional Facility."

"That's honestly amazing," I said, shaking my head.

She quickly collected herself. "Most people don't know that crazy story. But I thought it would be good for you to know that I really do understand what you've been facing here in Austin."

I nodded my head appreciatively and said, "Thank you for sharing your story. I know it can't be easy reliving all that."

She nodded and collected herself again.

I leaned forward slightly. "So how can you help us?"

The way things had been going lately, I wasn't exactly brimming with confidence, but Stephanie's background gave me a twinge of hope. At least she understood the underlying issues.

She told me the governor's office and ISDH were focused on controlling the HIV part of the disaster, and she attributed their resistance to involve DMHA to sheer lack of knowledge.

"I don't think it was intentional," she explained. "This is unlike any emergency response anyone has ever faced before. I think they really were challenged to figure out who to include."

"You've been to the Command Center?" I asked.

"Yes," she said. "I've been there a few times now. I even got into quite a heated debate with some of the state officials in front of the CDC in the back of that warehouse."

I'll bet.

"I had repeatedly stressed the need for all of us from the state agencies to listen to local voices when determining our approach and priorities, and one day I had just had it," she said. "I was sobbing by the time I left the Command Center. Thankfully, Dr. Walthall saw me and came over. 'I hear what you're saying,' she told me. 'Dr. Adams does too.' They told me they would support me whenever I stressed the importance of listening to people from the Austin community.

"My sense is that everybody at the Command Center wants to be in charge, and nobody is doing a great job of articulating what needs to be done." She paused for a second to collect her thoughts. "It feels as if the message is 'We're here to treat the HIV and contain the outbreak,' which I get from an emergency response standpoint. But nobody seems willing to take that next step to be really bold—to uncover some of the root causes of the outbreak, including substance use disorder."

I could sense her frustration. In fact, I'd lived it.

"We're dealing with economic depression, domestic violence, generationally low education levels, toxic childhood experiences, and a complete lack of resources," she continued passionately. I just nodded along. She was, after all, preaching to the choir.

"Nobody at the Incident Command Center seems to want to talk about these root causes of the hopelessness and desperation that lead to the drug use and sex work. We just keep painting over the water leak, you know?"

And it's a massive leak, I thought.

"On one hand," she continued, "they say they want economic growth and for Scott County to be a successful employer of people, but on the other hand, they seem to say they don't want to address the addiction epidemic. Those two things don't go together. They don't match."

I agreed with her wholeheartedly. Over the past several weeks, I had watched all the hard work and effort of my team and our local partners be systematically undone by an outside entity that seemed to consider *us* the outsiders.

Like Stephanie, I did feel supported by the top officials at the Indiana Department of Health. Just as Dr. Walthall had reassured Stephanie of her support, Dr. Adams took the time to listen to my opinions and then lifted my spirits by telling me to keep "fighting the good fight." Through their words and actions, it was clear they understood the complexities of this pandemic. But both Dr. Adams and Dr. Walthall operated out of Indianapolis, where Dr. Adams still served as a staff anesthesiologist for Eskenazi Health and Dr. Walthall was a pediatric emergency medicine physician for Riley Children's Hospital. They did their best to stay involved in Austin while also navigating those roles and the intricacies of Indiana's entire public health system.

But since those running the day-to-day operations at the Incident Command Center didn't appear interested in addressing the underlying socioeconomic issues that had contributed to the outbreak, Stephanie and I agreed to work together to coordinate efforts to address these needs. We set up our next meeting for the following week, a few hours before the meeting I had organized to discuss the community's mental health, substance use disorder, and recovery needs.

By the time Stephanie left my office, two things had become abundantly clear. First, the main emphasis of the governor's emergency response in Austin was to contain the HIV outbreak—"to get it out of the news." And second, the ICC's message to the local partnerships working in Austin seemed clear: "We are in charge. Do things our way or get out of our way."

I knew from experience that healing Austin was far too big a job for one person. I had been asking for help for over a decade. Now Austin was swarming with people trying to help.

The Pence administration had charged the Incident commander, Megan Sarvis, with the task of getting control of the HIV outbreak. DMHA deputy director Stephanie Spoolstra was coordinating the state's mental health and addiction responses. Dr. Joan Duwve was helping the ISDH find sustainable solutions for the addiction and medical responses, and Dr. Diane Janowicz was leading IU Health's HIV medical response. This left me operating between multiple decision makers from the state who didn't always seem to be in tune with one another.

In an effort to refocus the response on the underlying psychosocial and addiction issues, I organized a meeting on April 21, 2015, in the building where I had started my practice. Those in attendance represented the state and county health departments, DMHA, IU Health, Scott Memorial Hospital, Centerstone Behavioral Health, LifeSpring Behavioral Health, the Scott County Partnership, the Substance Abuse and Mental Health Services Administration (SAMHSA), the CDC, Great Lakes Addiction Technology Transfer Center (GLATTC), Mental Health America of Indiana (MHAI), churches, officials of city, county, and state government, and other organizations and individuals interested in being involved in the response. I told them, "This is our moment to put aside differences, to think more collaboratively."

I challenged them to consider the importance of modeling healthy relationships and warned them the resources in our rural community were too limited to sustain competing interests. "Our success depends on our ability to partner with the people of Austin to redefine this community as a place of compassion; where health and opportunity are available to every man, woman, and child regardless of their or our beliefs, circumstances, or economics."

The group agreed to begin meeting monthly and work together.

A few days later a gruff, gray-bearded guy in a fedora whom I had noticed at the meeting visited me at my office. Tom Cox represented the Great Lakes Addiction Technology Transfer Center (GLATTC). He told me that the kind of compassionate community for which I had advocated at the meeting has a name, evidence, and funding.

Recovery-oriented systems of care (ROSC), he explained, is a shared vision developed by a community that honors its people's unique strengths and culture to build a supportive, person-centered response ensuring that access to recovery, health, and wellness is available to all citizens.

Dan and Chris had shown that the hurting people of Austin wanted to have a role in their community's recovery, so the next week Tom and I met with Mental Health America of Indiana (MHAI) to discuss strategies to develop an active recovery community. We also knew people were likely to reject a system that, as Chris had said, tries to "parachute in to save the day." We knew developing a new system in Austin would take time and rely on a recovery community that didn't even exist yet. But it seemed the right course, so I began working in concert with the GLATTC and MHAI on developing a community-led ROSC.

The following week, the medical director of Indiana's Division of Mental Health and Addiction and I implemented an outpatient treatment protocol, including medication-assisted treatment

(MAT) to serve as an alternative plan to the existing six-to-eight-week waitlist for inpatient substance use disorder services.

She showed me research confirming treatment assisted by medications that curb cravings—like Suboxone and Vivitrol (naltrexone)—drastically cuts relapses, arrests, and death rates compared to abstinence-based programs.[4] In one study, three-quarters of people receiving MAT remained in care beyond a year.[5] This is critically important since relapse, and therefore death, decreases the longer someone remains in care. While nearly seven in ten people relapse within the first year of recovery, that rate decreases to three in ten after three years in recovery. After five years, the risk of drug use is no greater than in the general population.[6]

Though the results of these initiatives and the development of a Scott County Recovery Oriented System of Care (ROSC) would not be immediate, we were confident that we were on the right course. The problems in Austin had taken years to develop. So, too, would a viable, long-term solution. And it would work only if the people of Austin were involved in implementing *and* sustaining it.

CHAPTER 15

UNDONE

. . . .

If you can keep your head when all about you
Are losing theirs and blaming it on you,
If you can trust yourself when all men doubt you,
But make allowance for their doubting too . . .

RUDYARD KIPLING

RESPONDING TO A PUBLIC HEALTH DISASTER, I was learning, took a toll at home too. That spring I had been away from my family much more than I wanted to be. Although Melissa remained supportive, I felt us drifting apart as the weeks merged into months of rarely being together. I missed her and feared repeating old mistakes.

As April drew to a close, two separate response sites in Austin were also drifting apart. My clinic provided the daily medical care, relying on the support of IU Health's infectious disease specialists, the AIDS Healthcare Foundation (AHF), and the Indiana State Department of Health (ISDH). On the other side of our mere 2.6-square-mile town, the Community Outreach Center, located within the Incident Command Center, provided access to case management, insurance, birth certificates, HIV testing, substance abuse counseling, and the new syringe services program. While top-down directives from the Pence administration in Indianapolis sometimes led to tension and disconnect, the number of new HIV cases continued to decline as the number of people living with HIV who were engaging in care continued to increase.

The CDC lead, Dr. Phil Peters, said they were both impressed and relieved we had been able to quickly develop a system of care that worked in such a resource-poor area. Our system came under fire on May 7, however.

That morning began like any other. At home I reviewed a few patient charts before heading downstairs to the kitchen. Now that the situation in Austin seemed to be improving, I wanted to do something to connect with Melissa—to show her some of the love and support she'd so generously shown me. Knowing there are few things she enjoys more than waking up to a fresh cup of coffee, I started making some.

My thoughts were interrupted when I dropped Melissa's cup on the counter and spilled coffee everywhere. I cursed as my wife came into the room. She smiled and hurried over to help me clean up the mess.

In the process, I said, "I'm so sorry."

"It's just coffee," she countered.

"I mean for being gone so much lately," I said more directly.

"And not being here to help," she finished, holding up a towel soaked in coffee.

I nodded my head. "Exactly."

As she tossed the towel into the laundry, I poured her another cup more carefully.

"I miss you," I said, handing her a fresh cup of coffee, "and need you."

"Me too," she whispered, taking the cup with both hands.

"I'll start being here to help more," I promised. "I think things in Austin may finally be getting better."

She shifted to look up into my eyes and said, "I know you're trying to be sure that the people of Austin are taken care of. I love that about you."

She set her cup down, took my hands, and continued almost sternly, "Just make sure this sacrifice is worth it: Be the man Austin needs right now."

"I'm trying." I paused. "I just want you to know that your faith in me is what gives me the courage to even want to be that kind of person."

I left for the hospital feeling more encouraged than I'd been in weeks. After finishing my rounds, I headed to the Incident Command Center. Dr. Walthall and I had planned to meet after her regularly scheduled press conference. By the time I arrived at the back of the old warehouse, everyone else was gone. It was abnormally quiet, but the smell of coffee lingered, reminding me of Melissa.

As I approached Dr. Walthall, I could immediately tell something was wrong by the look of concern in her eyes. "Are you okay?" I asked.

She sighed and said, "This is just hard; I was hoping it wouldn't come to this."

"What do you mean?"

"The new AHF clinic at your office hit the news this morning, and IU Health is pretty upset about it."

"I don't understand."

Then she handed me a press release from AHF. I was stunned to read an announcement that AHF was opening a new HIV clinic in Austin in partnership with IU Health and my clinic.[1]

"Jen," I said, skimming it, "this is wrong. I have no idea what this is talking about."

"So AHF *isn't* opening an HIV clinic with you?" she asked.

"Absolutely not. I'm working with IU Health for that. AHF is only providing support for our community outreach and testing."

We both sat there in stunned silence for a moment, looking over the press release together.

Then she looked up at me and said, "IU Health is pulling out of your clinic. They had concerns about being so closely related to AHF, and this article sealed their decision."

"Seriously?" I held the release up. "But this information is wrong."

"I sincerely wish there was something we could do, Will," she apologized. "However, the damage is done. Although I've been doing my best to keep everything we planned together, AHF's involvement has made that very difficult."

"But they've done so much for my team and for Austin," I countered, thinking of all the funding Garith's organization had provided. "I just don't understand."

"I'm sorry, Will," she replied. "IU Health is going to be moving to the Community Outreach Center in a few weeks."

"What are my patients and my team supposed to do?" I asked.

"Can AHF help?" she asked.

"I don't know," I said. "We've never talked about them doing anything at the clinic because we had IU Health there."

"I'm so sorry," she said.

As she headed off to her next meeting, I lingered there alone for a few minutes. My thoughts echoed the abandonment I felt, as if spoken out loud in that silent, empty warehouse.

I headed back to my office, struggling to grasp what was happening. The Tuesday HIV clinic had been a central part of the response. I knew my team and I could eventually take over the work on our own, but to make that transition within the next two weeks didn't seem possible. It felt like we were being abandoned over a misunderstanding.

I immediately reached out to IU Health and apologized, explaining that the information in the press release was wrong and that we still depended on their support. Dr. Kara Wools-Kaloustian, medical director of IU Health's infectious diseases department, agreed to meet with me at my office in Austin at the following week's HIV clinic. That gave me a little hope that we could work through the conflict between IU Health and AHF.

Next, I contacted Garith, as well as Whitney Engeran-Cordova, the director of AHF's public health division, to let them know how upset I was that they had sent out this press release—particularly without running it by me. We talked through the unfortunate error, and Whitney agreed to fly in from California the following week to meet with Dr. Wools-Kaloustian.

"I'll do my best to make this right," Whitney promised me.

The following Tuesday, with much anxiety and tension, we proceeded with the HIV clinic.

Before we started seeing patients, I met with Drs. Walthall and Janowicz, my office manager, and a few of the CDC workers in my office.

"This response so far has worked incredibly well," Dr. Walthall agreed, "but the recommendation is to transition the clinical component of HIV care to a neutral location at the Community Outreach Center."

"Changing plans," I countered, "in the middle of an emergency response, especially when we've been so successful, isn't in our community's best interest." I then reiterated the three requirements I had repeatedly insisted on since our first meetings: that every aspect of the response be patient centered, sustainable, and directly connected with local resources.

"IU Health's plan is not patient-centered," I continued. "Moving to a temporary location isn't sustainable. Plus, there's no local involvement there. It doesn't meet any of those requirements. I've been here for over ten years. I will continue to be here after everyone else leaves. This is *our* community and these are *our* patients. We had a direction at the very beginning of the outbreak before Governor Pence even issued the emergency order. I see no reason to deviate from that path. My team always puts our patients first, we are sustainable, and we are part of this community. Our patients know they can call us anytime, and we'll be there for them."

Dr. Walthall looked at me for a moment and said, "The only thing I can say is the decision to transition has been made."

Dr. Janowicz interjected, "It's not our intent whatsoever to add additional hurdles for the patients to overcome. We recognize a change in location is something new to them and something they have to accommodate, and we're trying to help them out as much as possible. We simply feel it's best to provide HIV care in the most neutral location we can."

What's so "neutral" about the government-run Command Center? I thought. I tried to remain calm.

"I don't think what you are saying is true in an evidence-based sense," I said. "Integrated models work best, not separate locations for various services. I have spent my career trying to remove barriers from people receiving care. I cannot, in good conscience, support any plan that unnecessarily puts barriers in place."

I reminded them both of what Dr. Janowicz herself had written in an article for *Time* magazine: "Local providers will need to be trained to care for the HIV-infected patients—only by transitioning care to the community will the treatment paradigm be sustainable."[2] Yet it seemed the decision had already been made.

As I left my office after the meeting, I saw Garith and Whitney waiting in the hallway. Whitney walked over and gave me a big hug, reassuring me, "Don't worry. We've got your back, Dr. Cooke." We arranged for the three of us to meet with Dr. Wools-Kaloustian during lunch. Once that was settled, I got busy seeing patients.

The morning HIV clinic proceeded with a quiet intensity. Everyone seemed on edge, so Garith and Whitney stayed in my office to make things less awkward. Dr. Janowicz and I kept our distance from each other as we focused on caring for the patients. I breathed a sigh of relief as the last patient of the morning checked out.

The weather was nice, so Dr. Wools-Kaloustian agreed to meet with us out front. Whitney started things off. "First of all, Dr. Wools-Kaloustian, on behalf of the entire AHF organization and with the greatest respect for the work IU Health is doing in collaboration with Dr. Cooke, I want to apologize for the unfortunate press release. That was a mistake. I assure you, AHF is only in Austin by the invitation of the City of Austin and Dr. Cooke."

Dr. Wools-Kaloustian remained quiet. She seemed to be studying Whitney's sincerity. She said, "We are also here by Dr. Cooke's invitation and had intended to implement what we call the Kenya Model, based on our years of experience assisting Kenya's delivery of HIV care. Our intention was to eventually hand the HIV care off to Dr. Cooke and his team. We'd then offer telemedicine support as we do in Kenya."

Whitney said, "AHF actually provides a lot of support to Kenya. In fact, I just got back from there last week."

As they continued to talk, we discovered that Whitney and Dr. Wools-Kaloustian had both worked at the same clinic in Africa. They shared a few stories, which defused much of the tension. After some discussion, Dr. Wools-Kaloustian agreed events had gotten out of hand. She and Whitney discussed "hitting the reset button" and finding a way forward.

Talk about divine providence, I thought.

But the "reset button" Dr. Wools-Kaloustian agreed to turned out to be solely between AHF and IU Health—not *my* team.

She told me, "We feel it is too much to ask that you and your clinic's infrastructure continue to support the infectious disease clinical response given the obvious strain it is putting on you and your clinic. In addition, this movement will allow patients to access the One-Stop Shop at the same time they seek HIV care."

I was at a complete loss. During the initial months of the HIV response, my office had sustained the brunt of the backlash, but by this point, the initial negativity surrounding the HIV clinic had given way to genuine gratitude. The truth was, having IU Health coming to my clinic once a week posed very little strain on my team. Since my office provided the only health care in Austin, we'd be caring for HIV patients throughout the week whether IU Health helped us or not. Withdrawing their support would actually make things *more* difficult for us and our patients.

There seemed to be more going on behind the scenes than what was being openly communicated. Earlier that week, Governor Pence had signed a compromised version of Representative Clere's bill, modifying the syringe ban. Under the new syringe services program law, a county wanting to start an SSP had to

1. prove it faced an HIV or hepatitis C epidemic driven primarily by intravenous drug use;
2. hold a public hearing;
3. adopt a local emergency declaration;
4. describe other unsuccessful actions it had tried;
5. ask the state's health commissioner to declare an official emergency; and
6. wait for the state to sign off on the plan.[3]

Even if approved, this process would have to be repeated every year to continue the program. The compromised bill did not address the underlying causes of substance use disorder by providing increased access to health care and social service professionals. Instead the focus seemed to be solely on reacting to the symptoms while ensuring the government maintained control. IU Health's sudden decision to pull out of the clinic seemed to reflect a similar desire to hand all control over to the state.

Megan Sarvis arrived toward the end of our lunch break and asked me to meet with her and Dr. Janowicz. Even though I felt discouraged, I agreed, hoping we could salvage our relationship. We stepped into an empty exam room and closed the door.

"Look, Dr. Cooke," Sarvis began, "I need you to understand that we are moving the HIV Clinic to the Community Outreach Center in two weeks."

"Let's not uproot something that's working," I implored them. "Can we just work through this?"

"We warned you about working with AHF," Sarvis continued. "IU Health was clear in the letter they sent you."

"What letter?" I asked.

"We sent you a letter," Dr. Janowicz said. "We told you we will not work with AHF, and we would leave your office before being associated with them."

Perplexed, I told Dr. Janowicz, "I have never seen a letter from you or IU Health."

"Yes, you have," Sarvis insisted. "Dr. Walthall delivered it to you."

I looked at Dr. Janowicz. "That never happened."

Sarvis insisted, "I know for a fact it did."

Dr. Janowicz looked as confused as I felt. Later, when I asked Dr. Walthall about the letter, she told me that she and Dr. Adams had decided it seemed too heavy-handed. Instead, they just advised me to keep IU Health and AHF separated. The system I'd worked out had done that—at least until the press release came out.

"Regardless," I said, not seeing any benefit in debating the letter, "we actually have an opportunity to slow down and work all this out now that Dr. Wools-Kaloustian has accepted AHF's apology."

"Actually," Dr. Janowicz countered, "we are still transitioning the HIV care to the Community Outreach Center."

"Look, Dr. Cooke," Sarvis continued matter-of-factly, "the governor tasked me with getting this HIV outbreak under control, and you have been interfering with those efforts." She let me process that for a moment and added, "We are no longer willing to work with you. Further, we feel having everything at the Community Outreach Center will allow us to operate the emergency response more efficiently."

I couldn't believe what I was hearing. The misunderstanding with IU Health and the potential loss of their clinical support had already upset me. Now my very involvement in the response was being rejected.

Sarvis leaned in and said, "I've instructed my team to hire a primary care provider to start seeing patients alongside our HIV specialists at the Community Outreach Center."

She let that sink in a moment. I looked over at Dr. Janowicz who just looked down to avoid making eye contact.

"I want to get this HIV outbreak under control," Sarvis continued. "I don't want to keep coming down here."

I started to say something but realized it wouldn't change anything. *How*, I wondered, *does she think she can replace the system that took us over a decade to develop?*

After years of fighting alone for Austin and praying for help, I was devastated that these new partners considered me uncooperative and unnecessary, and were tossing me aside. Now the sudden weight of losing everything our community leaders had worked for made it hard to breathe. My ears began to ring, and the walls of the room seemed to close in. Time slowed, overwhelming my senses—lights glaring, sounds blaring, eyes accusing. I had to escape.

I excused myself and breathlessly rushed down the back hall of my clinic to a quiet place away from everyone. There I slumped against the wall and slid to the floor with my face in my hands. Tears fell as I prayed, "Father God, I'm done."

I felt the insecurities and heartaches I'd experienced struggling alone for years in Austin swarm around me like bats. My old hopelessness crept in from the shadows. *I can't do this anymore. I'm tired of trying so hard.*

Had I failed? Again? It took me right back to that time years ago when I fled Austin and wound up in the middle of the Amazon.

My mind was reeling. But a question—gentle and unbidden—came to my mind from somewhere. *What has changed since then?*

I stopped to consider the answer. I had more help now. People were finally taking notice of the problems in Austin. And a lot of people who were desperately in need of care and attention were finally getting both. *Granted, I don't agree with all the ways they are getting it or with all the decisions being made . . .* That's when it hit me—the same realization I'd had in the jungle years before: *All things work together for good, for those who are called according to his purpose.*[4]

His purpose, not mine.

God hadn't changed. Once again, I had been the one to allow my focus to shift back toward "I, me, and mine." When I came back from the Amazon, I had made a commitment to put my own desires aside and follow God's lead. Melissa's words to me that morning echoed in my heart, *Be the man Austin needs you to be.* My job wasn't to make sure the response was successful or even to fight for my role in the response. My job was to simply care for the people of Austin. This wasn't about me or what I wanted. It was about them.

IU Health and Governor Pence's Incident Command Center suddenly seemed almost irrelevant compared to the decades of social and economic hardships inflicted on Austin's people.

I took a deep breath to center myself, then slowly let it out. I knew what I had to do. The governor's team was trying to control a disease, but that was like trying to control a leaking roof in the middle of a hurricane. As for the HIV experts . . . they knew a disease, but I knew Austin.

I would continue to try to work with Governor Pence's Incident Command Center and with IU Health, but I would only take responsibility for things I could control. If they were no longer willing to help my team provide local, person-centered HIV care, then I'd find another way.

Returning to the rooms where the HIV clinic was still going on, I asked Drs. Janowicz and Walthall to meet with me again before they left for the day. I would make one final request that we find a way to keep the progress we'd made together from being undone. After all the patients were cared for, we returned to my office.

"I just need you to understand that this is my community," I said calmly but assuredly, "and I am committed to providing the most comprehensive care possible for everyone here—including those living with HIV."

Dr. Janowicz replied matter-of-factly, "Our intention is to

continue to provide the highest standard of care at the Community Outreach Center."

"That care is already being provided here and should continue," I countered.

"We've been very, very appreciative of how gracious and generous you've been in sharing your space with us," she said, "but we've already explained why we are leaving."

"Then we have a lot to talk about," I told her. "This HIV response has been complicated. Your changing locations while we are both intending to provide HIV care seems to have legal ramifications." Thinking through that more, I added, "It would probably serve us well to consult a lawyer. I don't want anyone coming to my clinic to get into trouble over taking a patient's records or something."

We agreed to have a follow-up meeting and said our goodbyes.

The clinic, which had been a hub of activity for the past six weeks, suddenly felt very empty. I quietly made my way to my car and began to drive home. I was alone—again. But I didn't feel abandoned anymore. Something inside me had changed.

CHAPTER 16

THE TRAGEDY
OF BIAS

· · · · · · · · · ·

*You can't fool the body. It knows what's being done to it.
At the right time, it will take revenge.*

CHITRA BANERJEE DIVAKARUNI,
THE UNKNOWN ERRORS OF OUR LIVES

ON MY WAY TO WORK two days later, my office manager called
me in a panic.

"Dr. Cooke, Dr. J hacked our medical records!"

"What?" I blurted out.

"You heard me, Dr. Cooke. I'll show you when you get here."

I drove in silence the rest of the way to the office. *There has to
be some mistake*, I thought.

There wasn't. The report from our electronic health record
showed that Dr. Janowicz had logged into the system remotely
and, for three hours and thirty-five minutes, printed out hundreds of patient charts. We looked up the IP address stamped
to her activity and found it was from the campus of IUPUI in
Indianapolis. The records included every HIV patient we had seen
and even some patients who did not have HIV.

Why would she do this?

After consulting a lawyer, I sent Dr. Janowicz and IU Health a letter:

> You have been welcomed in my practice as a guest physician. We find your activities troubling and at the minimum they constitute unethical behavior. The numerous documents you accessed and printed over several hours contained confidential patient information. At this time, I have been advised I should no longer welcome you to see patients in my Rural Health Clinic. Your login credentials have been terminated. . . . Until this is resolved, I have also been advised IU Health physicians should not see my patients or work in my Rural Health Clinic.

I ended the letter by letting them know I would "continue the care of my HIV-positive and high-risk negative patients effective immediately."

Over the past several weeks, I had seen both the best and the worst of the human heart, but this was particularly demoralizing. It seemed clear to me and my team that the governor's office wanted us to get out of the way and let the experts they hired do their work.

"The experts may know more than I do about HIV," I lamented to Melissa that night, "but there's so much more to the practice of medicine than data and diseases."

I was working hard to study HIV, hepatitis C, and addiction medicine, but knowing how to care for a whole person within a unique socioeconomic system was another thing altogether. The experts didn't know my patients, and my patients did not know them. After more than a decade in Austin, people trusted my team and me. We had become a part of Austin, and together, we would find a way forward.

. . . .

"Dr. Cooke, do you have a minute?"

I looked up from my laptop to see Dr. Michael Wohlfeiler, chief of medicine for the AIDS Healthcare Foundation (AHF), standing at my door. In the wake of the IU Health pullout, he had flown to Austin to evaluate the situation. He'd spent the past few days with us and even assisted me in our Tuesday HIV clinic.

"Of course," I said, motioning toward a chair. "So . . . what's the verdict?"

He sat down and after taking a deep breath, said, "The first thing I want to say is how enormously impressed I've been with you and your staff. I have never met a more dedicated, caring group of people."

I smiled. "That's certainly nice to hear."

"However," he continued, "in the past two days, I've noticed a number of things happening that seem to be intentional attempts to undermine you, your practice, and your physician-patient relationships."

"Oh?" I leaned forward.

"Yes," he said, casting his eyes down at his notes. "For one thing, the HIV care coordinators are only located at the site of the IU clinic and are referring patients to that clinic exclusively."

"Yeah," I responded. "I had a feeling that would happen. The governor's team has made it pretty clear that they want the Command Center to be *the* go-to place for testing and treatment."

"Are you aware that when your community health worker went to pick up one of your patients for his appointment, someone from the Community Outreach Center was already there trying to drive him to the IU clinic?" he asked.

"No, I wasn't," I said, wondering which patients might have missed appointments that week.

"For what it's worth," Dr. Wohlfeiler interjected, "the patient requested specifically to be brought here."

I looked up. "Well, that's encouraging. They trust us, and I want to make sure we don't let them down." I shook my head. "I never imagined that when help finally came, they'd end up trying to steal my patients."

Something about his expression told me I might want to get used to it.

I'm not giving up, Lord, I silently prayed. *I'll remain faithful to You and this community whether alone or under fire.*

"When I got here this morning," Dr. Wohlfeiler continued, snapping me back to the moment, "there was someone stationed outside, intercepting patients, asking if they were here to see you for HIV treatment. If they said yes, she told them their treatment was now being provided through the IU Health clinic and then she offered to transport them there."

I honestly didn't know whether to laugh or cry. On the one hand, what IU Health was doing was infuriating. But picking off defenseless patients one by one in front of my clinic . . . that bordered on absurd.

"And earlier today, one of your patients came to the clinic with his wife and told us they were visited at home by someone who told them they needed to start going to the IU Health clinic. The patient's wife also said she received an hour-long phone call from—" he scanned his notes with his finger until he found the name he was looking for—"Dr. Diane Janowicz of IU Health." He looked back up over the top of his reading glasses. "She convinced them to leave your clinic, Dr. Cooke, and to be seen by her at the IU Health clinic instead."

I leaned back in my chair, ran my hands through my hair, and said, "I can't believe they are trying so hard to keep people from coming to my clinic."

"In all my years of doing this, I've never seen anything like it, Will," Dr. Wohlfeiler said. "Your patient and his wife said they were both confused, as I'm sure many others are, and they didn't know where to go anymore."

I shook my head in frustration. This is exactly what I was trying to avoid. *The goal should be to make it easier for people to get help, not harder.*

"How did my staff handle that?" I asked.

"Your nurse told him he had the right to go wherever he wanted, and you would always be available to him if he wanted to come back."

Perfect. I relaxed. "That's the exact message I've always preached to my staff."

"I have to tell you, Will," he said, "I wanted to jump in and tell the patient he needed to leave the IU Health clinic and come back to see you. But your team was completely professional. They didn't pressure him at all."

I took solace in the fact that my team had responded with integrity and acted in the best interest of our patients, even though I was discouraged by the rest of Dr. Wohlfeiler's report.

"Look, Will," he said, leaning forward, "I can understand why you're distraught over what is happening. You want what's best for your patients. You and I both know that having a local provider is the most cost-effective, sustainable, evidence-based choice and the one most patients prefer."

I agreed with him wholeheartedly. I knew I'd support each patient's right to choose where and how they received care. But for there to be a choice I needed to ensure my clinic would withstand this bewildering attack.

"What can I do?" I leaned forward.

"Well," he said, putting his notes away, "for starters, I'm going to report back on what I've found here. The IU Health clinic is only once a week and otherwise has no physical presence in Scott County, correct?"

"Yes."

"The IU Health clinic only takes care of HIV, right?"

"Correct."

"And as far as I can tell, they're not connecting patients to local primary care docs?"

"They haven't hired anyone yet, so my office still provides the only primary care available in Austin."

He shook his head. We both knew how critical the primary care piece was. The people needing care for their HIV often had other medical conditions as well, and all were dealing with mental health and addiction issues. Primary care that was available every day was vital to our patients' success. Isolated specialists commuting from Indianapolis to offer a clinic once a week could not offer that.

As frustrating as it was to have IU Health working against me, I knew I had the support of AHF, and the Indiana State Department of Health was working to keep me involved. Even more importantly, our newly discovered Austin-based faith partners were becoming better equipped and organized to assist people with their basic needs of food and clothing, and partners like Centerstone Behavioral Health System, Get Healthy Scott County, Scott Memorial Hospital, the Great Lakes Addiction Technology Transfer Center (GLATTC), and Mental Health America Indiana continued to rally around my efforts to build a compassionate community and a patient-centered response. I determined not to let IU Health's actions distract me from working with those willing to lay the foundation for a new system of care that acknowledged value in all people—people like Jane.

· · · · · · · · · ·

One of the most important ways that AHF helped me was by enabling me to send Jill and Sherry, two community health workers, outside the four walls of the clinic to find and connect with forsaken people. We'd offer them food, clean clothes, condoms, and compassion. We'd also make sure they were connected to the syringe services program where they'd have access to sterile syringes and Narcan and could get tested for HIV and hepatitis C.

Every few weeks, Jill and Sherry had been checking on an energetic, wide-eyed twenty-six-year-old with straight, sandy hair named Jane. She was doing her best just to survive and stay out of sight so she wouldn't be arrested on a drug-related offense.

They were never quite sure where they'd find Jane. Often she was near a notorious drug house on the north side. Occasionally, they'd find her wandering aimlessly, carrying an oversized purse that held all her worldly possessions. More often than not, they'd have to ask around to locate and check on her. Sometimes Jane couldn't be found at all, causing Jill and Sherry to fear the worst. My aunt Sally went missing like that as I was growing up, and just like my aunt, Jane would eventually show back up without any explanation of where she'd been or what she'd been doing. But there are only a few things a young homeless woman without an education or resources can do to survive in a place like Austin. Jane finally let my community workers test her for hepatitis C and HIV, and when both tests came back positive, she seemed unfazed.

The people we worked with rarely thought of anything beyond how to get through the next few hours, let alone the consequences of living with untreated HIV. Most people using drugs seemed content with the idea of dying before they hit their midthirties. "Death," they'd say, "couldn't be any worse than the hell of living."

Over time, by exhibiting patience, compassion, and understanding, Jill, Sherry, and the ladies at the syringe services program slowly earned the trust of people like Jane. The day Jane told them she wanted treatment for her HIV, they drove her straight to my office and brought her back to a room to see me. Her clothes were dirty and much too big for her tiny frame. Her matted hair and unwashed face both hung dejectedly. Her recent methamphetamine use caused her to squirm and pick at one of the many pockmarks that covered her skin, scattered among the track marks on both arms. She was so small, she looked like a helpless, home-less child.

"Hey, Jane," I said quietly. I gave her some space and moved slowly as I sat down. She didn't say anything.

"I'm so glad you came in today," I continued. "I know this is all pretty scary, but I want you to know that we are here to help you in any way that we can."

She kept her head down, but I could see her eyes peek up and look at me through the strands of hair that covered her face.

"I'm sorry things have been so hard for you, but I want to help you. Is that okay?"

She nodded, still eyeing me suspiciously.

"How long have you been using drugs?"

She shrugged, and her eyes disappeared again.

I lifted a hand slightly and leaned in slowly. "That's okay," I reassured her. "I just want to understand so I know how to help you."

Her eyes cautiously reappeared.

I leaned in more to try to look directly into her sheepish eyes. "How can I help you?"

"Do you have anything to eat or drink?"

I stood a little too quickly, and she pulled her arms in tightly around her tiny frame. "Sure," I said gently, realizing I'd startled her. "I'll be right back."

Once in the hall, I rushed to the closet where we kept food and drinks for patients and came back with a Gatorade, cheese crackers, a protein bar, and some pudding.

As she ate, she relaxed and started talking more freely.

She told me her parents had divorced when she was two, and her mom quickly remarried. Her stepdad—whom she suspected used and sold drugs—emotionally abused her and her mom. When she was around five, her mom fled her abusive husband, taking Jane's two brothers and moving in with family back in Hazard, Kentucky. Jane was left behind to live with her dad.

She told me all she could remember from that period of time was a sense of abandonment. She remembered feeling like she had done something wrong and was being punished. That feeling intensified when she turned seven and her dad started molesting her. When she turned ten, she told her dad's girlfriend what was happening, but instead of helping, the woman turned on Jane.

"My dad's girlfriend hated me so much." Jane shuddered. "I just learned to keep quiet."

While eating her snack, Jane had just rattled off nine out of the ten adverse childhood experiences (ACEs). The concept of ACEs came out of a groundbreaking study in the 1990s that examined the effect of abuse, neglect, and household challenges like domestic violence and the loss of a parent on the health and well-being of children.[1] Predictably, the more experiences like these the children were subjected to, the greater the toll on their mental health. What surprised researchers was how ACEs affected the children's physical health, noting, "individuals with an ACE score higher than six [have] a lifespan almost two decades shorter."[2] These early toxic events had seeped into the very makeup of the child's mind, body, and spirit, increasing not only the rate of mental illnesses but also the death rate from virtually every disease studied, including heart and lung diseases, stroke, cancer, diabetes, and infectious diseases like HIV/AIDS.

Growing up surrounded by so much chaos and toxic stress, the most lasting lesson Jane learned before finishing elementary school was that the world was not a safe place.

Jane finished her pudding by running her fingers around the inside of the plastic cup and licking her fingers. She got up, threw her trash away, and sat back down. She appeared much more comfortable now.

"That woman was awful," she continued. "She'd call me ugly and tell me that no one would ever love me." She paused and wiped a few tears away. "I remember every single waking minute of it."

People with post-traumatic stress disorder don't just get over the trauma. It becomes part of them, and even if they are not consciously aware of its effects, their bodies and minds never forget, which forever alters how they interact with the world around them. To them, trauma isn't just the memory of something terrible that happened; it's the ever-present terror that followed them out of the nightmare when they were supposed to wake up. The threat does not remain buried in the past, it lives on with them, hiding behind the next corner or behind the eyes of the stranger coming toward them.

Jane told me she started using weed and vodka at twelve. "Drugs and alcohol made me a whole different person. I used them to escape reality and go off into a whole world of my own. It was nice," she added, smiling to herself.

After her mom moved back to Austin when Jane was a teenager, Jane went to live with her. She spent the next few years watching her mom be abused by a variety of men.

"She must have been depressed or something," she recalled. "She wasn't much more than a walking corpse. I mean, as a kid, I couldn't understand why Mom couldn't just love me. That's all I wanted." She paused to wipe away more tears. Then she took a deep breath and blew it out slowly, first looking up at the ceiling and then back at me. She seemed more comfortable making eye contact now.

"Dr. Cooke, all I ever wanted was just one person to love me." She let out a frustrated laugh and shook her head.

"Then when I was in my late teens, I found OxyContin. That was different." Her brow furrowed. "It made me feel safe, like everything in my rotten, f— up life was okay. And even though it wasn't, I didn't care. I liked feeling like it was." The tears started falling again. This time she didn't even bother to wipe them away as they dropped onto her leg.

"After I graduated, Mom found out I was using drugs and kicked me out, and then things got worse. I couldn't keep a job and had no place to live. So I'd stay at drug houses or with different guys." She wiped her nose with her shirt. "I hated myself, my life, my parents . . . I hated everything and everyone."

She looked up at me pleadingly. "I just wanted all the pain to go away, so I started using whatever I could get my hands on. The day I injected Opana, I knew I'd found what I'd been looking for."

She dropped her head again. "But the reality and pain always come back even worse." Her voice got quieter as she continued. "I did anything I could possibly think of for a fix. I lived from drug house to drug house. I sold my body for drugs and eventually went to jail for robbing stores to support my habit." She let out a quiet chuckle. "Even jail was better than the life I had on the street. I was safe from abusive men, I took a shower, and I had food. It was like a break from life."

She paused, shook her head, and looked at me again. "Once I got out the first time, my addiction became extreme. I didn't even care whose needle I used to shoot up with. We'd use dirty rainwater. The only thing that mattered was that rush and escape."

Jane said she was hospitalized with sepsis from abscesses three times and almost died twice. She didn't care. Even finding out she had HIV didn't matter.

Curious, I asked, "What made you come in?"

She paused and thought about that for a minute. "You know those ladies that keep coming and checking on me, and the ones at the needle exchange?"

I nodded.

"They seem to really care about me, and it made me think. If they really *do* care, maybe there's something about me worth saving after all."

I smiled and reached out my hand. She cautiously reached out and grasped mine.

"We do care, Jane. The pain and suffering you've experienced have been unfair. You are a good person who just got covered up and lost in all the chaos. We are here to help you rediscover what it means to be you so that you can live as the beautiful, shining person I know you are."

"I wanted to be a good person," she whispered.

She looked up. We saw each other through tear-filled eyes; not as doctor and patient or service provider and person in need—just two humans who had made some mistakes, who had been broken, and who wanted to be better.

It's not something you'll ever read in a medical book or learn during rounds, but it's a powerful truth: Sometimes just knowing another person cares—especially when you've lost your will to care for yourself—can pull you back from the brink of destruction.

· · · · · · · · · ·

Several weeks later, Melissa accompanied me when I attended an HIV training conference in Chicago. One morning at breakfast, I decided to sit next to an older black physician I noticed sitting alone. We talked for a few minutes and then the subject invariably turned to the drug-related HIV outbreak in Austin.

He looked at me and said, "You know, my people have been dying from drugs for decades, and nobody wanted to do a thing about it, except lock them up because they're black. But let a few white folk contract HIV, and suddenly drug use is a health-care crisis. That's not right. But it is what it is." He took a sip of coffee.

I was shocked. I had been so busy scrambling to do everything I could to help my rural white patients, I hadn't even considered how bias had harmed the black community.

He challenged me, "You should research the so-called war on drugs." He shook his head and rolled his eyes as he exhaled sharply. "Huh, that turned out to be more like a war on the people who frightened those in charge."

That night, Melissa and I sat in bed with my laptop between us. We had decided to accept the challenge leveled by my colleague. The first thing we discovered was that in 1971, President

Richard Nixon became the first public official to use the phrase *war on drugs*.[3] I was shocked to read Nixon's domestic policy chief John Ehrlichman claim drug laws allowed the federal government to police black people. Ehrlichman boasted:

> We knew we couldn't make it illegal to be either against the war or black, but by getting the public to associate the hippies with marijuana and blacks with heroin, and then criminalizing both heavily, we could disrupt those communities. We could arrest their leaders, raid their homes, break up their meetings, and vilify them night after night on the evening news. Did we know we were lying about the drugs? Of course, we did.[4]

"Have you ever heard this before?" I asked Melissa.

"I'm just as appalled as you," she responded.

We went on to read how the very first laws aimed at making narcotics illegal in 1914 were pushed through with unfounded racist claims like, "Most of the attacks upon the white women of the South are the direct result of a cocaine-crazed Negro brain."[5]

A few minutes later, Melissa frowned and said, "This doesn't seem to be the best stuff to read before going to sleep." I agreed and shut my computer a little harder than I intended. We settled into bed, and Melissa began reading something less upsetting.

As I lay there, I remembered how stunned my brother and I had been when the Maryland basketball star Len Bias overdosed on cocaine just two days after being drafted by the Boston Celtics. Years later Duke basketball coach Mike Krzyzewski said, "He would have been one of the top players in the NBA."[6]

When I got up the next morning, I read more about Bias's death and discovered that even though he'd overdosed on powder cocaine, the media responded with hundreds of stories about crack cocaine—the form of cocaine more often associated with impoverished black communities.[7]

Policy makers took notice as well. In a major speech less than two months after Bias's death, President Reagan said, "We must affect not only supply, but demand,"[8] focusing the war on drugs, not just on reducing supply, but also on aggressively prosecuting the people using them.

The resulting Anti-Drug Abuse Act that Reagan signed into law in 1986 leaned heavily on the criminalization of drug use while doing nothing to increase access to treatment. This new law established mandatory minimum sentences for the possession of as little as five grams (the weight of a sheet of paper) of crack cocaine, versus five hundred grams (a little more than a pound of flour) for the powder cocaine associated more with white people.

Within three years of implementing mandatory sentences, the incarceration rate in the United States surpassed all other countries in the world, and though black Americans accounted for only 15 percent of drug use in the United States, they represented a staggering 74 percent of prison sentences for drug offenses.[9] By 1992, more black men were in prison on drug-related charges than in college. In fact, by 2010, even adjusting for population, the United States had incarcerated five times as many black men as South Africa had at the height of apartheid (4,347 vs. 851 per 100,000 people).[10]

I'd gone to Chicago to learn more about treating HIV, but it was there that my eyes were opened to how racially motivated drug laws have harmed poor, urban, black communities. Ironically, physician bias against prescribing opioids to black Americans ended up skewing the current opioid crisis toward white Americans.[11] But when the legacy of the drug law began disrupting poor, rural, white communities like Austin, a different national tone emerged.

In response, President Trump declared the national opioid crisis a public health emergency in October of 2017. He said, "Nobody has seen anything like what is going on now,"[12] but the truth is, we have. The only difference is that President Trump's answer was to increase access to life-saving substance use disorder treatment while President Reagan's response was to punish members of African American communities with prison time.

I'm convinced that this change in national policy was influenced by Dr. Jerome Adams, who had just become the US surgeon general, and with whom I worked closely during the Scott County HIV crisis while he served as the Indiana State Health commissioner. Since his younger brother, Phillip, has struggled with substance use, he understands better than most how people get stuck in the vicious cycle of hopelessness, drug use, incarceration, restricted opportunities, and poverty. Dr. Adams has spoken openly about his brother's struggle:

> One of the most frustrating things is being surgeon general of the United States and feeling like you can't help your own brother. . . . I've watched my brother over and over and over again come out of incarceration with the best of intentions, determined that this is the time things are going to be different. And then he goes back to a neighborhood where the people who were selling him the drugs are still around and the bad elements are still around, and he can't get a job, or he gets a job that's paying minimum wage and he can't even afford the transportation back and forth to the job, and ultimately he ends up in a situation where he throws his hands up and says, "Why am I even trying?"[13]

It's the same story I've seen lived out in the lives of my patients in Austin. It turns out that poor rural white and poor urban black communities have much more in common than we'd been led to believe. After all, patients like Tyler and Jane faced many of the same roadblocks as many black Americans, like Phillip Adams.

The conversation I'd had with my colleague in Chicago was still in my thoughts the following month when I ran across a *New*

York Times article that analyzed the growing interest in providing treatment rather than punishment to those who abuse drugs. I told Melissa about it after our kids had left the dinner table one night. "Listen to this quote from Michael Botticelli, a former national drug czar," I said.

Because the demographic of people affected are more white, more middle class, these are parents who are empowered. They know how to call a legislator, they know how to get angry with their insurance company, they know how to advocate. They have been so instrumental in changing the conversation.[14]

As I looked up from my phone, I told Melissa, "I'd like to believe this article reflects how much we have learned from our past mistakes, but I don't blame that doctor who challenged me to look into this issue for feeling it reflects racial bias."

"Clearly he was right to point out the history of the drug law," she said.

"And the inconsistency in the way the government has responded," I added.

I looked down at my phone again. "I was struck by something a UCLA professor said in the article too." I skimmed through it once more until I found the paragraph:

This new turn to a more compassionate view of those addicted to heroin is welcome. But one cannot help notice that had this compassion existed for African Americans caught up in addiction and the behaviors it produces, the devastating impact of mass incarceration upon entire communities would never have happened.[15]

I sighed, putting my phone back in my pocket. "This is the same sort of unacknowledged bias, where society tries to control and police people they fear, that has ravaged places like Austin for decades."

As we began to clear the dishes, I thought about Jane and others like her, people whose PTSD had left such a profound and pervasive mark on their lives. *How much greater must that effect be on an entire population?* The answer was right there in the morbid statistics showing that black Americans—much like those who've experienced multiple ACEs—die younger and have higher rates of death than their white American counterparts for virtually every disease, including heart and lung diseases, stroke, cancer, diabetes, and infectious diseases like HIV/AIDS.[16]

Diseases and disasters do not create disparities and inequalities, I realized; they expose the cracks of injustice we've ignored. To heal our land, we have to do more than blame the resulting damage on the people huddled along these fissures, and even more than simply patch up the divide. New cracks will undoubtedly emerge, causing even more damage until we are willing to dig deeper to repair the fractured foundation we've built communities upon in pursuit of a more perfect union.

CHAPTER 17

STUBBORN ROOTS

. . . .

Hold fast to the mountain, take root in a broken-up bluff,
grow stronger after tribulations, and withstand
the buffering wind from all directions.

ZHENG XIE

IT HAD BEEN MONTHS since I'd last heard from Tyler, the young man who was helping us track down people to be tested for HIV. A few weeks after he had come in for testing, I asked Sherry and Jill if they'd seen him around, but they hadn't. We often found missing patients by checking the Scott County Jail roster. Even though people who are arrested are innocent until proven guilty, that doesn't keep their mug shots from being posted online for the world to see. That's how we located Tyler. Mystery solved.

A few weeks later, his name showed up on my appointment schedule.

I walked into his exam room, and after exchanging a few pleasantries, I asked him to catch me up.

"Well, the night I got released from jail I went to stay with my parents. I felt like I just needed to escape. So I took some Seroquel and didn't wake up for two days."

"Seriously?" I replied, wondering how much of the anti-psychotic he'd taken to be out of it that long.

"Yeah, and when I finally woke up, I walked into where my parents were, slammed my hand down hard on the table, and said: 'Somebody get me help right now.'"

"Good for you!" I encouraged him.

"So my parents drove me to the Salvation Army in Fort Wayne, and I stayed there for a while." He paused, looked down, and then back at me seriously.

"While I was there, they tested everyone for HIV. I didn't think anything of it since I'd tested negative with you a while back, but I'd kept sharing syringes with people." He lowered his head.

"Did you test positive, Tyler?" I asked gently.

Tears filled his eyes, and he nodded.

"How do you feel?" I asked.

He looked up at me. "Like I got hit in the face with a baseball bat."

A few weeks later, Tyler relapsed and started injecting again. Even so, he continued to religiously take his HIV medication and make his HIV appointments every month. One day, he stopped in for an unscheduled visit with me. When I walked into the room, he was pacing and agitated.

"What's up, man?" I asked.

Tyler continued to pace as he spoke. "I obviously need help, Doc. I can't do this. I'm not strong enough! I can try and try and try, but I just can't do it. I decide to do right, but I don't end up doing it; I decide not to do all that craziness, but then I do it anyway. My promises to myself and to my people mean squat." He cursed and grabbed his hair with both hands and squeezed his eyes tightly closed. "I feel like a crazy person." Letting go of his hair, he started to pace again. "There's something wrong with me, something deep down, like I'm rotten inside or something and that thing always wins."

I recognized that Tyler had just paraphrased the lamentation of the apostle Paul from Romans 7:15-23, which begins: "I want to do what is right, but I don't do it. Instead, I do what I hate" (NLT).

Tyler collapsed in a chair, put his head in his hands, and wept. I walked over and put my hand on his shoulder and said, "I hear you, brother. Let it out."

Tyler heaved great waves of emotions as his tears fell to the ground. I could feel his distress over not being able to control his dark urges to use drugs.

As his breathing slowed, I grabbed the box of tissues and sat down next to him. He grabbed a few to wipe his face as he leaned back and took a few slow breaths.

"Wanna tell me about it?" I asked.

"Was planning to see my kids this past Saturday," he began. "Everything was lined up, and I was so excited." He sighed and added, "I love them, Doc. I really do." He let out a few more sobs and then collected himself. "But that morning I found out my buddy got ahold of a big stash of Opana, so what did I do?" He threw up his arms. "I blew off my kids and got high all day. What's wrong with me, man?" He stared at me pleadingly.

"You're not a bad person, Tyler," I reassured him, "but you can't do this alone." I paused. "Can we get you help?"

"I'm too tired to try right now, Doc," he said defeatedly.

"The fact that you are so tired shows how hard you are trying, Tyler. At least let us get you somewhere safe to rest and recover," I pleaded.

"Not right now, Doc," he said. "I appreciate it, but not right now."

I leaned back in my chair and exhaled deeply. "I understand," I said. Though truthfully, I didn't. Tyler had so much going for him—kids, a sharp mind, a tender heart, and a personality that could win over even the harshest cynic in a heartbeat. If he could just break free from the Opana.

As I walked Tyler out, we stopped by our community outreach office where I grabbed a box of Narcan and handed it to him. "Be safe, Tyler," I cautioned him. "Use the syringe program, never use alone, and above all, let me know when you're ready to get help."

. . . .

As the weeks wore on, the pressure continued. At one point, the state came in to ensure my practice wasn't responsible for over-prescribing narcotics. Although I had expected an inquiry, it was still stressful. Their investigation found that we actually prescribed fewer narcotics than most practices in the state. More importantly, they were reassured that—consistent with my office's policy on medications—we did not prescribe Opana, the drug most directly responsible for the HIV crisis.

More and more struggling people found help at my office. The confidence I had in my team and our partners to meet the needs of our community deepened. The years I'd spent struggling to sink roots into harsh, barren soil were finally starting to pay off. For one of the first times in my life, I felt proud of the rugged hillbilly legacy passed down to me through my mom's family. The feelings of futility I'd fought against year after year were being replaced by confidence and optimism.

Those stubborn roots allowed me to withstand the chaos and uncertainty of operating at the epicenter of an unprecedented health-care crisis. We'd endured the clamoring for control and attempts to push my team aside while keeping the community and our patients at the center of the care we provided.

The primary care provider that the state hired had to be let go after a few weeks when they realized he was prescribing pain pills and Xanax. Regrettably, to avoid further controversy, IU Health decided to pull out of Austin completely. In the end, my clinic emerged as the only site, not only for primary care, but for HIV care as well.

By late June 2015, the CDC reported 172 cases of HIV associated with the outbreak in Austin. A remarkable 86.4 percent were engaged in care, compared with 39 percent nationally.[1] The CDC and state health department were blown away. The preconceived notion that people who inject drugs would not take care of themselves had been disproven.

A CDC study of the new syringe services program (SSP) reinforced this fact by finding that 86 percent of people who injected drugs reported using it. That number climbed to 98 percent among people living with HIV who still injected drugs.[2] Meanwhile, data confirmed that drug use had decreased since the SSP opened, with hundreds of people accessing recovery services, proving that alienated, highly stigmatized people are willing to take responsibility for their health when care is offered in a way that feels safe, respectful, and compassionate to them.

When the official sixty-day emergency response ended in late May, the state told us they were going to pay for a third-party community organizer to assist us in transitioning out of the emergency phase into something that was sustainable.

Instead, Megan Sarvis led a series of planning meetings in mid-June at the Command Center. Sheriff McClain, the Scott County Health Department, my team, and others all advocated for our local Scott County Partnership to take the lead role moving forward. But this local consensus kept getting shot down by Sarvis, who insisted that the Scott County Health Department had to be in the lead. Ultimately, the meetings and Governor Pence's emergency response expired without any clear transition plan for the community.

In an ironic twist, when the Community Outreach Center closed on June 30, 2015, the Scott County Health Department transitioned the SSP to my old office on the north side of town. They continued to provide case management, insurance navigation, immunizations, and other services. To improve collaboration, I invited one of the HIV care coordinators stationed there, Tiffney Mack, to come connect with patients at my office once a week. Although the worst of the HIV crisis appeared to be behind us, we knew there was a lot of work still to be done and additional ways we could serve our patients. During the height of the outbreak, we discovered that nearly 85 percent of the people living with HIV were also infected with hepatitis C,[3] as were hundreds of others who did *not* have HIV. A cure that took only eight to twelve weeks was available, but Indiana, like most states at the time, prohibited primary care doctors from prescribing hepatitis C treatment without a consultation with a specialist. Even then, treatment was approved only for patients with advanced stages of liver damage. No other infectious disease had these sorts of restrictions. I bristled at yet another strike against my patients and determined to find a way to get people the care they needed and deserved.

Working with Dr. Duwve, I connected with Dr. Marwan Haddad at Community Health Center, Inc., to join his HIV and hepatitis C Project ECHO (Extension for Community Healthcare Outcomes). The concept is simple but genius. Using teleconferencing technology, an expert interdisciplinary team routinely mentors community-based health-care providers in underserved areas, and over time, the participating providers become experts themselves. Dr. Duwve and I successfully lobbied the state to recognize this Project ECHO as the consult needed to grant my patients hepatitis C treatment.

As it happened, the first HIV case I presented to the Project ECHO team was Jane.

· · · · · · · · · ·

Since coming under our care, Jane had stopped injecting, and her HIV viral load had become undetectable. She even got a job and secured a new place to live. Then one day, she showed up at the clinic with a positive pregnancy test. As Jane was the first pregnant HIV-positive patient I had worked with, I presented her case to the ECHO team to ensure that I was doing everything right.

They determined that no changes were required, and for the next four months, Jane continued to take her meds, and her viral load remained undetectable.

She had been terrified that she might pass the HIV along to her baby. But I assured her that if she kept taking her HIV medications and we prepared to take extra precautions when she delivered, her baby would be safe. The only real danger I could foresee was that her placenta was in the way of a vaginal delivery. If she went into labor before we had planned, both she and her baby would be at risk. An unplanned emergency delivery in this setting would also increase the baby's exposure to Jane's blood. But up to this point, thanks to Jane's conscientious effort, everything had been going according to plan.

Then three months before her due date, I received an emergency call shortly after 2 a.m.

"Dr. Cooke, this is labor and delivery. We need you here ASAP."

Trying not to disturb Melissa, I whispered back hoarsely, "What's going on?"

"Jane, your HIV-positive patient, was brought in by EMS with severe abdominal pain. She's only at thirty weeks, and she's bleeding."

"I'll be right there," I said. "Call in the surgery team."

I frantically threw on some clothes and grabbed my keys. In spite of my best efforts to be quiet, Melissa had heard my half of the call and wandered into the hall to check on me.

"Everything okay?" she asked, groggily.

"It sounds pretty bad," I replied, giving her a quick kiss goodbye.

"Drive safely," she called after me.

"I will," I promised, rushing out the front door.

Doing almost a hundred—at night, in the rain—was *not* driving safely. I squeezed the steering wheel with both hands as I raced past a semitruck. The thought of what was waiting for me at the hospital pulsed a wave of dread through my body and urged me on. My yellow hazard lights flashed against the falling rain as I glanced in the rearview mirror, half-expecting to see flashes of red and blue. Silver streaks pierced my headlights as the cold rain fell, causing the highway to shine and hiss as I drove. Thankfully, it wasn't cold enough to freeze. Still, at this speed, a single puddle could easily send my car hydroplaning.

Lord, help me get there in time.

I forced myself to relax my grip enough for the color to return to my knuckles.

Focus.

I hit the number just under Melissa's on my phone's favorites list and waited for the labor and delivery nurse to pick up. After ten rings I became concerned; after fourteen, I was about to hit the "end call" button when a flustered voice answered, "Labor and delivery, how can I help you?"

"Hey, it's Cooke. How's she doing?"

I could actually hear Jane screaming in the background, and my heart broke.

Just a few weeks prior, she had seemed so relaxed and at peace during her visit with me. I remember her saying, "I'm so excited about having this baby. I never thought I'd get my life back together, but here I am—off drugs, working, and about to start a family. I'm so excited about what comes next."

The memory of Jane's smiling face was shattered by the sound of her continued screaming. This was the unplanned emergency I had dreaded.

"She's still bleeding and experiencing a lot of pain," the nurse continued.

She then gave me Jane's vital signs and the baby's heart rate. Both were showing signs of severe stress. My heart sank, and I gripped the wheel tighter. We'd have to deliver her as soon as I got there to have any chance of saving them both.

"Type and cross her, add a second bag of fluids, and give her a one milligram dose of Dilaudid and 4 milligrams of Zofran, both IV," I said, fighting to keep the fear out of my voice. "Is the surgery team there?"

"Someone is back there setting up," she answered. "We should be ready on your arrival."

"Great. And you've got the HIV meds for the baby ready?" I asked.

"Yes," she answered. And then with more concern than I think I'd ever heard from her, she pleaded, "See you soon?"

"Yes, I'm getting off at the Scottsburg exit right now."

As I got off the expressway, the streets were mostly vacant. I'd be there in just a few minutes. The closer I got, the more vivid the reality of the situation became. Jane would be the first person living with HIV to deliver at our twenty-five-bed critical-access hospital.

I tried to reassure myself that we had prepared for this ahead of time when we had clear heads and hearts. Not preparing but just waiting to scramble when something like this happens would have been reckless. The nurses, the pharmacist, and I had been meeting for weeks to plan for Jane's eventual delivery. We had practiced each step of her and her baby's care: how to manage Jane's delivery, how to clear away Jane's blood from the newborn, how to administer the HIV medications required to protect the infant.

But tonight was nothing like we had planned.

I finally arrived at the hospital, parked, and raced through the rain with my jacket pulled up over my head. My heart pounded with each stride I made toward the familiar emergency room doors that, tonight, seemed strangely ominous.

My mind whirling with worst-case scenarios, I said a quick prayer as I pushed my way through the doors where my nightmare was about to cross over into reality.

We scrambled, knowing Jane and her baby were in grave danger. She had continued to bleed and cry out in pain, and we all feared for the safety of her and her baby. I phoned surgery to make sure the team was ready and asked the nurses to prepare Jane for an emergency C-section. As we rushed to the operating room, I took her hand. Our eyes met; I noticed hers still held a flicker of hope.

I left Jane's side to change into scrubs. On the way, I made a quick call to the CDC Perinatal HIV Hotline, which is available to clinicians 24/7. The doctor on the phone confirmed that my plan met standard treatment guidelines. She emailed me updated information on the medications I planned to give the baby. Her availability on the phone made me feel less alone.

I rushed back to the operating room. As I began to scrub my hands, I noticed them trembling under the flowing water. *Lord, guide our hands and our minds.* When I entered the operating room, I felt the weight of everyone's worried eyes settle on me. I knew that we were all thinking the same thing: These two precious lives were literally in my hands. I noticed the anesthesiologist putting Jane to sleep as I donned my surgical gown and gloves and took my place at Jane's side. Everyone was in place, and in a few moments we'd know if we'd be able to save them or not. The anesthesiologist nodded to me, signaling Jane was ready. I nodded back, said one last silent prayer, and asked for the scalpel.

Within a few minutes, I had delivered Jane's three-pound, five-ounce baby girl. I quickly cut the umbilical cord and carried her over to the warmer. The infant was blue and not making any attempt to breathe, so we began to wipe away Jane's blood as we vigorously stimulated the baby in an effort to jump-start her breathing.

Nothing.

I took hold of the stump of the baby's umbilical cord to feel for her pulse. It was there but too slow. I motioned to the nurse to begin providing the baby breaths with an Ambu bag resuscitator. After a few breaths, I felt the heart rate start to speed up. Almost immediately the baby's skin became pink, and a moment later she began to cry. What a beautiful sound!

With one disaster averted, I returned my attention to Jane. The anesthesiologist confirmed her vital signs were stable. After all the excitement and rush to deliver Jane's baby, the post-birthing repair seemed almost mundane. Mom and baby were doing well.

The rain had slowed to a lazy drizzle by the time I left the hospital an hour later. I took the back roads home, grateful for the new life I'd seen—both in the baby Jane held in her arms and in her own eyes as she gazed into her daughter's face.

CHAPTER 18

A MORE
EXCELLENT WAY

. . . .

The world is overcome not through destruction,
but through reconciliation. Not ideals, nor programs, nor conscience,
nor duty, nor responsibility, nor virtue, but only God's perfect love
can encounter reality and overcome it.

DIETRICH BONHOEFFER

JUST OVER SIX MONTHS AFTER the first cluster of HIV cases was uncovered in Austin, but less than ninety days after Governor Pence signed the emergency order, everyone involved in the state-led emergency response had packed up and gone home. Their jobs were done. Meanwhile our work—the work of daily caring for and providing support and resources to the underserved people of Austin—continued. Although the immediate crisis had abated, we needed to develop a community-wide model to combat stigma and remove the barriers to accessing care faced by people struggling with poverty and substance use disorder.

Those battling substance use disorder in Austin still faced seemingly insurmountable obstacles to recovery. Many families struggled to pay for necessities like rent, food, and utilities, and one in three children in Scott County lived below the poverty line.[1] The criminalization of drug use compromised people's willingness to seek help. If arrested, they would lose their Medicaid insurance

221

coverage. If convicted, they would be classified as felons, which would make it nearly impossible to find jobs. Locking people away only made their return to society more difficult and second chances nearly impossible. In fact, studies show that many caught up in compulsive drug use overdose within the first two weeks of release.[2]

My bout with depression had taught me the simple act of getting out of bed could become a herculean task. For people living with substance use disorder as well as serious depression, anxiety disorder, bipolar disorder, or PTSD, seeking treatment was nearly impossible. Not only that, but there weren't many mental health resources available to people with substance use disorder. All this kept local families lost in the shadows of poverty and despair.

Despite these obstacles, I knew people would participate in recovery if given an opportunity that felt safe. If we could develop a secure bridge to help patients overcome their substance use disorder and make a fresh start, I was convinced people in recovery would actively maintain and expand that bridge for others.

• • • • • • • • • •

The lunch hour crowd was dwindling in the small café facing the Scottsburg town square. Carolyn King and I were finishing our meal with Tom Cox (representing the Great Lakes Addiction Training and Transfer Center) and Stephanie Spoolstra (deputy director of the state's Department of Mental Health and Addiction), along with the director of the IU Addiction Medicine fellowship and a federal representative from the Substance Abuse and Mental Health Services Administration. Carolyn and I felt we needed help resurrecting our county's spirit of collaboration.

"We lack resources," I told the group, "which makes it critical that we find ways to collaborate." Our server laid down our bill and began to quietly clear our table.

I nodded to Carolyn, who was sitting next to me. "Carolyn is the one who proved how successful Scott County can be when partnerships are built." Together, she and I began explaining how, more than twenty-five years before, Scott County had been nationally recognized for the collaborative program Kids Place.

"Over the past few years," Carolyn added, furrowing her brow, "with the economic downturn, we lost grants and programs that addressed things like childcare, domestic violence, teen pregnancy, and workforce development. Even the Kids Place closed. All of this has strained our collective system, and yet the spirit of teamwork prevails."

"An example of that," I added, "has been the work we've accomplished through the Scott County Partnership. That includes the Get Healthy Scott County coalition, representing agencies from every sector in the county, which is focused specifically on improving health indicators such as drug prevention, education, and poverty."

"Somehow," Carolyn picked back up, "Governor Pence's Incident Command Center missed our strong history of collaboration. The administration seemed to listen more closely to political influences that were not inclined to invest in social services."

Everyone nodded.

"It's not unusual for chaos to reign in a crisis," Carolyn continued. "I saw this happen when I took over the federal recovery efforts after the tornadoes that devastated Henryville, Indiana, in 2012. Various groups try to assume leadership. People worry that no one is in charge. However, once the chaos receded, we brought local partnerships together, and calm was restored. Now that the emergency response has ended, we believe Scott County is ready."

Our group began discussing ways for the entire community to get behind helping those battling substance use disorder. Stephanie pledged the support of Indiana's Division of Mental Health and Addiction (DMHA), and the representative from the Substance Abuse and Mental Health Services Administration (SAMHSA) agreed to hire a nationally recognized, professional facilitator she knew to help the splintered factions spread across the county reunite around a common purpose.

As we wrapped up, I looked at everyone around the table and smiled. "Thank you for hearing our concerns. Carolyn and I believe our community deserves the opportunity to develop our own way forward."

A few weeks later we held a successful two-day leadership summit at Scott Memorial Hospital. By the end, we had developed a countywide consensus to focus on recovery by working through the Scott County Partnership.

Carolyn, Stephanie, and I smiled as we found each other after the last meeting. We exchanged hugs, and Carolyn told Stephanie, "Thank you for not buying into the chaos narrative. We are grateful that you believe in us and are helping us pull this off!"

Stephanie replied, "This whole mess has taught me how vitally important it is to invest in and empower local coalitions and resources long before a crisis strikes. I'm not willing to play politics with people's lives."

· · · · · · · · · ·

Even before the crisis, Joel and Peggy Nunley were hard at work trying to make a difference in Scott County. Year after year, I worked alongside Dr. Joel at the free community health fairs he and his wife organized a couple of times a year and remember him telling me, "People who struggle aren't any different from others. We all share this commonality of being human, to need connections with others."

The son of a small-town doctor, Joel learned about the powerful grip of opioids during high school when he'd sneak them from his dad's clinic for a quick high. He hid his substance use disorder well enough to be accepted to Oklahoma University School of Medicine. But while there, his drug use worsened to the point that he found himself gulping down hydrocodone cough syrup before a lecture on the dangers of addiction.

During his third year of medical school, he got caught forging his dad's prescriptions. A sheriff's deputy told him to either go to treatment or go to jail. Fortunately, his medical school allowed him a three-month leave of absence to go to Talbott Recovery Treatment Center in Atlanta.

Although Dr. Joel relapsed the day he graduated, he still began his family medicine training at Oklahoma University. He couldn't escape the pull of the pills, even after his program director caught him lying to sneak home and use. Then one day Dr. Joel had a strong urge to pick up the Bible.

He once told me, "I turned to the book of 1 John and couldn't stop reading. I got into the third chapter and suddenly felt emotions I hadn't felt in years. The drugs had numbed everything. Now for the first time, I saw myself as a sinner in need of grace. Through tears, I asked Jesus to save me."

The following day, he confessed he had been lying and changed his attitude about participating in rehab.

"I knew Jesus was my redemption from my addiction, my loneliness, and my sins," he explained. "But I also knew God's deliverance didn't absolve me of my responsibility to follow through with treatment."

About five years after moving to Scottsburg, Joel and his wife, Peggy, started City on a Hill Church with a small mission-minded group, which reached out to disconnected people.

A year and a half before the 2015 HIV outbreak in Austin, Joel received the prestigious Doc Hollywood Award from the Indiana Rural Health Association for his service to Scott County.

No one was better prepared than Dr. Joel and Peggy to facilitate an unlikely collaboration between faith, government, healthcare, and secular organizations and pull off a one-day celebratory event in our community.

Leading up to what they called the Day of Hope, the Nunleys worked with Scott County churches to hold weekly prayer walks. Excitement grew as hundreds of people from across the region converged to walk in unity and pray for the people of Austin.

National media showed people making their way through the streets blowing horns, chanting, praying loudly, and carrying signs. This expression of sincere compassion, support, and faith was inspiring and appreciated.

One night, my family and I attended a prayer walk in Austin. It felt good to march alongside those who were praying in support of our community. But once in a while I winced when we heard small clusters of people shouting things like:

"Bring the criminals to light, Jesus, and send them to prison where they belong!"

"Begone, devils! In Jesus' name, we command the drug dealers to be driven out of this town!"

"Open the eyes of the prostitutes to see the sin in their lives and turn from their wicked ways!"

I knew many of the so-called "prostitutes" were in fact homeless young women—many with children—resorting to whatever they had to do to survive. These desperate people needed access to a compassionate community, not a threat that they'd be run out of their hometown. As we marched through the poorer neighborhoods, I imagined my family eating dinner in one of the houses while people shouted and blew horns just outside our window. I didn't want anyone thinking they were seen as the enemy.

Later, when I shared these concerns with Dr. Joel, he agreed. "The people of Austin are not the enemy. The battle for our community will only be won through authentic Christian love, not fear or intimidation."

He began to thumb through his Bible looking for something as he continued, "I didn't know all the people who came to the prayer walks, but I sense many may have had differing motives—to look good or to feel good, maybe. Or they may have been genuinely in prayer, but not adding to that the genuine godly love that demands selfless service."

He handed me his Bible and pointed to a passage that read, "If a brother or sister is naked and destitute of daily food, and one of you says to them, 'Depart in peace, be warmed and filled,' but you do not give them the things which are needed for the body, what does it profit? Thus also faith by itself, if it does not have works, is dead" (James 2:15-17).

As I prayed about this later that night, I had to be honest with myself and with God. I knew that up until about eight years before, the act of praying alone would have given me a sense of spiritual accomplishment. I would have felt accepted by my peers within the church and would have believed I'd acted compassionately. *I have done my part; now it's time for God to do His part.* I think I'd also have assumed it was time for "those people" to respond to the Spirit of God and take responsibility for their sins.

I now saw—to paraphrase C. S. Lewis and Søren Kierkegaard— that our prayers are not meant to move God to action but to move us to action.

When the Day of Hope took place on July 25, 2015, Dr. Joel and Peggy led a parade of people holding banners and waving from Austin High School to Austin City Park. Several hundred more people had come to enjoy the beautiful sunshine, activities for children, food, and music at the park. The state health department set up MASH tents, volunteers from the Scott County Health Department provided immunizations, and my Foundations Family Medicine staff provided free physicals, health education, and testing for HIV and hepatitis C. The Day of Hope was con- sidered a huge success; to me, it was a public representation of the many compassionate people in Austin who had quietly been reaching out to the vulnerable in our town for years.

● ● ● ● ● ● ● ● ● ●

At the height of the crisis, dozens of people, organizations, and churches with no local presence contacted me every day offer- ing help. I asked a friend and longtime Austin resident, Billy Snowden, to help me organize the community involvement. It was people like Billy and his wife, Dana, who had been doing the challenging work of bringing hope to the marginalized in our community long before the news of the HIV outbreak captured the world's attention. I knew they were the ones who would continue doing it after the lights and cameras left, and the dust had settled.

Billy and Dana Snowden lived in one of the most rundown parts of north Austin during the early 2000s but filled any room they entered with optimism. Their bedroom window framed the portrait of a neighborhood filled with despair. Through it, they witnessed crime, drug use, and prostitution. Each year, things grew worse, and they became increasingly afraid. They tried and failed to sell their house several times, hoping to move to raise their young family somewhere safer. In the end, Billy decided that God had a reason to keep them there.

Occasionally, someone would knock on their front door and ask for food. The Snowdens even bought a small pantry to make sure they had food available to hand out. They also began holding BLOCK (Bringing the Love Of Christ to Kids) parties for the local children. One day, a neighbor invited them to bring food to several sex workers he let wash clothes at his house. They hadn't eaten for days. Billy had already seen a lot of heartache while living in north Austin, but he carried the suffering of those women with him for days.

Billy began walking for exercise and found himself praying as he circled the neighborhood. As his burden for the people in Austin grew, he shared his heavy heart with a coworker named Brent Calloway, who joined him on his walks.

After a few months of planning, they held an outreach event for the community, specifically targeting people struggling with substance use disorders, those involved in sex work, and those living in poverty. They served lunch, distributed clothing, served dinner, and showed a movie. It was so successful they continued the program every other Saturday. People would stop in for a while to eat and talk with Dana, Billy, and Brent before going on with their day.

Shortly thereafter, Dana and Billy shifted their focus to leading a Kids Club ministry on Sunday nights, while Brent continued the Saturday outreach event. Soon agencies working with the families in Austin began calling Billy and Dana to help with other struggling families.

In 2011, they began leading Sunday morning services for the community and transformed Kids Club into a combined adult and children's ministry they named H2O—Hope To Others. And hope is exactly what the Snowdens offered.

H2O received local support from a few like-minded churches, like Dr. Joel's City on a Hill, to feed people, provide transportation, hand out backpacks filled with school supplies, host special community events, clothe people, deliver Thanksgiving baskets, and buy presents for children who had never known the wonder of finding a gift with their own name on it on Christmas morning.

As the outbreak was beginning to subside, Grace Covenant Church in downtown Austin donated a church building to Billy and Dana's H2O ministry, complete with a large sanctuary, kitchen, offices, and a backyard. It has since served as a recovery center where people can hang out in a safe and sober space, and Billy and Dana make sure the kitchen is always stocked.

Meanwhile, Brent Calloway's biweekly Saturday event ministry continued to feed, clothe, and teach people about God. In 2013, Brent felt called to full-time ministry in another community. By then, there were enough people helping that the biweekly Saturday meals and ministry continued after he left, run largely in part by another longtime Austin couple, Debbie and Jerry Ousley.

Debbie and Jerry expanded this work into a mobile ministry called Oasis of Hope. Besides meeting people's physical needs, they never passed up the opportunity to pray with people. Debbie would drive the streets, passing out ice-cold water in the summer and coats in the winter, and minister to women in the county jail. She once told me how she even fed a young homeless family secretly living in a boat parked behind someone's house. People felt loved in her presence and quickly learned to trust her.

One day in 2014, Debbie asked another longtime Austin couple, Becky and Paul Thomas, to help prepare meals for the North Austin community. The Thomases didn't hesitate and began working with the Ousleys preparing food. Becky would walk the neighborhood telling people, "Supper is ready," and over time, the two couples built relationships as they fed the hungry and talked with them about Jesus.

Less than a year later, the Snowdens, the Ousleys, and the Thomases found themselves at the heart of the unprecedented HIV outbreak in Austin. Sadly, most of the people to whom they ministered were affected, either directly or indirectly. As I sought local allies during the HIV outbreak to help meet some of my patients' basic needs for safety, food, clothing, and shelter, I partnered with these couples. We discovered we met people's needs more effectively when we collaborated than when we operated alone.

One day, Debbie stopped by my office for an appointment because she had a few health concerns. None of us were prepared for the results of the tests: metastatic breast cancer. She underwent a double mastectomy to remove the cancer and started chemotherapy. She and her husband shifted their focus to fighting for Debbie's life.

Though the ministry of Oasis of Hope was carried out by more than just Debbie, the influence of a single passionate person is nearly impossible to replace. Her presence had a unique power to draw people in and change lives. Since Becky Thomas was already working closely with Debbie, she agreed to continue the work Debbie had started with Oasis of Hope to ensure anyone who needed it got at least one warm meal each week. Sadly, Debbie died on June 30, 2016. Yet, through Becky and many others, her influence lives on.

I reached out to AIDS Healthcare Foundation to request financial assistance to help Becky establish a community kitchen, and they agreed. Becky applied for and received nonprofit status, naming the new organization Food 4R Souls. Pastor Harold White invited her to use some space his Church of the New Covenant wasn't using to feed the north Austin community. AHF and my office offset the cost to renovate the kitchen, get appliances, and buy enough food to feed around two hundred people weekly.

By September 2015, Food 4R Souls was ready to provide dinners to the Austin community. Becky wondered how she'd get enough help to feed so many people, but as soon as she put the word out, twenty local churches came together to assist her.

Members of my staff and I occasionally stopped by. One evening, I surveyed the room, nodding to a few familiar faces who caught my eye. As I made my way to sit at one of the cafeteria tables, I noticed one of my HIV patients who had missed her appointment earlier that day.

"I came here looking for you since you didn't show today," I teased her.

She just smiled and said, "I completely forgot. But I do need to get in there to check my levels." She assured me she was doing well, and I reminded her to stop in the office on Monday.

My staff and I do a lot of "hovering" with the help of community partners like H2O and Food 4R Souls.

Local healing can develop only from within a community. Outside organizations made a huge difference in connecting us with resources during the outbreak, but ultimately, for any change to be sustainable, it must be uniquely grown from within. This requires invested community partners being given the resources, opportunity, and time to grow deep roots.

Long-lasting contributions, I believe, also come from efforts made from the right motivation. The Nunleys, Snowdens, Ousleys, and Thomases had diverse backgrounds but were joined in a common purpose. Paul tells believers in 1 Corinthians 12 that we each have varied gifts and, therefore, have distinct roles to play. But at the end of chapter 12, Paul says something interesting that could be easily overlooked. He says he wants to tell us of a "more excellent way."

He starts chapter 13 by explaining that lasting impact does not come through words, speeches, or meetings ("though I speak with the tongues of men and of angels"); it does not come through knowledge or a great master plan ("though I have the gift of prophecy, and understand all mysteries and all knowledge"); it does not even come through faith alone ("though I have all faith, so that I could remove mountains"); nor does it come through great humanitarian efforts ("though I . . . feed the poor, and though I give my body to be burned").

Paul says the only thing that causes lasting change is godly love. Without this type of love, we are nothing. All else fails and fades away. Ultimately, we are called to simply show the love of God to hurting people. But is this type of love truly "simple"? After all, it requires us to leave our stories, reputations, plans, ideologies, and efforts to enter the strange and disorienting worlds of other people.

I have encouraged patients who lack a sense of community to find a church where they feel safe. It grieves me when they come back after experiencing the opposite. For example, it took months for one young lady I know to build up the courage to go to church. Once there, she felt a group of women looking at her. Eventually one approached her and said, "We don't dress that way here. You should leave and come back when you're dressed right."

Dr. Joel told me that when he was Scott County Jail chaplain, some guys didn't like chapel because others had come into the jail and shamed them, saying things like, "You deserve to be here. Things won't ever change until you get right with God!" But when Dr. Joel shared his own wayward past and how Jesus had helped him, the men's defenses came down.

The gospel reminds each of us that we are all both deeply broken and deeply loved. And from that, we can bring hope and healing to others. That has been my motivation, and I believe it's what drives people like Randy, who helped in practical ways during the crisis. I'd met Randy earlier in 2015 when the medicines he took to control the HIV he had lived with since 2002 had stopped working. He had withered to a hundred pounds and was close to dying when he was finally hospitalized. While in the hospital, he had heard about the HIV outbreak and, although he had never used drugs, decided he had to get strong enough to help. Working together, we found the right combination of medications, treated the opportunistic infections that had set in due to his weakened immune system, and restored his health.

Randy believed taking his HIV medication was part of his service to God because, as Randy told me, "It's how I can be strong enough to help my hometown in any way I can." This stands in stark contrast to patients who've been told by friends and religious leaders that they can "pray the HIV away."[3] All that does is increase barriers to treatment and contribute to the transmission of HIV. He soon became a regular volunteer at the City on a Hill community events, serving food at Food 4R Souls and driving a bus for H2O to share faith, hope, and love with others. He insists that, when it comes to people of faith, we don't need "benchwarmers"; we need "players in the game."

Randy understood that, although Austin was no longer in the nightly news, the fight to save the worn down and weary—people like Tyler—continued.

CHAPTER 19

LEARNING TO THRIVE

· · · · · · · · · ·

*The original, shimmering self gets buried so deep that most of us end up
hardly living out of it at all. Instead we live out all the other selves,
which we are constantly putting on and taking off like coats
and hats against the world's weather.*

FREDERICK BUECHNER,
TELLING SECRETS

SHORTLY BEFORE THANKSGIVING, Tyler walked into my office. The last time I'd seen him months before, he had just gotten back on Opana and was really struggling. This time, however, he was in high spirits.

"Got me a girl, Doc," he announced before I could even sit down.

"Really?" I said, raising my eyebrows.

He showed me her Facebook photo on his phone. "Her name's Hannah. She thinks I'm a 'nice-looking guy,'" he said using air quotes.

"That's great, Tyler," I began.

Then before I could say another word, he blurted out, "She came to Austin last week to meet me, and we decided to get married!"

Whoa. I paused, then asked, "Does she know about your HIV?"

"Yep." He smiled, adding, "And I told her I'm in recovery."

"But you're not," I corrected him.

"I've been using Suboxone, Doc," he beamed.

"From where?" Suboxone was prescribed as part of a medication-assisted treatment program.

His smile faded a little. "Yeah, about that. I've been buying them off this buddy I know who gets them from Louisville."

"So you're not injecting?" I asked, opting—for the moment—not to delve into either the legal or medical ramifications of what he'd just told me.

"Not as much," he hedged.

"And in your mind, that means you're in recovery?" I pushed.

"It's not as bad as what I was doin'," he assured me.

This was the most positive I'd seen Tyler about modifying his drug use in a while. Granted, I had concerns, but bearing in mind Dan Bigg's mantra of "any positive change," I opted not to slip into lecture mode.

"Hannah's in it for real though," he added.

"In what?" I asked.

"Recovery!" he said excitedly. "She's got a job and everything."

"That's really great news, Tyler. I'd love to meet her sometime. In fact, why don't you bring her to your next appointment?" At least that way, I figured, I could have a chance to talk with both of them about the best way to manage Tyler's HIV—and hopefully, with her support, get Tyler engaged with a real recovery network.

A few weeks later, Tyler brought Hannah with him to his appointment.

"Doc," he grinned, putting his arm around the beaming brunette seated next to him, "this is Hannah." Then after a brief pause, his smile widened and he added, "My wife."

"Wait, you guys are already married?" I blurted out, hoping the stunned look on my face didn't read to Tyler as negative.

"That's right," Tyler said, holding up Hannah's left hand to show me the ring.

"Wow," I said, sitting down. "You guys sure move fast."

"We were meant for each other," Tyler beamed.

"He's the sweetest guy I've ever known," Hannah said, smiling lovingly at Tyler. "And the best friend I've ever had."

After exchanging a few pleasantries, we talked about Tyler's HIV and the concept of U=U. I offered to prescribe Hannah pre-exposure prophylaxis (PrEP), a pill she could take daily to protect herself if his viral load ever became detectable again, if he stopped taking his medicine, or if she wanted an added sense of protection. She declined, opting instead to trust the science behind U=U.

Then out of nowhere, Hannah said, "Tyler overdosed the other day."

"What?" I looked at Tyler for an explanation, but he just waved it off.

"Yeah," Hannah continued, "he's been using more, and when he was out the other night, I called to check on him. He literally OD'd while he was on the phone with me." She elbowed him sharply, causing him to curse. Then he shook his head and chuckled. Personally, I didn't see the humor.

"Luckily," she continued, "his low-life friends brought him out of it."

"And I promised her I wouldn't do it no more," Tyler interrupted, trying to fend off a lecture from me.

"Yeah," Hannah replied warily. "We'll see."

· · · · · · · · · ·

Patients like Tyler reminded me that we still had plenty of work to do, but by the end of 2015, I was encouraged by how much progress had been made. We were confident by then that we had identified every HIV-positive person in Austin, and all were being offered treatment as well as access to treatment for substance use disorder and harm reduction services. By the following spring, the crisis that elicited a response from every level of government had settled into a new normal in Austin.

Stephanie Spoolstra, Tom Cox, Carolyn King, and I felt the next step was to organize a recovery-oriented system of care (ROSC) centered in our community. So Tom, Carolyn, and I began working with the Great Lakes Addiction Technology Transfer Center leadership team to develop a ROSC for Scott County. The entire Get Healthy Scott County leadership got behind our efforts.

After a few months of planning, we held a community-wide ROSC at Hope To Others in Austin on April 21, 2016—exactly one year from the meeting I had held to rally the different stakeholders around the concept of a compassionate community. Believing people in recovery with lived experience would be the key to creating a new recovery-oriented community, Billy Snowden and I reached out to those we knew personally and through social media, asking them to spread the word.

It worked. We had a great turnout at the summit, and the participants who had moved away from Austin to get healthy brought a wealth of invaluable knowledge and experience. One of my favorite memories is of Sheriff McClain working through one of our action items with a group that included people in recovery and at least one person I knew to still be actively using drugs. I also explained to the crowd that we needed recovery coaches.

Not long after the summit, Melissa Thompson contacted me to say she was interested in becoming a certified recovery coach. Having been in treatment since June 2014, she wanted to help others break free from the lifestyle she once felt held her captive. "At first," she told me, "I was worried about returning to Austin since it's where I'd come to use drugs."

"I'm so glad you decided to come back to help," I told her. "If we are going to be successful, we need you and others with lived experience to meet people where they are and give them hope. What convinced you to come back?"

"You asked me," she said with a bluntness that surprised me.

"But why did you agree to come?"

Again, she answered matter-of-factly, "God."

I motioned for her to elaborate. She continued, "He seemed to be calling me to return to Scott County. It was as if God was telling me, *You prayed to be of service; that's where people need you.*

In the months after the ROSC summit, the message spread and momentum built. Mental Health America of Indiana began training people to be peer recovery coaches. Our county went from having three struggling recovery support groups to offering a total of eighteen well-attended meetings throughout the week. The number of people in recovery increased by over 1,000 percent. Scott County suddenly accounted for over 20 percent of all the certified peer recovery coaches in the entire state—more than any other county, including more urban regions like the Indianapolis metro area.

Melissa Thompson was soon working out of my office as a recovery coach for Centerstone, a mental health and substance use disorder treatment center, specifically helping connect people released from jail to support and recovery services.

The first thing she tells clients now is: "You never have to use again." Not long ago she told me how she watched one of her clients in recovery speak before several hundred people. Her client repeated those same words.

"I was crying," she said. "My boss was crying."

. . . .

In August 2017, Kelly Dean joined the Scott County syringe services program (SSP) in Austin as the prevention outreach coordinator. She brought plenty of lived experience with her. Kelly's drug use began after her father died of a massive heart attack when she was twelve. Kelly progressed from smoking and drinking to experimenting with LSD and methamphetamine, leading to multiple arrests for possession and public intoxication as well as a DUI.

After completing probation, Kelly put herself through nursing school, becoming a licensed practical nurse. When she kept injuring her back by lifting patients, a doctor began prescribing her an opioid painkiller, hydrocodone. Kelly quit taking it while pregnant, but the pain continued, and she quickly resumed taking it after giving birth. When Kelly's family doctor wouldn't give her a higher dose, she found a pain clinic in a nearby town. She tried to quit multiple times, but withdrawal proved too horrible to bear.

To help her get through her shifts at work, she started using methamphetamine again, which soon progressed to Opana. Kelly began skipping work and lost her job. Feeling hopelessly trapped in her addiction, she even let her nursing license expire. Soon Kelly was injecting every day. She recalls sharing a dull needle for a week and a half with two people. Eventually she was arrested for possession of methamphetamine and other charges, for which she spent forty days in the Scott County Jail. While incarcerated, she missed the start of the HIV outbreak in Scott County.

She reached out to her mom—who had always bailed her out in the past—for help. Instead, she got an ultimatum: Get treatment, or never call again. But there was still nowhere to go for treatment in Scott County. So without the support and resources people higher up the socioeconomic ladder—like Dr. Joel Nunley and Stephanie Spoolstra—often have, Kelly found herself sleeping on a cot in a shelter in Louisville called The Healing Place.

While she was there, she learned that the CDC investigators who had tested her in the county jail were looking for her. As a nurse, Kelly knew this wasn't good news. Although she was HIV negative, her test results showed she had hepatitis C. She'd cared for people with liver failure resulting from this disease as they died a slow, painful death, and she was terrified.

After graduating from the recovery center, she stayed in Louisville, where she tried to find a doctor to treat her hepatitis C. Unfortunately, she was told to come back when she had better insurance.

She returned to Scott County with the resiliency she had lacked before. Soon afterward, she came to see me for an appointment and said, "I didn't get clean to get cirrhosis and die." I told her the virus was the last holdover from a life she had left behind, and we'd help her get free of it. We worked through what was at the time an arduous appeal process to get her access to the hepatitis C treatment, which healed her of the disease.

Filled with a passion to help people that was born out of her own brokenness, Kelly helped start a recovery group and began, as she puts it, "weaving my way back into the community."

During a recent visit, Kelly told me she loves working at the SSP. Many of her clients are people she's known all her life—some she used to get high with back in the day. "There are times when young people, younger than my kids, come in to the SSP," she once told me. "They're adults, but I want to shake them, and say, 'Oh, don't do this. Don't get started, because I've walked this road. You don't have to do this.'"

She says people often ask her, "Why don't they just stop?" Others have asked, "Is it a choice or a disease?" Her answer: "We all chose to do it at one time. But at a certain point, we lose our choice. It's like a must. And unless you've been there and walked in it, you don't know."

• • • • • • • • • •

People in recovery began to work their way into key positions throughout the county. This forced those who had never associated with (and who in fact often held strong biases against) people who use drugs to work with and interact with individuals who had been actively using just a few years before. This intimate interaction allowed fear and stigma to be replaced with respect and friendship. It also provided help and hope to those people who were still struggling.

Tiffney Mack escaped the chaos of drug use to become the HIV care coordinator who works with me in Austin. We collaborate closely to find ways to ensure all patients have what they need to be successful in caring for their HIV. Tiffney's and my experience of working with Adam, a young man trying to transition back home from prison, was typical of the type of challenge we face. I met with Adam when he first came into the clinic. He told me, "They just opened the door and sent me back to where I messed up." He shook his head. "I was better off locked up, man. I ain't got a job or nothin'."

"Do you have any supportive people to help you?" I asked.

"Not a soul. Everybody I know's messed up on dope."

"Would you be willing to talk to someone here?" I asked.

"Anything. I just want help."

I excused myself and found Tiffney talking with a client on the phone.

"We can find you a rehab bed when you're ready," I heard her say. "Just stay safe until then, okay?" She looked over at me and nodded to let me know she saw me.

"I love you too. Hang in there."

She hung up and said, "That was Ashley. She's doing better. I think she'll be willing to go to rehab soon."

"That's great," I said. I knew Ashley had been struggling that year after testing positive for HIV and losing her kids to foster care.

"Listen," I said, "I have a patient who just got out of prison and is really struggling. Do you think you could talk to him?"

She walked down the hall toward Adam's room with me and said, "Coming out of prison was probably the most scared I have ever been. I had always messed up everything in my life and I didn't want to mess up again. There's really no help for people to establish a better life when they come out. They're just thrown right back into the hell they came from."

I shook my head and asked, "How did you do it?"

We paused outside of Adam's room. "My faith in God and the love my husband, Tommy, showed me," she responded with a gentle smile. "Even though he'd never used drugs, he educated himself about substance use disorder and helped me when I didn't know how to help myself."

I knocked as we entered the room. "Adam, this is Tiffney."

They shook hands, and I left to see another patient. When I caught up with Tiffney later, she said she'd connected him with a recovery group and would be checking on him in a few days.

"Thank you," I said. "Adam seems like he really wants to do well. I enjoyed talking with him, but there was no way I'd be able to help him be successful without you."

"Most people who use drugs are some of the best people you will ever meet," she said. "They just got lost along the way."

"How do you convince people to see Adam as a person and not just see his tattoos, history of drug use, and prison record?"

She said, "I tell them, 'I was in the exact same place a few years ago. I was lost, broken, shattered, sick, addicted, angry, resentful . . . not knowing how to get out of the madness. Today I help people find their way out. Then they help others find their way out too.'"

Tiffney never envisioned herself capable of being addicted to drugs. As she was growing up, she saw her mom and other family members drink constantly while doing and selling drugs. Drunken fights, frequent arrests, and constant chaos marked her childhood. Tiffney vowed to never drink or do drugs like her family. She wanted a different life.

She told me, "That trauma I suffered as a child was embedded deep inside me. We grew up where you didn't talk about the bad stuff. You just stuffed it away. You didn't let anyone outside of the family know the things that happened inside of it. I never knew what a healthy relationship was."

By fifteen, while her friends partied, she dropped out of high school so she could work full-time to help support her family. After working all day, she'd come home to get her brother off the bus, help him with his homework, fix dinner, and make sure he was safe.

"I resented my mom and the rest of my family for the life they forced us to live. But she was also the only mom I knew. So, in a way, it was just normal."

When she had enough money, Tiffney moved in with her boyfriend, believing she was leaving the world she hated behind forever. As she discovered, no matter how bad the place we grew up was, we return there when "life happens." When that relationship ended poorly, she moved back home with her mom. Old insecurities and haunting heartaches dating back to childhood tormented her. With no one in her life she could depend on, she turned to her mom for help. Tiffany's mom offered her the only thing that helped her cope with life.

She told me her mom introduced her to crank (methamphetamine). "I loved it," she said. "It gave me energy, helped me lose weight, made me forget about everything I didn't want to feel."

By the time she was twenty, her whole family was making, selling, and using crank together. Years passed. She married a man caught up in the same lifestyle. They had a baby together.

"I was looking at my son one day," she said, "and realized I was just repeating the cycle. I saw myself through his innocent eyes and I knew I had to change."

When her husband refused to give up using and selling drugs, she filed for divorce and distanced herself from her dysfunctional family and their chaotic drug use.

Although she struggled, her life slowly began to improve. She met Tommy, who turned out to be a wonderful father and supportive partner. Then, around 2006, she had a nagging backache and went to see a doctor, who prescribed hydrocodone.

Tiffney said, "I told the doctor they made me sick. But he insisted I should just keep taking them and I'd get used to it. I knew deep down it wasn't a good idea."

After a few weeks, the nausea went away and she found that the pain pills gave her energy. But they also seemed to silence a craving she described as a sort of "hurting" inside her she didn't realize was even there. At twenty-five, she was being prescribed 240 oxycodones, 240 hydrocodones, 90 Xanax, and 90 Somas each month.

"I was pretty bad off," she told me. "I would usually sell about thirty pain pills to pay for the visit and my meds. Every dollar I could get my hand on went to get more pain meds. Still, it wasn't enough. If anything, it made things worse. Every time the pain pills started to wear off, that hurting was always there. I just wanted it to go away."

She suffered in silence for a long time. She said, "I would cry all day long while Tommy was at work. Then I would try to hold it together around him and pretend I was okay."

Finally, he asked Tiffney where all the money was going. She told him about her problem with pain pills and that she needed help.

"He supported me," she said with tears in her eyes. "He took me to rehab. But when I went to Narcotics Anonymous and everyone was high, I relapsed pretty quickly." In late 2011, she gave up, leaving Tommy and her kids. "I didn't care about anything or anyone. I just wanted to be dead. I felt completely worthless." Despite telling herself she'd never return to the needle, she finally succumbed. She told me, "I knew I would never shoot up again—until thirty seconds before I did it."

Her feelings of hopelessness deepened, and she even tried to overdose a couple of times to end her suffering.

"My life was pure craziness," she said, "until I got arrested." That had never happened before.

She resolved to straighten out her life when she got out of jail; instead, after moving back in with her mom, she relapsed and attempted suicide. Ultimately she was arrested and sentenced to ten years for selling drugs within one thousand feet of a church.

Once incarcerated, she was placed within a therapeutic community program separated from the rest of the prison. She was almost kicked out because she bucked against so many rules. Over time, however, the woman she bunked with became like a mother to her.

"I respected her," Tiffney said. "I recognized that she had qualities I wanted."

Her new mother figure, a person with lived experiences similar to her own, began to mentor her.

"She loved God and she loved herself," Tiffney said. "I wanted to be able to love myself."

"My friend in prison," Tiffney continued, "told me, 'Acceptance and surrender are two of the biggest parts of recovery, peace, serenity, and getting better.'"

Tiffney memorized a passage from Alcoholics Anonymous' Big Book:

> Acceptance is the answer to ALL of my problems today.
> When I am disturbed, it is because I find some person,
> place, or situation—some fact of my life—unacceptable
> to me, and I can find no serenity until I accept that
> person, place, or thing, or situation as being exactly the
> way it is supposed to be at this moment.[1]

Tiffney said she read those words over and over. She came to believe that acceptance was the key to her recovery.

"But I still could not forgive myself," she admitted. "Who was I to forgive myself when I had caused so much harm to the people I loved? I felt like my suffering was justified. I made them suffer. So I should suffer too."

Her new mother figure helped her accept that she couldn't change what had already happened. She told Tiffney, "Nothing is permanent, and everything changes. You can either accept what is happening and what has happened while choosing a peaceful state of mind or you can continue to fight against it and be miserable. Practicing acceptance prepares you for whatever might still happen."

Though he lived in New York and was unable to visit her, Tiffney's father also supported her by sending her weekly letters that included Scripture and other support. Like her mentor in prison, he encouraged her to forgive herself. "When God forgives you," he told her, "your sin is as far as the east is from the west. You don't get to choose to hang on to it. God has the final say."

Tiffney's breakthrough happened when she embraced God's forgiveness. "When I accepted that God could forgive me," she said, "I found that I could forgive myself."

She spent time studying Scripture to help her learn to surrender her struggles to God. As she slowly began to feel closer to Christ, the discontentment and tension inside of her began to fade. Tiffney also worked through the resentment she felt toward family members. In particular, she realized her mom's upbringing had been even more traumatic than her own, but in spite of that, she clearly loved Tiffney and her siblings dearly. Forgiving her mom was much easier than forgiving herself had been. Tommy started bringing her kids to visit her in prison and to participate in the counseling offered by Tiffney's program. When she finished that program, she helped other women going through it.

Tiffney always knew she liked helping people. That was an important part of who she was that had been covered up by all the chaos in her life. She began serving as a recovery coach before becoming a care coordinator in Austin, making sure our patients have access to medical care, health insurance, and their medications.

"I'm able to help people who may have never had anyone show them kindness and compassion," she told me. "Sometimes just giving them some food or a jacket or even someone to talk to is enough to show them that we care. Then when they're ready for treatment, they trust me to help. They are 'my people.' I genuinely love them. I get to make a difference in their lives."

Tiffney and I work closely, not just to treat people's HIV, substance use disorder, and sickness, but to treat people like whole people. Working together has been really eye-opening. We are able to work together as a physician and a person with lived experience to help break generational cycles of substance abuse disorder and disease.

Tiffney says, "Working in addiction is really hard. It is mentally challenging. It is draining. Putting in hours and hours and days and days of work into someone who decides they don't want help anymore and ends up continuing to shoot dope is heavy. Sometimes you feel completely defeated. But we encourage each other to keep going. Working together makes it easier to keep going and to never give up on a single person. That is a beautiful thing."

. . . .

In September 2017, Centerstone Behavioral Health System and I worked together to open an inpatient recovery center for women in Scott County. The twenty-one-bed Centerstone Recovery Center for Women has since helped people from all over the state change their lives. Once they complete the program, some move into transitional housing, others return home, and a few eventually train to become certified peer recovery counselors. These counselors use their lived experience to help others still lost in chaotic drug use discover a safe path to recovery.

By helping people replace their corrupted concepts of self, home, and community with more healthy, stable, and positive ones, we increase their chance of maintaining long-term recovery. Life itself spirals upward or downward based on our foundational belief of the world being either safe or unsafe. That understanding is stitched into the very fabric of who we are by our earliest experiences, often preceding our earliest memories and long before our first life choices. If our basic survival and safety needs are met, we are better equipped to move on to experience healthy relationships and more likely to feel esteemed by self and others; to pursue knowledge, art, and culture; and then to find purpose and meaning in our life.[2]

If our basic survival and safety needs are not provided for, we are less equipped to experience healthy relationships and more likely to move on to social, emotional, and cognitive impairment; to maladapt by adopting risky coping behaviors; to develop disabilities, diseases, and social problems; and then to find early death.[3]

When partnering with those patients whose basic needs were not met, we talk about building recovery capital, which is like cultivating a healthy garden. We begin by returning to the basics of establishing a healthy self by focusing on nutrition, exercise, sleep, meditation, and healthy behaviors. This acts as the soil in the garden. Then we nurture a healthy home as the garden's environment. The home must be supportive, stable, and sober because who we live with influences who we become. Next we add a healthy community to buffer us from the world and to infuse us with resilience. This recovery community acts as a fence around the garden.

As Ecclesiastes points out, life is easier when a partner walks along beside us encouraging our progress, warning of pitfalls, and helping us up when we fall.[4] A community's peer recovery coaches are the people who have bravely blazed a trail out of the wilderness of chaotic drug use and returned to help others. As they help more people find a safe way to recovery, even more people return to help others still lost. Over time, the path becomes worn with use, making it easier to find and safer to travel.

This leads to a harvest of healthy purpose and meaning. Those seeking recovery can't be forced to bloom but that result will grow naturally from a life nourished on recovery capital. This is similar to the Japanese concept of *ikigai*, which has no direct English translation, but roughly means "what gets you out of the bed in the morning." It's a sense of purpose that blossoms when you can overlap what you love, what you do well, what the world needs, and what you can make a living doing. Once the growth of purpose and meaning emerge, fruit begins to be produced and the risk of relapse decreases drastically.

Recently, Kelly Dean worked with Melissa Thompson and Tiffney Mack to found the Scott County Recovery Community Organization called THRIVE (Teach. Heal. Recover. Involve. Value. Encourage.). THRIVE quickly opened a Recovery Community Engagement Center staffed by people from the recovery community, the Scott County Health Department, and my office, so people in recovery who need help have a safe, sober, supportive place to go. They then partnered with Toby Deaton, chief deputy of the Scott County Sheriff's Office, and me to develop a rapid response peer support program. Now peer recovery coaches are invited to respond along with first responders to overdose calls. Once there, the officer allows the overdose victim an opportunity to meet with the peer recovery coach for support. If the victim is willing, a beautiful thing can happen: The responding officer, peer recovery coach, and I work together to rapidly get them into our local residential recovery center.

Like me, Kelly, Melissa, and Tiffney have walked a journey from feeling broken and alone to actively making Scott County a safer place. My friends in recovery have transformed our community. We need more people like them who willingly display their precious scars so that those who feel broken know it is okay to not be okay, it is safe to ask for help, and recovery is always possible.

CHAPTER 20

GOLDEN SCARS

· · · · · · · · · ·

In a few years, all our restless and angry hearts will be quiet in death,
but those who come after us will live in the world which our sins
have blighted or which our love of right has redeemed.

WALTER RAUSCHENBUSCH

HOPE DANCES DANGEROUSLY CLOSE to the edge of heartache.
Although Jane's baby girl spent months in the neonatal intensive care unit, by the time she turned two, she was healthy and
HIV-free. Even though Jane had kept all her prenatal checks, was
employed, and had stopped injecting drugs, she still occasionally
used stimulants. As a result, the Department of Child Services
removed the baby and placed her with Jane's mom.

This inadvertently left Jane homeless since her mom's house
was the only stable place she had to stay, and she was not allowed
to live with the baby. Jane relapsed, stopped taking her HIV medications, and disappeared. Having no place else to go, she slept in a
barn for a while and spent some time in Scott County's jail.

A few months later, she showed up at my clinic gaunt, shaky,
and tired. She sat alone, nervously scribbling in a coloring book
as I entered her exam room. When she glanced up, I was troubled

to see that the flicker of hope I'd noticed right after she had given birth was gone. She returned to her coloring as if she didn't care that I was there. The page was a mess. Her trembling hand had violently sprawled random colors across the page with total disregard to the picture underneath.

"Can we try to get things back on track?" I asked.

She didn't look up as she shrugged and continued her mad attempt to cover up the outlined image from a fairy tale with hectic lines of colors.

"Jane, I can't imagine what you've been going through." I paused, choosing my next words carefully. "But hiding the pain under the chaos of drugs isn't going to end well for you or your baby."

She stopped, closed her eyes, and whispered, "I don't care."

The tear that snuck out betrayed her.

"Can I at least get you somewhere safe and supportive for a while?" I asked. "Maybe you can start to sort things out while you're there."

She half-heartedly agreed, and I helped her find a recovery house. With no social support, however, as soon as she got out, she relapsed and ended up in jail again.

Seven months later, she was released. Unfortunately, jail rarely equips people with the resiliency they need to cope with toxic stress in healthy ways or connects them with community resources to support their transition back home. If anything, having a jail record or felony makes an already challenging life even harder. Worse, the lost tolerance to drugs during incarceration often results in death from overdosing within the first few weeks of release.

Jane, however, had someone waiting to help her. Melissa Thompson enrolled Jane in a reentry program called Emerge and served as her recovery coach. Melissa promised Jane she would love her even though Jane couldn't love herself yet.

So even when Jane began to start using again a couple of

months later, she knew she had resources and a recovery network to reach out to for help. As part of this process, Melissa brought her to talk with me. Jane said, "I'm ready. I don't want to suffer from the pain of my addiction anymore, and I never want to go back to being the person I was."

This time, I admitted Jane to the Centerstone Recovery Center (CRC), where I started her on Suboxone to treat her addiction. I also restarted her HIV medication.

When she graduated from the intensive inpatient program, we moved Jane into our transitional housing. Melissa came with her to her next office visit with me. Jane told us, "Thank you both for not giving up on me, even when I'd given up on myself."

As Melissa hugged her, I said, "We believe in you, and we care about you, Jane."

"The two of you showed me that I was worth love," she continued, wiping away a tear. "And the CRC programs—they helped me see my self-worth. I used to scrub myself so hard in the shower that I would bleed because I felt I would always be nasty and contaminated. Now I know that my past does not define me."

Today Jane surrounds herself with stable, sober, supportive people willing to pull her up, not drag her down. She routinely attends her support group meetings and church.

I've heard her tell people, "I can love myself because God has forgiven me and I have forgiven myself. I have gone from a needle junkie and prostitute to a productive member of society. I feel comfortable in my own skin."

She's now reunited with her daughter and married to a man who cherishes her. Recently she gave birth to a healthy baby boy. What once seemed like a fairy tale to her—finally finding that family she longed for her whole life—has come true.

Jane wants others to know all things are possible with faith, hope, and love: "Even though I live with two diseases—HIV and substance use disorder—I know I am worth love. I am worth anything any other human being is worth."

. . . .

In some ways, Tammy's story is similar to Jane's. After I helped her get off OxyContin during her first pregnancy in 2010, she had two more daughters. All three were taken from her by the Indiana Department of Child Services (DCS) and placed in foster care while Tammy continued to battle her substance use disorder.

In 2015, she was one of the nearly two hundred people who contracted HIV from sharing syringes. Although she was thrilled to discover there was safe and effective treatment for her HIV, when I also offered to help with her addiction, she told me she wasn't ready.

It was important to keep her alive until she was. So I gave her Narcan to carry, counseled her never to use alone, and referred her to the syringe services program (SSP).

Not long after that, Tammy overdosed.

"But by the grace of God, I was given Narcan and survived," she told me when she came to see me for help. "Dr. Cooke, not everyone gets a second chance. I want to take advantage of what I've been given. I don't want to live this way anymore."

I quickly got her into the Centerstone Recovery Center where I could integrate her treatments for HIV, substance use disorder, anxiety, and depression. She didn't look back.

I saw her regularly over the next year as I continued to treat her HIV and substance use disorder. During one appointment she told me, "Man, did that place save my life!"

About a year after the outbreak, Tammy and her husband had reunited with their three daughters. With their family intact and stable, they came to see me for a prenatal visit. This time, their family was thriving, and in the summer of 2017, I was honored to deliver their fourth child, a little boy.

Tammy's fear of passing the trauma of her own dysfunctional childhood on to her children is rapidly fading and is being replaced with a new hope for the future. At a recent wellness check, she told me she hopes that by sharing her story, she will encourage other people struggling with substance use disorder to seek help. "People need to know there is help, if you truly want it," she said, "and with help, all things are possible."

Remembering those frustrating early years working in Austin when I had virtually nothing to offer people like Tammy makes these life-changing moments even more meaningful.

· · · · · · · · · ·

After receiving his diagnosis in 2015, Jude braced himself for the difficult task of telling his girlfriend he had tested positive for HIV. To his relief, she didn't leave him and was supportive. Though he stopped sharing needles, his drug use continued, and several drug-related arrests followed. While in jail, he began working toward sobriety again, and after his release, he started coming to my office for medication-assisted treatment and changed his environment by moving in with his mom.

Jude later told me that his mom was his best friend. "She never turned her back on me," he said. Others, however, were not as kind. Family members disowned him, and friends shunned him for having HIV.

Often when I see Jude, whether in the clinic or in the community, he has his guitar with him. It's his most prized possession. With it comes the power to overcome the substance use disorder that has held him captive since his teen years and left him with the lifelong legacy of HIV.

Someday, Jude plans to write a song about his struggles with substance use disorder and HIV. "Music has helped me at a very hard time in my life," he said. "I could be a real voice for a lot of people here. I have a story to tell."

· · · · · · · · · ·

Not every story ends the way we wished it would. In the spring of 2016, I saw a post on Facebook from Tyler's mom asking for prayer. A few weeks later, Hannah appeared in my office. She was in tears—the worst had happened. She told me the story from the beginning.

"Tyler and I got into an argument one night over his reckless drug use," she explained. "The next day, he tracked me down asking for a ride to Scottsburg. I agreed, but I was still furious with him. He had me park at the car wash in Scottsburg and told me to stay in the car. I asked what he was doing, and he told me to just stay in the car. I said, 'Whatever,' and he left. I was so mad at him I did a shot of heroin to calm down while I waited and ended up falling asleep."

She said the police woke her up. "As soon as the officer had pulled me out of my car, he got another call about some lunatic screaming and actin' a fool out in front of Campbell's Motel. Of course," she scoffed, "it was Tyler!"

I handed her a box of tissues. She blew her nose and continued. "We was both being attended to by the police at the same time. I ended up being charged with needles, and he was charged with public intoxication."

She said that Tyler served fifty days and then went back to Fort Wayne for rehab while she continued serving time in jail. Tyler stopped by the jail to visit her when he got back from rehab.

"He looked real good, Doc," she said. "He looked healthy." She paused briefly, then glanced up at the ceiling and shook her head. It was through anguished sobs that she told me the rest of the story.

About a week later, Tyler was "shooting up" with a few people when he overdosed. Afraid of being arrested, the people he was with dragged him outside and threw him in a ditch rather than call 911. He lay there clinging to life all night. The following morning, a police officer on patrol found his bruised body. Miraculously, he was still alive. He fought for his life in the ICU all day, but eventually, he lost. He was just thirty years old.

"If any of those boneheads had carried Narcan, my husband might still be alive," Hannah forced out through clenched teeth. "That Good Samaritan law is supposed to protect people like my husband," she said, after her tears had subsided. "What good is it if the police still issue a warrant to arrest the people who called?"

What she said put a face to tens of thousands of people who overdose and die each year because the people they are with are afraid to call for help.

After Tyler's death, I started Hannah on a form of medication-assisted treatment to help her overcome her own addiction. She got a job and has continued to do well since. To this day, she remains HIV free and is off drugs, mourning the loss of Tyler and wishing for better laws to protect those who do the right thing by calling 911 to save a life.

. . . .

Two years after Chris Abert helped with the historic response to the HIV outbreak in Austin, he sat in a courtroom in Lawrence County, two counties over from ours, waiting to hear the fate of the local SSP. The courtroom was packed, and the air was alive with anticipation.

Though Indiana law was changed in response to the HIV outbreak so that sterile syringes could be provided to people who inject, the local county commissioners could approve an SSP for only one year at a time. The Indiana Recovery Alliance (IRA), headed by Chris, had overseen the program in Lawrence County, and the year was up. They hoped that the SSP would be approved for another year.

Chris felt the IRA had made significant strides in the short year they'd been given, a view shared by others who came to testify and show their support. SSP data from the previous year was shared, showing the success of the program, including fifty overdose lives saved by community-distributed Narcan, a significant reduction in the transmission of hepatitis C, and the prevention of any reported cases of HIV.

A commissioner from the neighboring county spoke to support the renewal so the two counties could work together. Superior Court Judge Michael Robbins even reversed his usual role to plead his case to the commissioners.

"After 60 years of this war on drugs," Robbins stated, "if we think that we can arrest, prosecute, and have guys like me send [people who use drugs] to prison to work our way out of this epidemic, then we are bigger fools than I think we are. There is no silver bullet," he continued, "but we need new solutions, and this happens to be one of those. Does this save lives? Of course it does. Does it save us from budgetary problems? Of course it does. The question is: What are our moral obligations to those people each of us represent? I believe it is to try new solutions to this confounding problem that we as a society have created."[1]

Chris Abert told the commissioners how heartbreaking it was to work with people as young as fifteen but added that the IRA gives them hope, since "dead people can't recover."

Four members of the county health board testified about the importance of renewing the SSP from a public health perspective. One member, who had acted as the county coroner, said his testimony in support of the SSP wasn't based on an opinion of whether it's working, but instead was "based on facts." Shawna Girgis, the mayor of Bedford, which was the county seat, wrote a letter urging the commissioners to consider the irrefutable thirty-plus years of scientific evidence backing SSPs and to follow the recommendation of their own county's health board to approve the renewal.

The only testimony against the program came from the county prosecutor who suggested people who inject could just access livestock syringes at a store called Rural King.

Finally, the moment of truth came. County Commissioner President Gene McCracken made a motion to renew the SSP and asked for one of the other two commissioners to second the motion.

He looked over at commissioners Rodney Fish and Dustin Gabhart, but they remained silent, leaving Commissioner McCracken with no choice but to rule against the motion to renew the Lawrence County Syringe Services Program.

Everyone in the courtroom seemed dumbfounded. Commissioners Fish and Gabhart both said they could not separate the drug issue from the public health benefit of a syringe program.

Commissioner Fish added he didn't know any public-sector answers to these problems. Instead, he quoted 2 Chronicles 7:14: "If My people who are called by My name will humble themselves and pray and seek My face and turn from their wicked ways, then I will hear from heaven, and will forgive their sin and heal their land." He said he came to his conclusion to stop the program after considerable prayer, stating, "It was a moral issue with me."[2]

And with that quotation from the Word of God, hope fled the room, as did Chris Abert. Overwhelmed by emotion and compassion for those he felt had just received a death sentence, he shouted to the commissioners as he left, "You are killing people!"

I was taught early to live a life guarded against the evils of the world. My imagination was enough to keep me from exploring those dark places. I have since discovered that "the acknowledged shadow may be terrible enough. But it is the unacknowledged one which is the real killer."[3]

Fish seemed to miss the message of the very verse he quoted. "If My people," refers to followers of God. So when the verse continues ". . . will humble themselves and pray and seek My face and turn from their wicked ways," God is asking Christians, "who are called by My name," to humbly seek Him—He isn't condemning the outcast, sick, and needy.

Somehow, Christ's message of meeting needs and rejecting the status quo has been lost. Love has the power to transform lives and communities. But entrenched forces resist change, maintaining the socioeconomic gradient, marginalizing people, and imposing control. They seek to define us by our race, gender, and class; by our past, where we came from, and what we look like; and by our successes, failures, and performance. No one, however, has the right to overlook the intrinsic value in every person.

We think of the human heart as having light and dark, good and evil. But in actuality, what we often experience most is simply acceptance or rejection. Modern social media is fueled by this fact with "likes" and "dislikes." Our desire for acceptance and aversion for rejection can be exploited by groups and personalities without us even being aware of it. We can get caught up supporting causes that have nothing to do with our personal values—or worse, are unknowingly contrary to them—to gain a sense of acceptance, security, and superiority.

Christ consistently railed against humanity's attempts to equate rule following to morality. Instead, He condensed all the laws down to their simplest form as expressions of love.[4] Scripture clearly states, "Owe nothing to anyone—except for your obligation to love one another. If you love your neighbor, you will fulfill the requirements of God's law."[5] Yet we keep falling into the same old trap of following religious and political rules or charismatic leaders instead of the more difficult path of caring for our neighbors, who may be different from us.

In fact, Christ seemed always to focus on meeting people's physical needs first. In all of the verses I found concerning Jesus healing someone, He required nothing from the person beforehand. Yet we often place criteria on when we will meet hurting, hungry, desperate people's physical needs.

Meera Bai is a public health nurse who works at a safe injection site in Vancouver, where they have never lost a patient to a drug overdose. She tells the story of caring for one of her regular patients to help people understand why she feels compelled by her Christian faith to do this work:

Another regular . . . chats with me in the treatment room as I dress his abscess, trying not to cringe away from the overwhelming odour he emanates. "It would have been my anniversary with my wife today, if she hadn't gone missing. We've both been down and out, but she took care of me out here. Now, I got nobody to talk to. This is the first human touch I've had today." I look up, startled. I am wearing gloves, holding my breath, cleaning his sores with a ten-inch sterile Q-tip. Even this, my deficient attempt to heal, is taken as love by a man desperate for human connection. I am ashamed.[6]

The Rev. Edwin Sanders, who founded the Metropolitan Inter-denominational Church in Nashville in 1981, was once asked how, as a member of the clergy, he could justify teaching people how to clean used needles.

His response: "I need live people to offer what I have in the work that I do."[7]

In Matthew 25, Jesus said if we fail at caring for the least among us, we lose everything. Chris Abert told me recently if he had to testify before the commissioners of Lawrence County again, he would put aside his mountain of evidence and data irrefutably proving SSPs work and just sincerely tell them: "We hang out with sex workers, bring people back from the dead, cure the sick, and minister to the outcasts. We love without judgment. . . . What work could be more Christlike?"

· · · · · · · · ·

Nine out of ninety-two counties in Indiana have instituted syringe services programs since 2015. The legislation permitting them expires in July 2021. State representative Ed Clere's attempts to extend the program failed to pass the Indiana legislature in early 2020.[8]

I firmly believe, based on the health outcomes and statistics I've seen, that the SSP has saved many lives. However, I know its future is ultimately in the hands of our public officials. For that reason, I concentrate my efforts on building our local recovery community, as well as other initiatives that are showing positive results. The Get Healthy Scott County coalition, for instance, has successfully started school-based drug and alcohol prevention programs such as Life Skills Training and Allstars. When local leaders followed up with the students, they discovered that the number of youth who reported using alcohol had decreased by nearly 70 percent, tobacco by 65 percent, marijuana by 60 percent, and prescription drugs by an incredible 81 percent.

Though hepatitis C is on the rise in counties all around us, through diagnosis, treatment, and prevention, we've decreased the number of new hepatitis C cases by over 76 percent.

A recent regional hepatitis A outbreak in 2018 and 2019 further demonstrates the progress we've made. While Kentucky experienced delays in responding to the outbreak, which sickened over four thousand and killed forty-three people, Indiana acted quickly. The Indiana State Department of Health (ISDH) deployed "strike teams" and proactively vaccinated food handlers and other at-risk populations. As a result, our state had only a quarter as many cases as Kentucky and, although still too many, only four deaths. Even more impressive, since the Scott County Health Department had been actively vaccinating people through the SSP since 2015, Scott County experienced only eight total cases of hepatitis A, all traced to other counties.

As of November 2018, all the people living with HIV are engaged in care, with 77 percent virally suppressed—compared to 54 percent nationally.[9] New HIV cases have plummeted by over 95 percent, and after CDC calculations predicted twenty-eight new cases of HIV per year, we've had no more than eight per year during 2017, 2018, and 2019. And we are no longer listed as the county with the worst health outcomes in Indiana.

We continue to try to expand access and opportunity to people in need. In the fall of 2019, my team also partnered with Wooded Glen Recovery Center, located just south of Scott County, where we are able to rapidly admit, detox, and provide recovery services for thirty days. Then in the spring of 2020, I hired Billy Snowden to be part of our team at Foundations Family Medicine, serving as our licensed clinical social worker.

We've witnessed a remarkable turnaround in Austin since the HIV outbreak of 2015. What was once a failed community is now thriving—largely in part to the efforts of the community itself to destigmatize poverty and substance use disorder, and to create safe places for people to access help.

Communities do not fail because the people within them fail. They fail because we allow those who stumble to be dehumanized. This only encourages people to hide pain and deny mistakes. Communities fail because we keep painting over the cracks in the foundations instead of being willing to accept the struggling among us as our neighbors. We must not banish broken people but rather reject a broken culture that forbids vulnerability.

Since sickness and death thrive where community fails, we must examine our own hearts instead of blaming and banishing those we disagree with, don't understand, fear, or dislike. During my own battle with depression, I learned for myself how damaging isolation is, not just to the human soul but to the very foundation of our communities. That experience changed me for the better. It allowed me to understand marginalized people and made me a stronger, more determined advocate for those who suffer.

Kintsugi is the Japanese art of mending broken ceramics with gold-powdered adhesive. Artisans do not discard broken jars of clay, nor do they attempt to hide their brokenness; instead, they transform the shattered remains of what was into a new, more valuable vessel with the unique beauty that comes from highlighting its brokenness in gold. Likewise, I believe failures can make us stronger and more valuable. Shattered lives with rough edges can be filled with the golden glow of compassion. I like how Ernest Hemingway put it: "The world breaks everyone and afterward many are strong at the broken places."[10] If we discard, shun, or shame the broken, we will miss the restored beauty, strength, and purpose of those who bear golden scars.

We don't have to hide our cracks. By vulnerably sharing our own damaged selves without shame to be melded together with other broken people, we have the opportunity to bring unity and common purpose to our fragmented communities. We can transform our communities into unique masterpieces of healing that are healthier, more prosperous, and more beautiful than they were before.

HOPE REVEALED

· · · · · · · · · ·

The opposite of love is not hate; it's indifference.
The opposite of art is not ugliness; it's indifference.
The opposite of faith is not heresy; it's indifference.
And the opposite of life is not death; it's indifference.

ELIE WIESEL

I SOMETIMES WONDER what became of the young woman who surprised me by jumping into my car at the gas station. She opened my eyes to the existence of people I'd neglected to acknowledge. My life had been more comfortable when I didn't notice the young woman dropped off at the same corner several times a day, the barefoot and shirtless child playing near a woman rummaging through a trash can, or the thin, older man staggering along the railroad track drinking from a brown paper bag.

My discomfort caused me to cling to beliefs I'd been taught about life and about people who were different from me. I wanted the world to make sense and unwittingly tried to force these people to fit into the preconceived narrative I'd stitched together from my upbringing and training. It was easiest to not recognize nameless, faceless people as anything more than distorted shadows forced to live behind a veil of bias and stigma. After all, my worldview insisted that they must have brought that level of misery on themselves by making bad choices and living immoral lives.

The longer I worked in Austin, the more people like that young woman—authentic, flesh-and-blood people with feelings, hopes, and dreams—kept tearing their way through the veil, challenging what I thought I knew. At first, the thick threads of prejudice and ideology spread back across my mind, obscuring the fact that life and people are much more complicated than I acknowledged. The status quo requires predictability at the expense of insight.

The real world was turning out to be not nearly as tame and certain as I'd been led to believe. Somehow it was both a brutal, chaotic mess and a beautiful, inspiring work of art. The inner sense of wonder and terror I experienced in those vulnerable moments with vulnerable people turned out to be meaningful and life-changing. It was like witnessing the northern lights, an approaching storm, or the darkness of a solar eclipse. Or hearing about atrocities committed against nameless people in a strange land, or the rapid spread of a deadly disease across the globe. Something awakens in these moments that has been with us our entire lives: the understanding that we are more like those we consider "other" than we think.

Why do we allow these moments of awakened clarity and insight to be overwritten by stories that uphold bias, reaffirm stigma, and justify prejudice? In doing so, we lose touch with the authentic nature of life and people. It's as if hypnotic flakes of ordinary, mundane life gently settle over our hearts like snowfall. In the end, we are left with only a vague sense of something forgotten.

Sometimes it takes an extraordinary encounter to open our eyes to see ordinary people and truths. The truth is, as horrendous as the opioid and HIV crises have been for Austin, these calamities did bring the unseen people out of the shadows and into the light.

Today the individuals who once walked our streets in search of a "fix" or a meal are at the forefront of our town's efforts to build a community in recovery. The injuries caused by broken homes and systems are being healed so that all people can rewrite their narratives from a place of hope, not from shame and stigma. These brave souls are the true agents of change, and I consider them the heroes who are rewriting Austin's story.

· · · · · · · · · ·

The year 2020 taught us all that not only are our health care and support systems fragile, they are essential to the stability of our economy and way of life. The COVID-19 pandemic caused people to experience unemployment, isolation, food insecurity, and illness, which only exacerbated underlying issues already harming communities and lives.

Although overdose deaths in the US had plateaued in 2018 and 2019,[1] they surged again during the pandemic. By July 2020 they were already 13 percent higher than at the same time the previous year.[2] The American Medical Association announced in September 2020 that more than forty states had reported increases in the number of overdose deaths during the pandemic.[3] "In some cities, current estimates are that these deaths could far exceed those from Covid-19."[4]

Disasters and diseases do not create disparities; they reveal them. The tensions that build during times like these shatter our communities along preexisting fracture lines of injustice we've ignored.

In America, we are rightfully proud of our Constitution, proclaiming that all people have the right to life, liberty, and the pursuit of happiness. Yet we tolerate a system that denies equal access to safety, health, and opportunity. Under this system, how much life someone has access to is far too often based on their zip code, race, socioeconomic status, or what those in power think of them. This predictable outcome played out on a much larger scale during the COVID-19 pandemic when—as with every historic disaster—the disease, disability, and death disproportionately struck along the fault lines of race and socioeconomic class. Our communities suffer more than necessary because we've allowed them to be built on a divided foundation.

The resulting harms that arise from adverse health and socioeconomic factors, childhood trauma, and isolation represent a real national crisis. All communities can work together to reduce barriers and increase access to opportunity, health care, and social support.

We must stop squaring off against those who look, act, or believe differently than we do and become willing to seek first an unbroken foundation of commonality. A Spanish proverb says, "Habits are at first cobwebs, then cables." The same can be said of relationships. We become stronger when we find and reinforce the threads that bind us together as neighbors, citizens, and humans.

Allowing all faces a seat at the table so all voices can be heard doesn't threaten our union. It's the principle upon which our union was established. By presuming equality, unity, and goodwill combined with the freedom to speak our concerns without fear, communities can develop actionable solutions together that affirm our shared quest for safety, health, and opportunity.

We don't have to agree with or even like someone to defend their shared human right to life, liberty, and the pursuit of happiness. To me, that is the essence of the American spirit.

However, I'm often reminded that some people are unable to see hope through the relentless stress, despair, and barriers in their lives. Others have lost their belief that they can achieve the American dream because of mistakes and failures. To ensure that all people have access to health and opportunity, we must stop shaming and marginalizing people who make mistakes, struggle, and even fail. The truth is that none of us have it all together; we often fumble through life the best we can.

When we become comfortable allowing others to stumble, to do things differently, and to feel broken, we open ourselves to the privileged moments that are fundamental to being human: caring for each other with lovingkindness. I've found that it is in these moments that our sleepy hearts stir and we feel what it is to be alive.

So it is up to us to leave our comfort zones and reach across the divide to connect with people—not as different from us as we've been led to believe—in a way that feels safe and loving to them. For if we send the hurting, hungry, sick, and pressed-down people away without compassion, we are hiding hope from *those who are perishing*.[5]

None of us can do everything, but we can all do something. Times of darkness can also reveal those holding the sacred light of liberty. Each of us is personally responsible for and affected by the fate of every member of our community. We must ask ourselves and each other, *What are we willing to do to reduce suffering, to allow people we may not understand to try and fail, to respond by encouraging them to try again, to make it easier for them to succeed, and to make our communities a little better?*

Connection heals; isolation harms. Love has the power to transform broken lives and communities. That is the reason the Scott County recovery community uses a butterfly as its symbol. It could just as aptly have been a phoenix.

· · · · · · · · · ·

The small town of Austin came out of the Appalachian coal mines to become the canary in the coal mine for our nation. Austin has a message worth hearing. It's not a new one, but when our people came together, we proved that even struggling communities can be transformed and renewed. Let us willingly surrender to God everything to which we cling so desperately—ego, identity, honor, prestige. In so doing, we may sacrifice who we were or thought we were for who we are meant to be. It's the mystery of giving up our life to find it. Then we can transcend our lives and join a grander work with others to ensure that every single life has access to wellness, community, and the transforming power of faith, hope, and love.

There will always be disasters, but we can reduce their damage by healing the divides along which most of the damage occurs. We do not have to helplessly wait for the next humanitarian crisis. By investing now in infrastructure, health care, equity, and life-affirming programs, we can slow and even prevent the spread of disease, disability, and early death. Our nation's blood, treasure, and prosperity depend on what we do next.

Will the work be hard? Will we make mistakes along the way? If my story has convinced you of anything, you know the answer to both questions: Yes!

You may also question what you can do on your own. You are not alone. Once you begin, you will quickly find others doing this critical work. They will inspire you, as you will inspire them.

So take a moment before you close this book to commit yourself to this life-and-death cause. Working together, we can end a tremendous source of human suffering by bringing safety, health, and opportunity to every child on every street. The stakes are real. The time is now. Let's get started.

Acknowledgments

Writing a book is no easy task. Countless people influenced, inspired, and instructed me along this several-year journey. Publishing a book turned out to be even more challenging. This book wouldn't exist without the many experienced guides, mentors, and collaborators I've been blessed to work with. Although there's not enough space here to list everyone, I do want to acknowledge a few people by name.

Melissa, you have been an ever-present source of encouragement and inspiration. You've challenged me and forced me to grow, and even through my times of self-doubt, you have never given up on me. Bringing this story to publication has been a labor of love, one you've shared with me over the last few years. You've given so much of yourself editing and re-editing (and re-editing) this story that it has become infused with your gentleness, insight, and goodness. Your spirit breathes within these pages.

Mom and Dad, we don't get to choose our parents. But if we did, I'd choose you. Your unconditional love has shone brightly to help me through the darkest times. Mom, when things seemed impossible, it was your insatiable drive and stubborn persistence that stirred in me and refused to let me quit. Dad, it was you who taught me that everyone not only needs but deserves to feel safety and love. I hope you are proud of how that truth lives within these pages.

Laura Ungar, thank you for the hours of interviews you conducted with my patients, helping me to accurately capture their stories. You have been a great professor, researcher, collaborator, and friend. I'm honored to have your name on this book.

Steve Ross, my agent, you never stopped believing in me or this book. There were times when the challenges of writing and publishing felt insurmountable, but your spot-on advice, constant encouragement, and unyielding persistence pulled me through the few rough stretches. Thank you for believing in and advocating for me. I'm privileged to have you in my corner.

It's one thing to publish a book. It's an entirely different thing to nurture and cultivate a book into publication. I was initially apprehensive about trusting my story to a publisher, but when I started working with the **Tyndale Momentum** team of Jan Harris, Kim Miller, and Carol Traver, all my anxieties melted away and were replaced with a constant feeling of support, availability, and encouragement. They championed my voice and message in a way that humbled me while demonstrating their commitment to this book by working as hard to bring it to life as I did. Jan, Kim, and Carol, you have earned my respect as well as my eternal gratitude by collaborating to help me further develop my story, coach me in writing, and expertly guide me through the editing process. To you and everyone at Tyndale Momentum, thank you for making a seemingly daunting process feel safe.

To **my patients**, this story is as much yours as it is mine. I hope I've honored you in what I have written. Our journey together does not end with the conclusion of this book. I'm just as committed to seeing our community whole as I was when I first started back in 2004. Our stories are forever linked, and I'm proud of what we have accomplished together.

Without **my staff**, this book wouldn't exist. Your hands have held the hurting, fed the hungry, and delivered hope to the hopeless. Your hands have opened doors of hope, healed calloused hearts with compassion, and removed barriers to opportunity. As your hands hold this book, please know how much I admire and respect you for using them to defend, serve, and comfort those who've known only hands that harm. You are my heroes, and I'm blessed to work with each of you.

On June 9, 2019, my friend and mentor **Tom Cox** died from lung cancer. Although his death has left an irreplaceable void, Tom made an enduring imprint on Indiana and those who knew him. Without his influence and guidance, Scott County might never have succeeded in developing a recovery-oriented system of care (ROSC). His quiet leadership following Scott County's 2015 HIV outbreak enabled our recovery community to come together, draw strength from one another, and overcome obstacles. Then by faithfully working with our Get Healthy Scott County coalition, he mentored our budding recovery community into a fully realized and regionally influential recovery community organization, THRIVE.

Prior to his work with us, Tom had devoted over forty years of his life to advocating for people living with substance use disorder in Indiana. He was a founding member of the Indiana Addictions Issues Coalition, which fights stigma and defends the rights of people living with SUD. I'm grateful to have known Tom. May his gruff voice and powerful legacy be remembered through this book and through the countless lives and communities he helped.

While I was writing this book, my friend **Dan Bigg** tragically died of an accidental overdose in his Chicago home. He was only fifty-nine. His wife, Karen, said she believes he was trying to get relief from his chronic insomnia. Dan's family and friends, as well as the harm reduction and recovery communities, are in deep mourning. I'll not shy away from how ironic it is that this man—a champion of modern harm reduction and responsible for saving countless lives—lay dying with the antidote naloxone stacked in boxes a few feet away.

Dan remains one of my all-time heroes. More importantly, he was my friend. He changed the world around him for the better, and he changed me. The circumstances of his death do nothing to diminish that. I'll always remember him as the patron saint of harm reduction.

Ten Biblical Principles
of Harm Reduction

MY FIRST EXPOSURE to the concept of harm reduction was as a teenager growing up in the 1980s and early 1990s. The emergence of HIV/AIDS dominated the headlines, and my evangelical Christian church wrestled with how to respond. On the one hand, we were told to love our neighbors because Christ loved us first. On the other hand, we were warned that harm reduction strategies like condom and sterile syringe distributions enabled people's vices. Since then, I have wrestled with how to resolve the moral dissonance I felt rising between this religious instruction, my spiritual obligations, and eventually, my scientific training.

My experience was not unique. As sociologist Susan M. Chambré wrote when looking back at that time, "Religious traditions had a paradoxical impact on the social response to the epidemic: both a source of stigma and the basis of enormous concern and compassion. Some religious leaders used AIDS as an object lesson illustrating moral decline. Others preached compassion and emphasized the obligation to care for the sick and dying."[1]

As I sought to reconcile the contradictory messages I was hearing from my faith community, I turned to Scripture. Second Timothy 3:16-17 says, "All Scripture is given by inspiration of God, and is profitable for doctrine, for reproof, for correction, for instruction in righteousness, that the man of God may be complete, thoroughly equipped for every good work."

So I began to search for biblical principles of harm reduction. This list is the result of my personal exploration of what Scripture says. I share them here hoping for two outcomes.

First, to readers who share my faith and may be struggling with wanting to help but not wanting to enable: I hope you find comfort in this list.

Second, to readers who do not share my faith but want to invite people of faith into the harm reduction community: I hope this list allows you more understanding and equips you for a more productive interaction.

1. OBSERVE THE LAW OF LOVE: Love is to be the interpreter of law.

When Jesus was asked which of the Old Testament laws was the greatest He replied, "'Love the Lord your God with all your heart and with all your soul and with all your mind.' This is the first and greatest commandment. And the second is like it: 'Love your neighbor as yourself'" (Matthew 22:37-39, NIV).

Augustine insisted these twin commandments of love were the lens through which all Scripture must be interpreted. He wrote, "Anyone who thinks he has understood the divine scriptures or any part of them, but cannot by his understanding build up this double love of God and neighbour, has not yet succeeded in understanding them."[2]

The apostle Paul put it this way:

Let no debt remain outstanding, except the continuing debt to love one another, for whoever loves others has fulfilled the law. The commandments, "You shall not commit adultery," "You shall not murder," "You shall not steal," "You shall not covet," and whatever other command there may be, are summed up in this one command: "Love your neighbor as yourself." Love does

no harm to a neighbor. Therefore love is the fulfillment of
the law.
ROMANS 13:8-10, NIV

Jesus went on to give an example of how the law of love can
be applied: "[David] entered the house of God, and he and his
companions ate the consecrated bread—which was not lawful for
them to do" (Matthew 12:4, NIV). The sixteenth-century German
theologian and religious reformer Martin Luther wrote,

> Had the priest been disposed to refuse David the holy
> bread, had he blindly insisted on honoring the prohibitions
> of the Law and failed to perceive the authority of Love,
> had he denied this food to him who hungered, what would
> have been the result? So far as the priest's assistance went,
> David would have had to perish with hunger, and the
> priest would have been guilty of murder for the sake of
> the Law.[3]

He summed it up this way, "No greater calamity, wrong and
wretchedness is possible on earth than the teaching and enforcing
of laws without love."[4]

2. SEEK AND SAVE: Go to the people.

We must follow Christ's example of leaving our comfort zone
to seek those who may not yet be ready to embrace healthy choices.
Let us not forget that "God demonstrates his own love for us in
this: While we were still sinners, Christ died for us" (Romans 5:8,
NIV). Paul beautifully describes the example we are called to follow:

> Do nothing out of selfish ambition or vain conceit.
> Rather, in humility value others above yourselves, not
> looking to your own interests but each of you to the
> interests of the others.

In your relationships with one another, have the same mindset as Christ Jesus:

Who, being in very nature God,
    did not consider equality with God something to be
        used to his own advantage;
rather, he made himself nothing
    by taking the very nature of a servant,
    being made in human likeness.
And being found in appearance as a man,
    he humbled himself
    by becoming obedient to death—
        even death on a cross!

PHILIPPIANS 2:3-8, NIV

Although Christ was, is, and always will be God, he "gave up his divine privileges" (Philippians 2:7, NLT) and the glory of heaven to live among us as a man (John 1:14) and "to seek and to save" (Luke 19:10).

We must be like the Good Shepherd who left the ninety-nine to find the one to carry back home rejoicing (Luke 15:4-5). One of the most beautiful examples of meeting people where they are was when Jesus went to Samaria to meet a marginalized and traumatized woman at the well. When He asked her for water, she was surprised by His willingness to connect with and acknowledge her as a person. He was willing to understand her situation and pain, meet her on her terms, and offer her acceptance (John 4:4-41).

3. DO NOT CONDEMN: This leads to fear, and there is no love in fear.

God did not send His Son into the world to condemn the world, but that the world through Him might be saved.

JOHN 3:17

Judge not, that you be not judged. For with what
judgment you judge, you will be judged; and with the
measure you use, it will be measured back to you.

MATTHEW 7:1-2

Brothers and sisters, if someone is caught in a sin, you
who live by the Spirit should restore that person gently.
But watch yourselves, or you also may be tempted. Carry
each other's burdens, and in this way you will fulfill
the law of Christ [love].

GALATIANS 6:1-2, NIV

4. MEET PHYSICAL NEEDS FIRST: Providing food and other basics
meets people's needs, brings them together, and opens doors.

Christ seemed to focus on meeting people's physical needs first.
Though Jesus required nothing from people before He healed them,
we often lay out our conditions before we are willing to meet the
physical needs of people who are hurting, hungry, and desperate.

Jesus' brother James pointed out our responsibility to care in
tangible ways for those in need: "Suppose a brother or a sister is
without clothes and daily food. If one of you says to them, 'Go
in peace; keep warm and well fed,' but does nothing about their
physical needs, what good is it?" (James 2:15-16, NIV).

In many Scripture passages, we see Christ's desire to meet the
physical needs of those around Him: "Jesus called his disciples
to him and said, 'I have compassion for these people; they have
already been with me three days and have nothing to eat. I do not
want to send them away hungry, or they may collapse on the way'"
(Matthew 15:32, NIV).

5. LOVE OTHERS LAVISHLY: We should hate harmful behaviors
because we love those trapped in them (Mark 12:31).

St. Augustine encouraged a commune of nuns in AD 424 to
act with "love for the persons and a hatred for their vices."[5] Much

later, in his 1929 autobiography, Mahatma Gandhi wrote that we must "hate the sin and not the sinner."[6]

We can sometimes be so quick to condemn others' actions that we lose sight of them as people. Our fiery anger is like the brightness of the sun hiding the stars. But when we quiet all that heat, the stars creep out and we behold a beauty that was there all along. C. S. Lewis put it like this:

> I remember Christian teachers telling me long ago that I must hate a bad man's actions, but not hate the bad man: or, as they would say, hate the sin but not the sinner.
>
> For a long time I used to think this a silly, strawsplitting distinction: how could you hate what a man did and not hate the man? But years later it occurred to me that there was one man to whom I had been doing this all my life—namely myself. However much I might dislike my own cowardice or conceit or greed, I went on loving myself. There had never been the slightest difficulty about it. In fact the very reason why I hated these things was that I loved the man. Just because I loved myself, I was sorry to find that I was the sort of man who did those things.[7]

When Christ says to "love your neighbor as yourself" (Matthew 22:39), He implies that we are to hate the behaviors that cause harm in others' lives in the same way we hate those behaviors in our own lives.

As long as we require sick, hungry, hurting people to magically change before we offer assistance, we are failing to demonstrate the type of love God has called us to show—the sort of unconditional love we offer to ourselves.

6. DON'T BE SELF-RIGHTEOUS: Our own attempts at righteousness are like dirty rags (Isaiah 64:6).

God said He doesn't want our demonstrations, sacrifices, or efforts (Psalm 40:6; Isaiah 1:11; Hosea 6:6). He wants our hearts to be right with Him and for us to then share His love with others: "For the LORD sees not as man sees: man looks on the outward appearance, but the LORD looks on the heart" (1 Samuel 16:7, ESV).

There's a Latin phrase that seems to sum up this concept well: *esse quam videri*, which means "To *be*, rather than to *seem*."[8]

Jesus put it this way: "Woe to you, teachers of the law and Pharisees, you hypocrites! You are like whitewashed tombs, which look beautiful on the outside but on the inside are full of the bones of the dead and everything unclean. In the same way, on the outside you appear to people as righteous but on the inside you are full of hypocrisy and wickedness" (Matthew 23:27-28, NIV).

7. PUT PEOPLE BEFORE MORALITY: We must approach one another as humans first.

Christ boldly and repeatedly raised people above a rigid or legalistic view of moral principles. He demonstrated this in whom He spent time with and through the lessons He taught. When asked who our neighbor is, Christ told the story of how a good Samaritan helped someone whom the "religious" refused to help (Luke 10:29-37).

Jesus healed on the Sabbath, intentionally breaking a strongly held principle to demonstrate that people matter more than rules (Luke 13:10-17). He explicitly said, "The Sabbath was made for man, and not man for the Sabbath" (Mark 2:27). Christ had strong words for those who placed principles above people, saying they "made void the word of God" (Matthew 15:6, ESV).

8. RECOGNIZE ANY POSITIVE CHANGE: Look for progress, not perfection.

Scripture repeatedly calls us to perfection, but it also includes many reminders that we are only human and are doomed to fall short. As the apostle Paul wrote, " Not that I have already attained, or am already perfected; but I press on, that I may lay hold of that for which Christ has also laid hold of me" (Philippians 3:12).

At first glance, Jesus appears to take the completely opposite view when He calls for believers to practice the Jewish concept of *khumra*—"an elaborate system of rules and practices that were meant to keep people as far away from sin as possible."[9] This principle was born out of Deuteronomy 22:8, which says to build a rail around the edge of a flat roof to avoid being guilty of bloodshed if someone falls off the roof. Christ drew from His audience's knowledge of this concept when He delivered the Sermon on the Mount, by giving increasingly challenging examples of ways to avoid falling off the dangerous edge of sin. To avoid murder, Christ said we cannot be angry (Matthew 5:22); to avoid adultery, we cannot lust (Matthew 5:28); to keep our eye from leading us astray, we must pluck it out (Matthew 5:29); to keep our hand from sinning, we must cut if off and cast it away (Matthew 5:30); and to faithfully love our neighbor, we must love our enemy (Matthew 5:44). Finally He says, "You therefore must be perfect, as your heavenly Father is perfect" (Matthew 5:48, ESV).

Christ wants us to realize that piously practicing religious rules will never be enough to prevent us from sinning. He wants us to know that the very reason He came to earth was because we could not save ourselves from sin. As the apostle Paul says, we all "fall short of the glory of God" (Romans 3:23). This simple truth that we inherently accept about ourselves and even demand others to acknowledge is something we somehow reject in the lives of those we dislike or with whom we disagree. Even that shortcoming reveals how human we are and that we will always fail in a world of zero tolerance.

Scripture repeatedly calls us to perfection, promises abundance for obedience, reminds us we are still only humans doomed to fall short, and provides direction for our shortcomings. Moses told the Israelites that "there need be no poor people among you . . . if only you fully obey the LORD your God" (Deuteronomy 15:4-5, NIV). But a few verses later, Moses says, "There will always be poor people in the land. Therefore I command you to be openhanded toward your fellow Israelites who are poor and needy in your land" (verse 11, NIV). Moses is saying that ideally all Israelites would be prosperous, but since they were not perfect, there "will always be poor people in the land."

9. SEEK COMMUNITY CURES: Where community fails, addiction thrives.

Christ told the story of a son who left home after demanding his inheritance and then blew everything on "wild living" (Luke 15:13, NIV). But then he remembered his father's love. Some use this story to insist that people have to "hit rock bottom" before they will change. These critics overlook how vitally important it was that the son knew his father was there and provided a safe place for him to go. Does the following passage read like a father practicing "tough love"? "But while [the son] was still a long way off, his father saw him and felt compassion, and ran and embraced him and kissed him" (Luke 15:20, ESV).

Despite the father's mercy, it's important to note that the son's inheritance was still gone. The father did not further enable his son's irresponsible actions by removing the consequences of choosing to blow his half of the inheritance. We know this because he reassured his other son, "All that is mine is yours" (Luke 15:31, ESV). But the father never withheld his love from his hurting son.

Likewise, Scripture repeatedly says that we are to love one another. In fact, there are at least fifty-nine "one another" verses, including "love one another" (John 13:34; 1 John 4:7); "be kind to one another . . . forgiving one another" (Ephesians 4:32); and "encourage one another and build one another up" (1 Thessalonians 5:11, ESV).

10. SURRENDER TO THE GREATER: Be a part of the story; do not insist that you *be* the story.

A drowning person who is fighting and thrashing about is dangerous to everyone around him. But by surrendering to a rescuer, the person can be saved. We are not that different. Others are nearby to step in and help. But first we must learn to surrender control of our lives and our futures.

Galatians 2:20 (NIV) says, "I have been crucified with Christ and I no longer live, but Christ lives in me."

The first three steps in the traditional twelve steps of recovery from substance use disorder are designed to take participants through the process of surrendering:

1. We admitted we were powerless over alcohol—that our lives had become unmanageable.
2. Came to believe that a Power greater than ourselves could restore us to sanity.
3. Made a decision to turn our will and our lives over to the care of God as we understood Him.[10]

We do not become less of who we are by surrendering; we become who we were created to be. All our independent efforts, struggling, and striving prevent us from becoming all we are supposed to be. "Whoever wants to save their life will lose it, but whoever loses their life for me will save it" (Luke 9:24, NIV).

The Social Determinants
of Health

CARING FOR PEOPLE INVOLVES much more than addressing specific diseases. When we health-care providers address only an individual disease or the risk factors of a patient, we are not caring for the whole person. We also end up providing care in silos with poor collaboration.

Austin's opioid and HIV epidemics, along with the COVID-19 pandemic, put a spotlight on the rarely acknowledged but critically important psychosocial and socioeconomic factors that contribute to disease, substance use disorder, disability, and early death.

So, what puts people in communities like Austin at risk for disease, disability, and early death in the first place? The World Health Organization, CDC, and other organizations agree with over three decades of scientific evidence showing that health outcomes are directly impacted by social determinants. I've organized these factors into five basic categories:

1. **Health services:** Includes quality, availability, and affordability of health care.

2. **Personal behavior and stability:** Includes early childhood experiences, education, and type of work.

3. **Social environment:** Includes class, inequity, opportunity, and sense of community.

4. **Physical environment and security:** Includes access to food, transportation, and shelter; chronic toxic stress.

5. **Genes and biology:** Includes family history, sex, and age.[1]

About 80 percent of our overall health is thought to be determined by the first four categories of social determinants.[2] However, evolving research is revealing that our bodies remember and that our health is also affected by what happened to our ancestors and to us during our early development. This discovery has turned the world of genetics upside down. The age-old question of nature versus nurture has suddenly become much more complicated. Our environment (nurture) cannot physically change our genes, but it can change how those genes are expressed (nature). One example from nature can be seen in the development of a queen bee. Although genetically identical to the other bees, a new queen develops because she receives different nutrition than the other developing larvae.[3]

Likewise, the most important choices about who we become, our health, and our access to opportunity are not ones we get to make. They are decided for us by the health of the people around us and the places where we are born, grow, play, and live.[4]

Adverse Childhood Experiences and Toxic Stress

IN 1985, A DOCTOR FRUSTRATED by the dropout rate at an obesity clinic stumbled upon a discovery. Dr. Vincent Felitti, chief of preventive medicine at San Diego–based Kaiser Permanente, shared his experience in the Adverse Childhood Experiences Study, which the Centers for Disease Control and Prevention released in 2012.[1] His discovery came when he accidentally asked the wrong question while interviewing a patient.

"Instead of asking, 'How old were you when you were first sexually active?' I asked, 'How much did you weigh when you were first sexually active?'" Dr. Felitti recalls.

The female responded, "Forty pounds."

Flustered, the doctor repeated his question. He said the patient burst into tears and said, "It was when I was four years old, with my father."

Only then did Dr. Felitti realize what he'd asked—and the implications of the woman's answer. He started asking other patients about their childhood experiences and over the next few weeks was shocked to find that many of his obese patients had experienced childhood sexual abuse.

Dr. Felitti says his first thought was, *This can't be true. People would know if that were true. Someone would have told me in medical school.*

Dr. Felitti's initial findings captured the attention of an epidemiologist at the CDC. With that organization's support, Dr. Felitti and his colleagues began a large study that included more than seventeen thousand participants, evenly divided between males and females. All were from the middle class without barriers to health care. The prevalence of trauma during childhood was so shocking that one of the CDC researchers wept over the findings.[2]

As a result of the study, ten adverse childhood experiences were identified as having profound and lasting effects on a person's social and health outcomes. These experiences prevent children from having the sense of security and belonging that is critical to every person's well-being. These factors fall into three categories that can be remembered using ACE: Abuse, Challenges, and nEglect.

Abuse	Household Challenges	nEglect
Physical	Exposure to domestic violence	Physical
Sexual	Household substance abuse	Emotional
Emotional	Household mental illness	
	Parental separation or divorce	
	Incarcerated family member	

An individual's ACE score is determined by counting the number of these traumatic events that person had in childhood. People with an ACE score of 4 or more have usually grown up with chronic toxic stress and almost always have developed major risk factors for chronic disease and early death. Harvard University's Center on the Developing Child explains the devastating effects of ACEs: A "toxic stress response can occur when a child experiences strong, frequent, and/or prolonged adversity . . . without adequate adult support. This kind of prolonged activation of the stress response systems can disrupt the development of brain architecture and other organ systems, and increase the risk for stress-related disease and cognitive impairment well into the adult years."[3]

Repeated studies in virtually every state confirm that, as the number of ACEs increases, so does the risk of experiencing adverse health or social outcomes. These include substance use, poor job performance, obesity, mental illness, domestic violence, overdose, teen sexual behavior, suicide, being raped, liver disease, lung disease, heart disease, HIV, and more. The end result is startling: "People with six or more ACEs died nearly twenty years earlier on average than those without ACEs."[4]

Research into ACEs dovetails with the work psychologist Abraham Maslow did in the 1940s, when he first laid out his hierarchy of needs, which begins with basics like food, shelter, and sleep and eventually leads to self-actualization (reaching one's potential) and self-transcendence (yielding oneself to something greater).

Maslow believed that if people were not striving for the higher needs, it was because their lower needs were going unmet. Rather than moving up toward actualization and transcendence, these people were descending toward disease, disability, and early death.

What if we consider the possibility that substance use disorder is a way for people who have experienced toxic stress, unmet needs, and inequality to cope with real physiologic changes?

What if their drug use is a way to artificially stimulate their brains to provide their needed feelings of love, belonging, and relief from their constant fears and insecurities?

In that case, we'd have to admit that isolation harms while connection heals. Addiction cannot be cured in seclusion; it requires community, purpose, and meaning.

If we see someone struggling and invest in them, we provide them with the security and safety they need to overcome fear and choose growth. However, we must also give them the freedom to make mistakes and the assurance that it is okay not to be okay.

THE TWO TRAJECTORIES OF LIFE

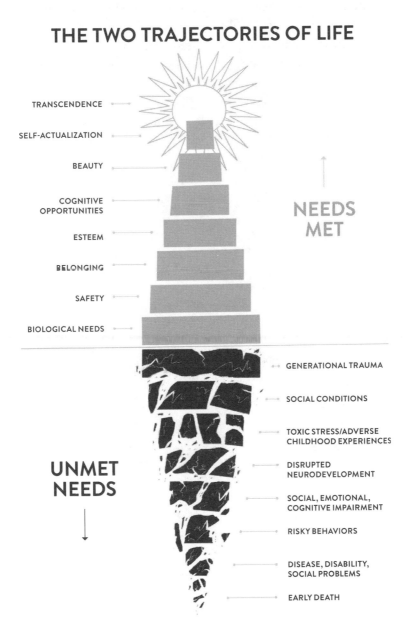

TRANSCENDENCE

SELF-ACTUALIZATION

BEAUTY

COGNITIVE OPPORTUNITIES

ESTEEM

BELONGING

SAFETY

BIOLOGICAL NEEDS

NEEDS MET

GENERATIONAL TRAUMA

SOCIAL CONDITIONS

TOXIC STRESS/ADVERSE CHILDHOOD EXPERIENCES

DISRUPTED NEURODEVELOPMENT

SOCIAL, EMOTIONAL, COGNITIVE IMPAIRMENT

RISKY BEHAVIORS

DISEASE, DISABILITY, SOCIAL PROBLEMS

EARLY DEATH

UNMET NEEDS

Rather than fearing mistakes, Maslow suggested that people need "to plunge in, to do the best that one can, hoping to learn enough from blunders to correct them eventually."[5]

If we convince ourselves that marginalized people are intrinsically broken because they are lazy, immoral, corrupt, or ignorant, we absolve ourselves of any responsibility to them.

But if we see them as ill people within a sick system instead of bad people making bad choices, we realize that we must act.

Additional Resources

ADVERSE CHILDHOOD EXPERIENCES
Centers for Disease Control and Prevention (CDC)
https://www.cdc.gov/violenceprevention/acestudy/index.html

Harvard University's Center on the Developing Child
https://developingchild.harvard.edu

Substance Abuse and Mental Health Services Administration (SAMHSA)
https://www.samhsa.gov/child-trauma

Robert Wood Johnson Foundation
https://www.rwjf.org/en/library/collections/aces.html

HIV
Understanding the basics of HIV
https://www.cdc.gov/hiv/basics/whatishiv.html

HIV and AIDS timeline
https://npin.cdc.gov/pages/hiv-and-aids-timeline#1980

Ending the HIV epidemic
https://www.hiv.gov/federal-response/ending-the-hiv-epidemic/overview

Treatment and prevention guidelines
https://clinicalinfo.hiv.gov/en/guidelines

PRESCRIPTION DRUG DISPOSAL
Guidelines
Federal Drug Administration
"Where and How to Dispose of Unused Medicines"
https://www.fda.gov/ForConsumers/ConsumerUpdates/ucm101653.htm

"Disposal of Unused Medicines: What You Should Know"
https://www.fda.gov/Drugs/ResourcesForYou/Consumers/BuyingUsing
MedicineSafely/EnsuringSafeUseofMedicine/SafeDisposalofMedicines
/ucm186187.htm

Search for local drug disposal locations
Drug Enforcement Administration's Diversion Control Division, (800) 882-9539
https://apps.deadiversion.usdoj.gov/pubdispsearch/spring/main
?execution=e1s1

SUBSTANCE USE DISORDER
Understanding the epidemic by CDC
http://www.cdc.gov/drugoverdose/epidemic/index.html

HHS strategy for fighting opioid crisis
https://www.hhs.gov/about/leadership/secretary/speeches/2017-speeches
/secretary-price-announces-hhs-strategy-for-fighting-opioid-crisis
/index.html

Behavioral health treatment services locator
https://findtreatment.samhsa.gov

"CDC Guideline for Prescribing Opioids for Chronic Pain"
https://www.cdc.gov/drugoverdose/prescribing/guideline.html

Components of comprehensive drug treatment
https://d14rmgtrwzf5a.cloudfront.net/sites/default/files/images/colorbox
/treatmentcomponents.jpg

"Finding Quality Treatment for Substance Use Disorders"
https://store.samhsa.gov/system/files/pep18-treatment-loc.pdf

Recovery community organization toolkit
https://facesandvoicesofrecovery.org/blog/publication/recovery-community
-organization-toolkit/

SAMHSA opioid overdose prevention toolkit
https://store.samhsa.gov/system/files/sma18-4742.pdf

SAMHSA Recovery-Oriented Systems of Care (ROSC) resource guide
https://www.samhsa.gov/sites/default/files/rosc_resource_guide_book.pdf

Notes

INTRODUCTION: FORGED BY FIRE

1. Stacy L. Rosenberg et al., "Stress and Asthma: Novel Insights on Genetic, Epigenetic, and Immunologic Mechanisms," *Journal of Allergy and Clinical Immunology* 134, no. 5 (November 2014): 1009–15, https://doi .org/10.1016/j.jaci.2014.07.005; Sara Karlovitch, "Socioeconomic Status Tied to Risk of Chronic Disease, Including Cardiac, Diabetes," *American Journal of Managed Care*, December 21, 2019, https://www.ajmc.com /view/socioeconomic-status-tied-to-risk-of-chronic-disease-including -cardiac-diabetes.

2. Aaron van Dorn, Rebecca E. Cooney, and Miriam L. Sabin, "COVID-19 Exacerbating Inequalities in the US," *Lancet* 395, no. 10232 (April 18, 2020), 1243–44, https://doi.org/10.1016/S0140-6736(20)30893-X.

3. The term *canary in the coal mine* developed from the now outdated practice of using the bird to detect and give advance warning of carbon monoxide and other toxic gases to workers entering coal mines. If the canary keeled over, the miners knew there were dangerous gases and would quickly leave the mine. Dean Reynolds, "Drug Abuse, Dirty Needles Fueling HIV Crisis in Indiana," CBS News, April 7, 2015, https://www.cbsnews.com/news /drug-abuse-dirty-needles-fueling-hiv-crisis-in-indiana/.

4. Brianna Ehley, "From Opioids to HIV—A Public Health Threat in Trump Country," *Politico*, October 21, 2017, https://www.politico.com /story/2017/10/21/opioids-hiv-public-health-threat-red-states-trump -243999.

5. "Vulnerable Counties and Jurisdictions Experiencing or At-Risk of Outbreaks," Centers for Disease Control and Prevention, accessed September 11, 2020, https://www.cdc.gov/pwid/vulnerable-counties -data.html. In 2019, the US Department of Health and Human Services

bolstered these findings by showing the trend to be nationwide, reaching far beyond these counties.

6. Sanjay Kishore, Margaret Hayden, and Josiah Rich, "Lessons from Scott County—Progress or Paralysis on Harm Reduction?," *New England Journal of Medicine* 380, no. 21 (May 23, 2019): 1988–90, https://doi.org/10.1056/NEJMp1901276.

7. Ehley, "From Opioids to HIV."

8. "Recent HIV Clusters and Outbreaks across the United States among People Who Inject Drugs and Considerations during the COVID-19 Pandemic," CDC Health Alert Network, Centers for Disease Control and Prevention, October 5, 2020, https://content.govdelivery.com/attachments/INSDH/2020/10/06/file_attachments/1564398/CDC%20HAN%20436%20HIV%20Clusters%20in%20US_October%205%202020.pdf; Lindsey Sizemore et al., "Using an Established Outbreak Response Plan and Molecular Epidemiology Methods in an HIV Transmission Cluster Investigation, Tennessee, January–June 2017," *Public Health Reports* 135, no. 3 (May 2020): 329–33, https://doi.org/10.1177/0033354920915445.

9. Kenneth D. Kochanek et al., "Deaths: Final Data for 2017," *National Vital Statistics Reports* 68, no. 9 (June 24, 2019): 6, 34–36.

10. Lenny Bernstein, "US Life Expectancy Declines Again, a Dismal Trend Not Seen Since World War I," *Washington Post*, November 28, 2018, https://www.washingtonpost.com/national/health-science/us-life-expectancy-declines-again-a-dismal-trend-not-seen-since-world-war-i/2018/11/28/ae58bc8c-f28c-11e8-bc79-68604ed88993_story.html.

11. Jen Christensen, "US Life Expectancy Is Still on the Decline. Here's Why," CNN, November 26, 2019, https://www.cnn.com/2019/11/26/health/us-life-expectancy-decline-study/index.html.

CHAPTER 1: WELCOME TO LITTLE HAZARD

1. Harvey Goodin was Austin's mayor when the music video was shot in 1983 and can be seen toward the end of the video (at 4:36), dancing shirtless while wearing a straw hat. See "John Mellencamp—Pink Houses," October 5, 2009, https://www.youtube.com/watch?v=qOfkpu6749w.

2. J. R. R. Tolkien, *The Two Towers* (New York: Houghton Mifflin, 1954), book IV, chapter 8.

3. *Biographical and Historical Souvenir for the Counties of Clark, Crawford, Harrison, Floyd, Jefferson, Jennings, Scott and Washington, Indiana* (Chicago: John M. Gresham, 1889), 241.

4. "Camp Austin," City of Austin website, https://cityofaustin.in.gov/history/wwii-pow-camp/.

5. "About Morgan Foods," Morgan Foods website, https://www.morganfoods.com/03_history.php.

CHAPTER 2: BLOOD AND TEARS

1. Michael S. Gottlieb et al., "*Pneumocystis* Pneumonia—Los Angeles," Centers of Disease Control and Prevention, *MMWR Weekly* 134, no. 5 (June 5, 1981): 1–3.
2. The newly discovered disease was initially called the 4H disease for the four risk factors: homosexual, Haitian, heroin, and hemophilia.
3. Susan Resnik, *Blood Saga: Hemophilia, AIDS, and the Survival of a Community* (Berkeley, CA: University of California Press, 1999).
4. Elton John, *Love Is the Cure* (New York: Little, Brown, and Co., 2012).
5. On June 19, 1983, Jerry Falwell said, "AIDS is not just God's punishment for homosexuals, it is God's punishment for the society that tolerates homosexuals." See Hans Johnson and William Eskridge, "The Legacy of Falwell's Bully Pulpit," *Washington Post*, May 19, 2007, https://www.washingtonpost.com/wp-dyn/content/article/2007/05/18/AR2007051801392.html.
6. L. L. Ainsworth and Claude D. Baker, "Effects of Illumination Changes on Infant Monkey Contacts with Surrogates," *Psychological Record* 32 (1982): 513–18.
7. I didn't realize it then, but the department was drawing on Maslow's hierarchy of needs, which posits that people's basic needs for security and love, along with food, water, and shelter, must be met before they will be motivated to develop further.
8. John 10:10.
9. Thomas A. Arcury et al., "Access to Transportation and Health Care Utilization in a Rural Region," *Journal of Rural Health* 21, no. 1 (January 2005): 31–38, https://doi.org/10.1111/j.1748-0361.2005.tb00059.x.
10. David Vine, "Tracing Paul Farmer's Influence," website of American University, Washington, DC, May 23, 2013, https://www.american.edu/cas/news/paul-farmer-influence-in-anthropology.cfm.
11. "A Place for Children Helps Parents, Too," *New York Times*, January 26, 1989, https://www.nytimes.com/1989/01/26/garden/a-place-for-children-helps-parents-too.html.

CHAPTER 4: SHARKS IN THE WATER

1. Malcolm Gladwell, *Outliers: The Story of Success* (New York: Little, Brown, and Co., 2008), 221.
2. Gladwell, *Outliers*, 268.
3. C. S. Lewis said, "I believe in Christianity as I believe that the Sun has risen, not only because I see it, but because by it I see everything else." C. S. Lewis, *The Weight of Glory and Other Addresses* (New York: HarperOne, 2001), 140.
4. See, for example, Indiana State Epidemiology and Outcomes Workshop,

The Consumption and Consequences of Alcohol, Tobacco, and Drugs in Indiana: A State Epidemiological Profile, 2009, Indiana University School of Public and Environmental Affairs, https://fsph.iupui.edu/doc/research -centers/2009%20State%20Epidemiological%20Profile.pdf.

5. Lee Ohanian, "Competition and the Decline of the Rust Belt," Federal Reserve Bank of Minneapolis, December 20, 2014, https:// www.minneapolisfed.org/article/2014/competition-and-the-decline -of-the-rust-belt.

6. The "marketing plan for OxyContin was to target the physicians who were the highest prescribers for opioids across the country." Art Van Zee, "The Promotion and Marketing of OxyContin: Commercial Triumph, Public Health Tragedy," *American Journal of Public Health* 99, no. 2 (February 2009): 221–27, https://doi.org/10.2105/AJPH.2007.131714.

7. Van Zee, "Promotion and Marketing of OxyContin."

8. Ashton Marra, "New Federal Data Confirms What We Already Know: Opioid Distributions Inundated Appalachia," website of 100 Days in Appalachia, July 19, 2019, https://www.100daysinappalachia.com /2019/07/new-federal-data-confirms-what-we-already-know-opioid -distributions-inundated-appalachia/.

9. Jane Porter and Hershel Jick, "Addiction Rare in Patients Treated with Narcotics," *New England Journal of Medicine* 302, no. 2 (January 10, 1980): 123, https://doi.org/10.1056/NEJM198001103020221.

10. US General Accounting Office, "Prescription Drugs: OxyContin Abuse and Diversion and Efforts to Address the Problem," December 19, 2003, https://www.govinfo.gov/content/pkg/GAOREPORTS-GAO-04-110 /html/GAOREPORTS-GAO-04-110.htm.

11. Van Zee, "Promotion and Marketing of OxyContin."

12. Sujata S. Jayawant and Rajesh Balkrishnan, "The Controversy Surrounding OxyContin Abuse: Issues and Solutions," *Therapeutics and Clinical Risk Management* 1, no. 2 (July 2005): 77–82, https://doi.org/10.2147/tcrm .1.2.77.62911.

13. USGAO, "Prescription Drugs: OxyContin Abuse."

14. "Oregon Board Disciplines Doctor for Not Treating Patients' Pain," *New York Times*, September 4, 1999, https://www.nytimes.com /1999/09/04/us/oregon-board-disciplines-doctor-for-not-treating -patients-pain.html.

15. Ben A. Rich, "Physicians' Legal Duty to Relieve Suffering," *Western Journal of Medicine* 175, no. 3 (September 2001): 151–52.

16. Sandra H. Johnson, "Relieving Unnecessary, Treatable Pain for the Sake of Human Dignity," *Journal of Law, Medicine & Ethics* 28, no. 4 suppl (March 2001): 11–12, https://doi.org/10.1111/j.1748-720X.2001 .tb00036.x.

17. National Pharmaceutical Council and Joint Commission on Accreditation of Healthcare Organizations, *Pain: Current Understanding of Assessment, Management, and Treatments*, December 2001, 17, https://www.npcnow .org/system/files/research/download/Pain-Current-Understanding-of -Assessment-Management-and-Treatments.pdf.
18. Laxmaiah Manchikanti, "National Drug Control Policy and Prescription Drug Abuse: Facts and Fallacies," *Pain Physician Journal* 10, no. 3 (May 2007): 399–424.
19. Sean Esteban McCabe et al., "Medical and Nonmedical Use of Prescription Opioids among High School Seniors in the United States," *Archives of Pediatrics and Adolescent Medicine* 166, no. 9 (September 2012): 797–802, http://doi.org/10.1001/archpediatrics.2012.85.

CHAPTER 5: FORSAKEN

1. C. S. Lewis, *The Problem of Pain* (New York: HarperOne, 2001), 161.
2. Fred Rogers, *You Are Special: Neighborly Words of Wisdom from Mister Rogers* (New York: Penguin, 1995), 120.

CHAPTER 6: SURRENDER IN THE AMAZON

1. Traci Pedersen, "Amazon: Earth's Mightiest River," Live Science, December 20, 2016, https://www.livescience.com/57266-amazon -river.html.
2. New International Version.
3. Deepak Chopra, foreword to *Nonviolent Communication*, by Marshall B. Rosenberg (Encinitas, CA: PuddleDancer Press, 2015), xiv.

CHAPTER 7: LESSONS NOT LEARNED

1. John Fauber and Kristina Fiore, "A Look Back: Abandoned Painkiller Makes a Comeback," MedPage Today, June 9, 2017, https://www .medpagetoday.com/psychiatry/addictions/65916.
2. "Endo Pharmaceuticals Announces Reformulated Version of Opana ER with INTAC Technology Designed to be Crush-Resistant Accounts for More than 90 Percent of OPANA ER Total Prescription Volume," press release, Endo Pharmaceuticals, September 6, 2012, https://investor .endo.com/news-releases/news-release-details/endo-pharmaceuticals -announces-reformulated-version-opanar-er.
3. Indiana Code 35-48-4-8.5.
4. Mary Wisniewski, "Painkiller Opana, New Scourge of Rural America," Reuters, March 26, 2012, https://www.reuters.com/article/us-drugs -abuse-opana-idUSBRE82Q04120120327.
5. Wisniewski, "Painkiller Opana."

CHAPTER 8: SCARLET LETTERS

1. Laura Ungar, "HIV Outbreak Tied to Painkiller, Dirty Needles," *Courier Journal*, February 25, 2015, https://www.courier-journal.com/story /news/local/indiana/2015/02/25/hiv-outbreak-tied-painkiller-dirty -needles/24000869/.

2. Ellsworth M. Campbell et al., "Detailed Transmission Network Analysis of a Large Opiate-Driven Outbreak of HIV Infection in the United States," *Journal of Infectious Diseases* 216, no. 9 (November 1, 2017):1053–62, https://doi.org/10.1093/infdis/jix307.

3. Philip J. Peters et al., "HIV Infection Linked to Injection Use of Oxymorphone in Indiana, 2014–2015," *New England Journal of Medicine* 375, no. 3 (July 21, 2016): 229–39, https://doi.org/10.1056 /NEJMoa1515195.

4. Bob Segall, "Inside Indiana's HIV Epidemic," WTHR, March 24, 2016, https://www.wthr.com/article/inside-indianas-hiv-epidemic.

5. Segall, "Inside Indiana's HIV Epidemic."

6. Ungar, "HIV Outbreak Tied to Painkiller, Dirty Needles."

7. John R. Nichols, Cecil P. Headlee, and Harold W. Coppóck, "Drug Addiction I. Addiction by Escape Training," *Journal of the American Pharmaceutical Association (Scientific ed.)* 45, no. 12 (December 1956): 788–91, https://doi.org/10.1002/jps.3030451206.

8. B. P. Smyth et al., "Lapse and Relapse Following Inpatient Treatment of Opiate Dependence," *Irish Medical Journal* 103, no. 6 (June 2010): 176–79, https://pubmed.ncbi.nlm.nih.gov/20669601/; Johan Kakko et al., "1-Year Retention and Social Function after Buprenorphine-Assisted Relapse Prevention Treatment for Heroin Dependence in Sweden: A Randomised, Placebo-Controlled Trial," *Lancet* 361, no. 9358 (February 22, 2003): 662–68, https://doi.org/10.1016/S0140-6736 (03)12600-1.

9. "Opioid Painkiller Prescribing," Centers for Disease Control and Prevention, July 2014, https://www.cdc.gov/vitalsigns/opioid-prescribing/index .html; M. Azadfard, M. R. Huecker, J. M. Leaming, *Opioid Addiction* (Treasure Island, FL: StatPearls Publishing, 2020), https://www.ncbi.nlm .nih.gov/books/NBK448203/; Kevin E. Vowles et al., "Rates of Opioid Misuse, Abuse, and Addiction in Chronic Pain: A Systematic Review and Data Synthesis," *Pain* 156, no. 4 (April 2015): 569–76, https://doi.org /10.1097/01.j.pain.0000460357.01998.f1.

10. Bruce K. Alexander, "The Myth of Drug-Induced Addiction," presented to the Canadian Senate, January 2001, https://sencanada.ca/content /sen/committee/371/ille/presentation/alexender-e.htm.

11. Congressmen Robert Steele from Connecticut and Morgan Murphy of Illinois visited in May 1971. See Alix Spiegel, "What Vietnam Taught Us about Breaking Bad Habits," NPR, January 2, 2012,

https://www.npr.org/sections/health-shots/2012/01/02/144431794
/what-vietnam-taught-us-about-breaking-bad-habits.

12. Lee N. Robins et al., "Vietnam Veterans Three Years after Vietnam: How
Our Study Changed Our View of Heroin," *American Journal on Addictions*
19, no. 3 (May–June 2010): 203-11, https://onlinelibrary.wiley.com/doi
/abs/10.1111/j.1521-0391.2010.00046.x.

13. Stanton Peele and Zach Rhoads, "Vietnam Vets Proved That Addiction
Is a Product of Life Circumstances," Filter, June 5, 2019, https://
filtermag.org/vietnam-vets-proved-that-addiction-is-a-product-of-life
-circumstances/#:~:text=In%20fact%2C%20over%2090%20percent
,at%20Washington%20University%20in%20St.

14. Hans Villarica, "The Chocolate-and-Radish Experiment That Birthed
the Modern Conception of Willpower," *Atlantic*, April 9, 2012, https://
www.theatlantic.com/health/archive/2012/04/the-chocolate-and-radish
-experiment-that-birthed-the-modern-conception-of-willpower/255544/.

CHAPTER 9: LOVE VERSUS FEAR

1. Rural Center for AIDS/STD Prevention, "Syringe Exchange: Indicators
of Need and Success," Indiana University School of Public Health, April
20, 2015, https://rcap.indiana.edu/doc/Policy%20Brief_Need%20for
%20SEP_Updated%20April%2020%202015.pdf. See table on page 5;
author excluded Hendricks and Parke because these counties' figures are
dramatically skewed by prison data.

2. "State Health Compare," SHADAC, http://statehealthcompare.shadac
.org/rank/117/per-person-state-public-health-funding#2,3,4,5,6,7,8,9,10
,11,12,13,14,15,16,17,18,19,20,21,22,23,24,25,26,27,28,29,30,31,32
,33,34,35,36,37,38,39,40,41,42,43,44,45,46,47,48,49,50,51,52/a/27
/154/false/location.

3. Indiana State Department of Health, *State of Indiana: Statewide
Comprehensive Plan*, April 2013, 42, http://www.in.gov/isdh/files
/Indiana_Comprehensive_Plan_with_SCSN_for_FY_2012-2015
_(April_2013_rev).pdf.

4. Indiana State Department of Health, *State of Indiana: Statewide
Comprehensive Plan*, 29, 43.

5. Indiana State Department of Health, *State of Indiana: Statewide
Comprehensive Plan*, 29.

6. Pence's positions were brought to light in the national media in 2016;
Megan Twohey, "Mike Pence's Response to HIV Outbreak: Prayer,
Then a Change of Heart," *New York Times*, August 7, 2016.

7. National Institute of Allergy and Infectious Diseases, "Science Validates
Undetectable = Untransmittable HIV Prevention Message," *NIAID Now*,
July 22, 2018, https://www.niaid.nih.gov/news-events/undetectable
-equals-untransmittable.

8. K. E. Nelson et al., "Human Immunodeficiency Virus Infection in Diabetic Intravenous Drug Users," *Journal of American Medical Association* 266, no. 16 (1991): 2259–61, https://pubmed.ncbi.nlm.nih.gov/1920726/.

9. National Commission on Acquired Immune Deficiency Syndrome, "The Twin Epidemics of Substance Use and HIV," July 1991, https://abuse-drug.com/lib/The-Twin-Epidemics-of-Substance-Use-and-HIV/executive-summary.html.

10. Heidi Bramson et al., "State Laws, Syringe Exchange, and HIV among Persons Who Inject Drugs in the United States: History and Effectiveness," *Journal of Public Health Policy* 36, no. 2 (May 2015): 212–30, https://pubmed.ncbi.nlm.nih.gov/25590514/.

11. Trang Quynh Nguyen et al., "Increasing Investment in Syringe Exchange Is Cost-Saving HIV Prevention: Modeling Hypothetical Syringe Coverage Levels in the United States," August 2012, XIX International AIDS Conference, Washington DC. See "Syringe Services Programs: Myth vs. Fact," amfAR, October 31, 2013, PowerPoint slide 12, https://www.amfar.org/syringe-services-programs-myth-vs-fact/.

12. AIDS Foundation of Chicago, "AFC Statement on Federal Funding Ban for Syringe Exchanges," https://www.aidschicago.org/page/news/all-news/afc-statement-on-federal-funding-ban-for-syringe-exchanges. See "Syringe Services Programs: Myth vs. Fact," amfAR, October 31, 2013, PowerPoint slide 12, https://www.amfar.org/syringe-services-programs-myth-vs-fact/.

13. AIDS Action Committee, "President Obama's Fiscal 2013 Budget Demonstrates Commitment to Ending HIV/AIDS Epidemic in America." See "Syringe Services Programs: Myth vs. Fact," amfAR, October 31, 2013, PowerPoint slide 14, https://www.amfar.org/syringe-services-programs-myth-vs-fact/.

14. B. Silverman et al., "First Federal Support for Community-Based Syringe Exchange Programs: A Panel Presentation by SAMHSA Grantees," Poster WEPE234, presented at the International AIDS Conference Poster Session, Washington, DC, July 25, 2012. See "Syringe Services Programs: Myth vs. Fact," amfAR, October 31, 2013, PowerPoint slide 7, https://www.amfar.org/syringe-services-programs-myth-vs-fact/.

CHAPTER 10: THE LAW OF LOVE

1. Laura Ungar, "Healing Austin: Town Races to Stop America's Worst Rural HIV Plague," *Louisville Courier Journal*, April 20, 2017, https://www.courier-journal.com/story/news/local/indiana/2017/04/20/healing-austin-part-two-troubled-city-tested/97735344/.

2. English Standard Version.

3. *The Power of Children*, Children's Museum of Indianapolis, https://thehistory.childrensmuseum.org/exhibits/power-children.

4. 2 Corinthians 6:17.
5. John Nicholas Lenker, ed., *The Precious and Sacred Writings of Martin Luther* (Minneapolis: Lutherans in All Lands, 1904), 161.
6. Luke 13:10-17.
7. Matthew 22:37-39, NIV.
8. Andi TenBarge, "Pence Orders Limited Needle Exchange to Stem Scott County HIV Outbreak," TheStatehouseFile.com, March 26, 2015, http://thestatehousefile.com/pence-orders-limited-needle-exchange -to-stem-scott-county-hiv-outbreak/20803/.
9. Ungar, "Healing Austin."
10. Jared Kaltwasser, "Early Intervention Could Have Prevented Indiana's HIV Outbreak," *HCP Live*, September 27, 2018, https://www.mdmag .com/medical-news/intervention-could-have-prevented-indianas-hiv -outbreak.

CHAPTER 11: VOICES

1. Will Cooke, Facebook, March 26, 2015, https://www.facebook.com /dad.cooke/posts/10203981044507593.
2. "HIV Outbreak in Indiana Raises National Awareness," Al Jazeera America, March 26, 2015, http://america.aljazeera.com/watch/shows/live -news/2015/3/hiv-epidemic-in-indiana-raises-national-awareness.html.

CHAPTER 12: ANY POSITIVE CHANGE

1. Paul D. Loprinzi et al., "Healthy Lifestyle Characteristics and Their Joint Association with Cardiovascular Disease Biomarkers in US Adults," Mayo Clinic Proceedings 91, no 4 (April 1, 2016): 432–42, https:// doi.org/10.1016/j.mayocp.2016.01.009.
2. Mark Mather and Paola Scommegna, "Up to Half of US Premature Deaths Are Preventable; Behavioral Factors Key," Population Reference Bureau (PRB) website, September 14, 2015, https://www.prb.org/us -premature-deaths/.
3. In fact, Dr. Jerome Adams, Indiana's health commissioner during the Austin outbreak and later US surgeon general, endorsed the use of Narcan in April 2018. See "Surgeon General Releases Advisory on Naloxone, an Opioid Overdose-Reversing Drug," Health and Human Services press release, April 5, 2018, https://www.hhs.gov/about/news /2018/04/05/surgeon-general-releases-advisory-on-naloxone-an-opioid -overdose-reversing-drug.html.
4. Tom Dreisbach, "How a Painkiller Designed to Deter Abuse Helped Spark an HIV Outbreak," NPR, April 1, 2016, https://www.npr.org /sections/health-shots/2016/04/01/472538272/how-a-painkiller -designed-to-deter-abuse-helped-spark-an-hiv-outbreak.
5. Lisa Girion, "FDA Allows Sales of Generic Opana Painkiller to Continue,"

Los Angeles Times, May 10, 2013, https://www.latimes.com/health/la-xpm -2013-may-10-la-me-0511-opana-20130511-story.html.

6. Dreisbach, "How a Painkiller Designed to Deter Abuse."

7. Author's adaptation from C. S. Lewis, *The Weight of Glory* (New York: HarperOne, 2001), 45–46. See also Justin Taylor, "There Are No Ordinary People; You Have Never Talked to a Mere Mortal," The Gospel Coalition, October 17, 2011, https://www.thegospelcoalition.org/blogs/justin -taylor/there-are-no-ordinary-people-you-have-never-talked-to-a-mere -mortal/.

CHAPTER 13: THE OTHER SIDE OF HELL

1. Sharoda Dasgupta et al., "Reported Drug Injection Behaviors Before and After an HIV Outbreak—Indiana, 2016" (poster presented at the HIV and Drug Use Session of the Conference on Retroviruses and Opportunistic Infections held in Boston, MA, on March 7, 2018), https://2jg4quetidw2blbbq2ixwziw-wpengine.netdna-ssl.com/wp -content/uploads/sites/2/posters/2018/1430_Dasgupta_967.pdf.

CHAPTER 14: A BROKEN BALLERINA

1. G. R. Clark, *Col. George Rogers Clark's Sketch of His Campaign in the Illinois in 1778–9* (Cincinnati: Robert Clarke & Co., 1869).

2. Samuel Harrod, "A Little Sketch of Pioneer Life in Scott County, Indiana," *Scottsburg Chronicle*, December 13, 1883. See https:// archive.org/stream/pioneerlifeinsco00boga/pioneerlifeinsco00boga _djvu.txt.

3. Harrod, "A Little Sketch."

4. Hilary Smith Connery, "Medication-Assisted Treatment of Opioid Use Disorder: Review of the Evidence And Future Directions," *Harvard Review of Psychiatry* 23, no. 2 (March–April 2015): 63–75, https://pubmed.ncbi.nlm.nih.gov/25747920/; Nora D. Volkow et al., "Medication-Assisted Therapies—Tackling the Opioid-Overdose Epidemic," *New England Journal of Medicine* 370 (May 29, 2014): 2063–66, https://doi.org/10.1056/NEJMp1402780.

5. Johan Kakko et al., "1-Year Retention and Social Function after Buprenorphine-Assisted Relapse Prevention Treatment for Heroin Dependence in Sweden: A Randomised, Placebo-Controlled Trial," *Lancet* 361, no. 9358 (February 22, 2003): 662–68, https://doi.org /10.1016/S0140-6736(03)12600-1.

6. Michael L. Dennis, Mark A. Foss, and Christy K. Scott, "An Eight-Year Perspective on the Relationship between the Duration of Abstinence and Other Aspects of Recovery," *Evaluation Review* 31, no. 6 (December 2007): 585–612, https://journals.sagepub.com/doi /10.1177/0193841X07307771.

CHAPTER 15: UNDONE

1. Elizabeth Beilman, "HIV Clinic, Pharmacy to Open in Austin," *News and Tribune*, May 7, 2015, https://www.newsandtribune.com/news /local_news/hiv-clinic-pharmacy-to-open-in-austin/article_08e12156 -f51d-11e4-8d2e-5f772962ed30.html.
2. Diane Janowicz, "Doctor Treating HIV Epidemic in Indiana: Much Remains to Be Done," *Time*, May 13, 2015, http://time.com/3853590 /indiana-hiv-epidemic/.
3. Indiana State Department of Health, "Syringe Exchange Program Guidance for Local Health Departments, Version 2.0," updated October 4, 2016, https://www.in.gov/isdh/files/ISDH%20SEP%20Guidance %20Version%202%200%20FINAL%20-%2010-04-2016-EC.pdf.
4. Romans 8:28, ESV.

CHAPTER 16: THE TRAGEDY OF BIAS

1. "Preventing Adverse Childhood Experiences," Centers for Disease Control and Prevention, reviewed April 3, 2020, https://www.cdc.gov /violenceprevention/aces/fastfact.html.
2. Vincent J. Felitti and Robert F. Anda, "The Relationship of Adverse Childhood Experiences to Adult Health, Well-Being, Social Function, and Healthcare," chapter 8 in *The Impact of Early Life Trauma on Health and Disease: The Hidden Epidemic*, ed. Ruth A. Lanius, Eric Vermetten, and Clare Pain (Cambridge, UK: Cambridge University Press, 2010).
3. Ed Vulliamy, "Nixon's 'War on Drugs' Began 40 Years Ago, and the Battle Is Still Raging," *The Guardian*, July 23, 2011, https://www.theguardian .com/society/2011/jul/24/war-on-drugs-40-years.
4. Dan Baum, "Legalize It All," *Harper's*, April 2016, https://harpers.org /archive/2016/04/legalize-it-all/.
5. See Alexander Cockburn and Jeffrey St. Clair, *Whiteout: The CIA, Drugs and the Press* (New York: Verso Books, 1998), 71.
6. Bob Ryan, "What Might Have Been," *Boston Globe*, November 18, 2003, http://archive.boston.com/sports/articles/2003/11/18/what_might _have_been/.
7. Jimmie L. Reeves and Richard Campbell, *Cracked Coverage: Television News, the Anti-Cocaine Crusade, and the Reagan Legacy* (Durham, NC: Duke University Press, 1994).
8. George de Lama, "Reagan Opens Drug Crusade," *Chicago Tribune*, August 5, 1986, https://www.chicagotribune.com/news/ct-xpm-1986 -08-05-8602260119-story.html.
9. Joseph J. Palamar et al., "Powder Cocaine and Crack Use in the United States: An Examination of Risk for Arrest and Socioeconomic Disparities in Use," *Drug and Alcohol Dependence* 149 (April 1, 2015): 108–16, https://dx.doi.org/10.1016%2Fj.drugalcdep.2015.01.029.

10. Lauren E. Glaze, "Correctional Populations in the United States, 2010," Bureau of Justice Statistics, US Department of Justice, December 2011, https://www.bjs.gov/content/pub/pdf/cpus10.pdf; Marc Mauer, "Americans behind Bars: The International Use of Incarceration, 1992–93," The Sentencing Project, September 1994, https://www.ncjrs.gov/App/abstractdb/AbstractDBDetails.aspx?id =152587.

11. Carlos Ballesteros, "Racism Might Have Spared Black and Latino Communities from Opioid Epidemic, Drug Abuse Expert Says," *Newsweek*, November 7, 2017, https://www.newsweek.com/racism -opiod-epidemic-blacks-latinos-trump-704370.

12. Ali Vitali, "Trump Calls Opioids 'Worst Drug Crisis in American History,'" NBC News, October 26, 2017, https://www.nbcnews.com /politics/white-house/trump-declare-opioids-public-health-emergency -n814536.

13. Andrew Joseph, "The Surgeon General and His Brother: A Family's Painful Reckoning with Addiction," *STAT*, December 7, 2017, https://www.statnews.com/2017/12/07/surgeon-general-and-his -brother/.

14. Katharine Q. Seelye, "In Heroin Crisis, White Families Seek Gentler War on Drugs," *New York Times*, October 30, 2015, https:// www.nytimes.com/2015/10/31/us/heroin-war-on-drugs-parents.html.

15. Seelye, "In Heroin Crisis, White Families Seek Gentler War on Drugs."

16. "Profile: Black/African Americans," Office of Minority Health, US Department of Health and Human Services, https://www.minorityhealth .hhs.gov/omh/browse.aspx?lvl=3&lvlid=61.

CHAPTER 17: STUBBORN ROOTS

1. Philip J. Peters et al., "HIV Infection Linked to Injection Use of Oxymorphone in Indiana, 2014–2015," *New England Journal of Medicine* 375, no. 3 (July 21, 2016): 229–39, https://doi.org/10.1056 /NEJMoa1515195. For national statistics, see "HIV Prevention in the United States: New Opportunities, New Expectations," Centers for Disease Control and Prevention, December 2015, https://www.cdc.gov /hiv/pdf/policies/cdc-hiv-prevention-bluebook.pdf.

2. Sharoda Dasgupta et al., "Changes in Reported Injection Behaviors Following the Public Health Response to an HIV Outbreak among People Who Inject Drugs: Indiana, 2016," *AIDS and Behavior* 23 (December 2019): 3257–66, https://doi.org/10.1007/s10461-019-02600-x.

3. Shari Rudavsky, "CDC: Indiana Has 'One of the Worst' HIV Outbreaks," *Indianapolis Star*, April 28, 2015, https://www.usatoday.com/story/news /nation/2015/04/28/indiana-hiv-outbreak/26498117/.

CHAPTER 18: A MORE EXCELLENT WAY

1. See "County Health Rankings & Roadmaps: Indiana," https:// www.countyhealthrankings.org/app/indiana/2013/rankings/scott /county/outcomes/overall/snapshot.
2. Shabbar I. Ranapurwala et al., "Opioid Overdose Mortality among Former North Carolina Inmates: 2000–2015," *American Journal of Public Health* 108, no. 9 (September 1, 2018): 1207–13, https:// doi.org/10.2105/AJPH.2018.304514.
3. Donald G. McNeil Jr., "Trump Plans to End the AIDS Epidemic. In Places Like Mississippi, Obstacles Are Everywhere," *New York Times*, March 18, 2019, https://www.nytimes.com/2019/03/18/health/trump -hiv-aids-blacks.html.

CHAPTER 19: LEARNING TO THRIVE

1. *Alcoholics Anonymous: The Big Book* (New York: Alcoholic Anonymous World Services, 2001), 417.
2. Mark E. Koltko-Rivera, "Rediscovering the Later Version of Maslow's Hierarchy of Needs: Self-Transcendence and Opportunities for Theory, Research, and Unification," *Review of General Psychology* 10, no. 4 (December 1, 2006): 302–17, https://doi.org/10.1037/1089-2680 .10.4.302.
3. Marilyn Metzler et al., "Adverse Childhood Experiences and Life Opportunities: Shifting the Narrative," *Children and Youth Services Review* 72 (January 2017): 141–49, https://doi.org/10.1016/j .childyouth.2016.10.021.
4. Ecclesiastes 4:9-12.

CHAPTER 20: GOLDEN SCARS

1. Bob Bridge, "Commissioners Terminate Needle Exchange," *Hoosier Times*, September 21, 2018, https://www.hoosiertimes.com/uncategorized /commissioners-terminate-needle-exchange/article_76a8b427-c6ea-51e6 -9cad-9de57040de08.html.
2. Maggie Fox, "Indiana County Stops Needle Program Meant to Halt HIV," NBC News, October 18, 2017, https://www.nbcnews.com/storyline /americas-heroin-epidemic/indiana-county-stops-needle-program-meant -stop-hiv-n811741.
3. Mary Midgley, *Wickedness: A Philosophical Essay* (London: Routledge & Kegan Paul, 1984), 126.
4. Matthew 22:37-39.
5. Romans 13:8, NLT.
6. Meera Bai with Jack Stackhouse, "Why I Help Addicts Shoot Up: A Christian Defense of Harm Reduction," *ChristianWeek*, October 15, 2010,

http://www.johnstackhouse.com/why-i-help-addicts-shoot-up-a-christian
-defense-of-harm-reduction/.

7. "Harm Reduction or Harm Maintenance: Is There Such a Thing as Safe
   Drug Abuse?" hearing before the Subcommittee on Criminal Justice,
   Drug Policy, and Human Resources, 109th US Congress, February 16,
   2005, https://www.govinfo.gov/content/pkg/CHRG-109hhrg22200
   /html/CHRG-109hhrg22200.htm.

8. John Boyle, "Southern Indiana Suffered a Big HIV Outbreak Due to
   Intravenous Drug Use. Now, Needle Exchange Programs Set Up to Fight
   the Disease Will Expire," *Chicago Tribune*, February 25, 2020, https://
   www.chicagotribune.com/midwest/ct-indiana-needle-exchange-hiv
   -20200225-bmf446tkynac7jaqbvp7vxuoyi-story.html.

9. Henry J. Kaiser Family Foundation, "HIV Viral Suppression Rate in
   U.S. Lowest among Comparable High-Income Countries," March 20,
   2019, https://www.kff.org/hivaids/slide/hiv-viral-suppression-rate-in
   -u-s-lowest-among-comparable-high-income-countries/.

10. Ernest Hemingway, *A Farewell to Arms* (New York: Scribner, 2008).

EPILOGUE: HOPE REVEALED

1. Josh Katz, Abby Goodnough, and Margot Sanger-Katz, "In Shadow of
   Pandemic, U.S. Drug Overdose Deaths Resurge to Record," *New York
   Times*, July 15, 2020, https://www.nytimes.com/interactive/2020/07/15
   /upshot/drug-overdose-deaths.html.

2. Katz, Goodnough, and Sanger-Katz, "In Shadow of Pandemic."

3. "Issue Brief: Reports of Increases in Opioid- and Other Drug-Related
   Overdose and Other Concerns during COVID Pandemic," Advocacy
   Resource Center of the American Medical Association, October 31, 2020,
   https://www.ama-assn.org/system/files/2020-09/issue-brief-increases-in
   -opioid-related-overdose.pdf.

4. Alex Wittenberg, "Amid Spike in Opioid Overdoses, Momentum for
   Reform Wavers," Bloomberg CityLab, August 31, 2020, https://
   www.bloomberg.com/news/articles/2020-08-31/as-opioid-overdoses
   -spike-reform-momentum-wavers.

5. 2 Corinthians 4:3.

APPENDIX A: TEN BIBLICAL PRINCIPLES OF HARM REDUCTION

1. Susan Maizel Chambré, *Fighting for Our Lives: New York's AIDS
   Community and the Politics of Disease* (New Brunswick, NJ: Rutgers
   University Press, 2006), 60.

2. Augustine, *On Christian Teaching* 1.86, trans., R. P. H. Green (Oxford:
   Clarendon Press, 1995).

3. Martin Luther, "Fourth Sunday after Epiphany: Christian Love and
   the Command to Love," *Luther's Epistle Sermons: Epiphany, Easter and*

Pentecost, trans. John Nicholas Lenker, (Minneapolis: Luther Press, 1909), 61.

4. Martin Luther, "Fourth Sunday after Epiphany," 60.

5. Augustine, "Letter 211," *The Works of Saint Augustine: Part II—Letters 211–270, 1*–29** ed. Boniface Ramsey, trans. Roland Teske (Hyde Park, NY: New City Press, 2005), 25.

6. Thomas Weber, *Gandhi as Disciple and Mentor* (Cambridge, UK: Cambridge University Press, 2004), 202.

7. C. S. Lewis, *Mere Christianity* (New York: HarperOne, 2001), 117.

8. *Merriam-Webster*, s.v. "esse quam videri," accessed October 5, 2020, https://www.merriam-webster.com/dictionary/esse%20quam%20videri.

9. Harmon Lewis, "Don't Act Like a Christian," Messiah Johns Creek blog, August 30, 2018, https://www.messiahjohnscreek.org/blog/2018/8/30/dont-act-like-a-christian.

10. *Alcoholics Anonymous: The Story of How Many Thousands of Men and Women Have Recovered from Alcoholism*, 2nd ed. (New York: Alcoholics Anonymous World Services, 1955), 59.

APPENDIX B: THE SOCIAL DETERMINANTS OF HEALTH

1. Adapted from Alvin R. Tarlov, "Public Policy Frameworks for Improving Population Health," *Annals of the New York Academy of Sciences* 896, no. 1 (December 1999): 281–93, https://nyaspubs.onlinelibrary.wiley.com/doi/abs/10.1111/j.1749-6632.1999.tb08123.x.

2. Tara O'Neill Hayes and Rosie Delk, "Understanding the Social Determinants of Health," American Action Forum website, September 4, 2018, https://www.americanactionforum.org/research/understanding-the-social-determinants-of-health/.

3. "Epigenetic Patterns Determine If Honeybee Larvae Become Queens or Workers," Queen Mary University of London, ScienceDaily, August 22, 2018, www.sciencedaily.com/releases/2018/08/180822130958.htm.

4. "Closing the Gap in a Generation: Health Equity through Action on the Social Determinants of Health," Commission on Social Determinants of Health, World Health Organization, 2008, https://www.who.int/social_determinants/thecommission/finalreport/en/#:~:text=Closing%20the%20gap%20in%20a%20generation%3A%20Health%20equity,of%20illness%2C%20and%20their%20risk%20of%20premature%20death.

APPENDIX C: ADVERSE CHILDHOOD EXPERIENCES AND TOXIC STRESS

1. Vincent J. Felitti et al., "Relationship of Childhood Abuse and Household Dysfunction to Many of the Leading Causes of Death in Adults," *American Journal of Preventive Medicine* 14, no. 4 (May 1, 1998): 245–58, https://doi.org/10.1016/S0749-3797(98)00017-8.

2. Jane Ellen Stevens, "The Adverse Childhood Experiences Study—The Largest, Most Important Public Health Study You Never Heard Of— Began in Obesity Clinic," *ACES Too High* blog, October 3, 2012, https://www.acesconnection.com/blog/the-adverse-childhood-experiences -study-the-largest-most-important-public-health-study-you-never-heard -of-began-in-an-obesity-clinic.
3. "Toxic Stress," Center on the Developing Child, Harvard University, accessed October 5, 2020, https://developingchild.harvard.edu/science /key-concepts/toxic-stress/.
4. David W. Brown et al., "Adverse Childhood Experiences and the Risk of Premature Mortality," *American Journal of Preventive Medicine* 37, no. 5 (November 1, 2009): 389–96, https://doi.org/10.1016/j.amepre.2009 .06.021.
5. Abraham H. Maslow, *Motivation and Personality* (New York: Harper and Row, 1987), 149.

About the Authors

WILLIAM COOKE, MD, is a fellow of the American Academy of Family Physicians (FAAFP), and the American Society of Addiction Medicine (FASAM). He has been credentialed as an American Academy of HIV Medicine Specialist (AAHIVS). He has received national recognition for his work serving the rural community of Austin, Indiana, with limited resources. Dr. Cooke's work has been covered by CBS, NBC, PBS, the BBC, *USA Today*, the *New York Times*, NPR, and others. He was named Family Physician of the Year by the Indiana Academy of Family Physicians in 2016 and the National Physician of the Year by the American Academy of Family Physicians in 2019. He joined the ranks of two US surgeon generals and a former secretary of the US Department of Health and Human Services by receiving the Ryan White Distinguished Leadership Award in 2019 as well. Dr. Cooke lives outside of Austin, Indiana, with his wife, Melissa, and six children.

LAURA UNGAR is a Louisville-based investigative and enterprise editor for the *Courier Journal* who previously worked for the USA TODAY Network, the *Hartford Courant*, and Kaiser Health News. She has won more than fifty national, regional, and local awards in her years as a journalist from organizations such as National

Headliners, the Association of Health Care Journalists, and Investigative Reporters and Editors. Ungar is also a 2020 recipient of the AAAS Kavli Science Journalism Award. She has covered the health beat for more than half her career, writing two award-winning series on Austin, Indiana.